Praise for
Psychedelics and the Soul

"I started dreaming of reading this book the day I met Simon. He was my guide through a week of intense psilocybin-assisted therapy. Toward the end, after I had peeled my face off and thrown it into the cosmic dumpster, the reverence I felt for this medicine was equal to the admiration and gratitude I felt for Simon's wisdom and support. That experience has stayed with me, like a numinous reservoir of awe that I carry with me wherever I go.

This is not just another book about psychedelics. *Psychedelics and the Soul* effortlessly transitions between our most current understanding of the transformative properties of plant and fungal medicines and the perennial truths embedded in our earliest myths. And while many books might focus on the archetypal images and intimate accounts of the psychedelic experience itself, few books put such a much-needed emphasis on integrating this knowledge into our day-to-day lives. We need books like this to remind us to offer something before we take, to inspire us to shed our skin, to teach us how to pray for a vision.

There are only a handful of people I would willingly go to the underworld with. Simon is one of those people. *Psychedelics and the Soul* will speak to the ancient parts of you. It may inspire you to answer a call. You might see sparks from an ancestral fire, you might hear healing songs, a precious boon; whatever it is, it's just for you and it will only reveal itself to you once earth and bone touch, once you start to sync yourself up with the unimaginably intimate rhythm of the longing you were born with, that real old longing . . . It's a monumental journey, and let me tell ya, it's good to have books like this to guide us along the way."

—DEVENDRA BANHART, singer-songwriter and visual artist

"Using cogent myths and depth psychology, Simon Yugler acts as a soulful guide to and through the liminal terrains of plant medicines and altered states. He clarifies how psychedelics have always been part of the paths of seeking and of healing and how they speak to us individually and collectively at this critical time of life on earth."

—MICHAEL MEADE, author of *Awakening the Soul* and *Fate and Destiny*

"Holy wow, I can't wait to recommend *Psychedelics and the Soul* to everyone I know. It's the perfect book at the perfect time. Kudos to Yugler for masterfully weaving the wisdoms of depth psychology, cross-cultural mythology, and reverence for Indigenous traditions as grounded in his own counseling, teaching, and psychedelic experiences. Nothing has been as helpful as depth psychology in my process of unpacking and integrating the major psychedelic experiences in my life. Yugler's book—specifically geared to seekers and guides—is an all-around excellent read for the novice and psychonaut alike."

—DAVID BRONNER, cosmic engagement officer (CEO) of Dr. Bronner's soap company

"Simon Yugler leads us into collaborative inquiry with Mythopoetic Integration, rewilding the archetypes and legends that have inspired our dreams and nightmares for millennia so that they may guide us through the murkiness of our own visionary states. This book is a generous invitation to invite poetry and myth back into the world of healing and plant medicine."

—SOPHIE STRAND, author of *The Flowering Wand* and *The Madonna Secret*

"With deep gratitude, I welcome this work. . . . Simon deftly navigates territory that is uniquely suited for psychedelics but is often missing from our maps and models of healing and integration. What an honor to explore psychedelic depth psychology with Simon as our guide."

—TOM ECKERT, founder of InnerTrek and architect of Oregon's Psilocybin Service Initiative

"An essential addition to the evolving psychedelic canon. . . . Operating somewhere between a cosmic adventure story and a finely tuned, well-grounded guide to psychedelic healing, the book zooms out and zooms in, moving gracefully between the individual and the collective, with a profound respect for diverse mythic and Indigenous traditions and their essential contributions to the human experience. . . . This cosmic-mythic-psychedelic 'tour de force' will entertain and enlighten readers from a wide array of professional disciplines."

—HARVEY SCHWARTZ, PhD, cofounder of Polaris Insight Center

"Simon's book is a generous gift in perilous times and an act of service to his community. By casting his net widely, he has drawn in a feast of stories and myths—both modern and ancient—to put at the soul's table. In the often murky waters of the psychedelic therapy world, he sees clearly. Like his subject, this book may well provoke a deeper relationship with the true living world around us, inside us, flowing through us. May it pass from hand to hand as an ally to those who explore the vast landscapes it describes, and to those who wish to aid them."

—TOM HIRONS, poet, storyteller, and founder of Feral Angels Press

"An accessible resource for psychedelic facilitators old and new—a sextant for navigating the collective unconscious—as our society both taps into ancient ways of knowing and explores new terrain through widespread psychedelic healing. Yugler helps shine a vital light on what lies beyond personal healing."

—DR. CHRIS STAUFFER, MD, associate professor of psychiatry at Oregon Health and Science University and psychedelic-assisted therapy researcher for the Department of Veterans Affairs

"Having worked with Simon leading psychedelic retreats in Jamaica, I have witnessed firsthand how his passion, education, and broad and deep mythopoetic knowledge combined with his astute clinical intuition provides the uncanny ability for him to accurately understand, relate, and bring guidance and meaning to psychological content typically beyond the remit and scope of the majority of therapists. With real examples of clients' psychedelic experiences interpreted through the mythopoetic lens, this book sets itself apart from others. I wholeheartedly recommend [it] as a must-have for all psychedelic practitioners."

—JUSTIN TOWNSEND, CEO of MycoMeditations

Psychedelics
and the Soul

Psychedelics and the Soul

A Mythic Guide to Psychedelic Healing, Depth Psychology, and Cultural Repair

Simon Yugler

North Atlantic Books
Huichin, unceded Ohlone land
Berkeley, California

Published by
North Atlantic Books
Huichin, unceded Ohlone land
Berkeley, California

Cover art: General Research Division, The New York Public Library. "Eutania faireyi, Fairey's Garter Snake." New York Public Library Digital Collections
Cover design by Jason Arias
Book design by Happenstance Type-O-Rama

Printed in the United States of America

Psychedelics and the Soul: A Mythic Guide to Psychedelic Healing, Depth Psychology, and Cultural Repair is published by North Atlantic Books, an educational nonprofit based in the unceded Ohlone land Huichin (Berkeley, CA) that collaborates with partners to develop cross-cultural perspectives; nurture holistic views of art, science, the humanities, and healing; and seed personal and global transformation by publishing work on the relationship of body, spirit, and nature.

North Atlantic Books's publications are distributed to the US trade and internationally by Penguin Random House Publisher Services. For further information, visit our website at www .northatlanticbooks.com.

DISCLAIMER: The following information is intended for general information purposes only. The publisher does not advocate illegal activities but does believe in the right of individuals to have free access to information and ideas. Any application of the material set forth in the following pages is at the reader's discretion and is their sole responsibility.

Library of Congress Cataloging-in-Publication Data

Names: Yugler, Simon, author.
Title: Psychedelics and the soul : a mythic guide to psychedelic healing, depth psychology, and cultural repair / Simon Yugler.
Description: Berkeley, California : North Atlantic Books, [2024] | Includes bibliographical references and index. | Summary: "An exploration of how psychedelic medicine can heal the soul that invokes the traditions of Jungian depth psychology, mythology, and Indigenous cultural wisdom"— Provided by publisher.
Identifiers: LCCN 2024009021 (print) | LCCN 2024009022 (ebook) | ISBN 9798889840640 (paperback) | ISBN 9798889840657 (ebook)
Subjects: LCSH: Hallucinogenic drugs. | Parapsychology. | Hallucinogenic drugs and religious experience. | Indigenous peoples—Religion.
Classification: LCC RM324.8 .Y84 2024 (print) | LCC RM324.8 (ebook) | DDC 615.7/883—dc23/eng/20240411
LC record available at https://lccn.loc.gov/2024009021
LC ebook record available at https://lccn.loc.gov/2024009022

1 2 3 4 5 6 7 8 9 VERSA 29 28 27 26 25 24

To my teachers, and to all ceremonial elders.

May your fires never go out.

And so long as you haven't experienced this:
to die and so to grow,
you are only a troubled guest
on the dark earth.

—GOETHE

Contents

Introduction

El Camino Rojo

*N*ight comes quickly in the jungle. The sun offers one last spectacular display of pink and golden light before being swallowed by the endless green
horizon. In the darkness, the jungle comes alive. A chorus of frogs and insects
harmonizes in an electric hum, forming a sonic tapestry that resounds with
the wet pulse of life. At night, animals and spirits roam this verdant expanse
where, in some areas, the level of biodiversity in one square hectare can rival
that of an entire country. The jungle breathes.

In this fertile darkness, the healers of the Amazon do their work.

In 2015 *I spent six weeks living in the Peruvian Amazon with a family
of traditional healers from the Shipibo tribe, a culture renowned for their
skills in healing and in working with* ayahuasca, *a powerful psychedelic
plant medicine used throughout the upper Amazon. This relatively brief
immersion in the Shipibo tradition set my internal compass firmly in the
direction of something many have called* el camino rojo: *the red road, the
healing path.*

*Those were some of the most challenging weeks of my life. Eventually,
downing a full cup of the thick, ominous ayahuasca brew every other night
became a less frightening prospect than consuming the arsenal of plant
purgatives our Shipibo teachers presented us. The strict* dieta *of unsalted,
bland, and nutritionally vacant food created a slow burn of calorie-restricted
introspection that alternated between ecstasy and torture, permeated by the
entrancing whir of amphibian chirping. Among frequent visitations from*

giant butterflies, enveloping rainstorms, and bioluminescent tree spirits, two things dawned on me.

The first was that it was not my place to be pouring cups of this powerful, ancient medicine for others to consume. After facilitating just one ceremony during that time, and feeling the immensity of the maestro's seat and the duties attached to it, I firmly understood the seriousness of this responsibility. Despite the prevalence of self-described "shamans" one can encounter across much of the Western world, the time and energy required to become a fully trained ayahuasquero could in some ways compare to a PhD, but with stakes much higher than student debt. That fact, combined with issues around legality and cultural legitimacy, caused me to think twice about claiming this mantle.

My second realization occurred when I came to see the tradition of depth and Jungian psychology as the closest thing Western culture had left to a living tradition of genuine soul work. Having immersed myself in the disciplines of anthropology, mythology, and depth psychology for most of my adult life, I could comfortably call that tradition my own.

I continued to study ayahuasca, along with other traditions of plant medicine and healing, many of which were a part of my life long before my journey to Peru. My path took me around the globe several more times as I became an experiential educator, leading immersive study-abroad semesters for young adults. Eventually I enrolled at Pacifica Graduate Institute to study depth psychology, and I became a psychotherapist specializing in psychedelic integration, Internal Family Systems therapy, and men's work. During the height of the COVID-19 pandemic, I, like so many others, found the cornerstones of my life—an engagement to my then-partner, old friendships, and best-laid plans—dissolving into an ocean of uncertainty. After months spent navigating the underworld of heartbreak, I accepted a position in Jamaica at one of the world's leading psilocybin retreat centers, serving as a psychedelic therapist and retreat leader. All of this built upon a decade of travel and time learning from Indigenous peoples across the world. I've witnessed full-power hakas in Maori maraes, stared into the shifting coals of ceremonial fires, and danced with Shona spirit mediums in the throes of possession. These *experiences taught me things that changed the very bedrock of my being, shifted how I relate to the human and more-than-human world, and upended my understanding of what is real.*

Most of this book exists because of the kindness and generosity of Indigenous people who trusted me enough to share from their hearts. I am forever in their debt.

Now, I watch the white winter sun slip behind the forested hills that cradle downtown Portland. Gazing out massive floor-to-ceiling windows overlooking the Willamette River, I am struck by the natural beauty of this beloved, troubled city. Sitting on the top floor of a colorfully painted high-rise, I am surrounded by sixteen people, some lying under blankets while wearing eyeshades, others breathing silently in a meditative posture. They are some of the first people in the United States to experience a legal psi-locybin mushroom journey. As I stare out across the valley that holds my hometown, I can look behind the skyscrapers and glimpse the very hillside where I first took this medicine almost twenty years ago. Today, as a psy-chedelic therapist and educator helping to train some of the nation's first legal psychedelic guides, I can only feel a sense of completion and stillness, a body of settled satisfaction, and a full heart after a long journey home.

Psychedelics and the Soul

Psychedelics are not about improving mental health. There, I said it. Psychedelics are not about having a slightly better day at the office, boosting your productivity, or optimizing your portfolio of cryptocur-rencies. There's no guarantee that psychedelics will make you happy or make your life easier. They might help you discover a life more rich with meaning, saturated in wonder, or centered in truth. But this is not an easy road. Myth tells us there is no getting something for noth-ing, no reward or wisdom that is not duly earned. Unless you have a burning desire to sit for seven years beside a druid's fire, peer into black temple doorways, descend into the underworld, break bread with serpents, shed your skin, and learn to feed eagles from your fingertips, this path isn't for you. Within these pages you won't find easy methods for self-improvement or tips for an exciting new career. What you will find, however, are ten stories that speak to the soul, and stories from my own life and practice that I hope will serve you, no matter where you are on this spiral road.

A new generation of psychedelic healers, therapists, educators, researchers, and business leaders is emerging. Laws are changing, prohibitions are loosening, and modern culture is beginning to molt its skin in favor of something that is increasingly strange and uncertain. On many counts, this is cause for celebration. Yet amid the collective effervescence of the "psychedelic renaissance," what if something is getting lost? The word *psychedelic*, coined by British psychiatrist Humphry Osmond, is often said to mean "mind-manifesting." Yet if we follow the trail of language back to its roots, the Greek word *psyche* actually refers to the soul, while *delos* means to reveal or make manifest. Psychedelic, therefore, literally means "soul-revealing," a necessary distinction that sets our compass squarely in the direction of this inner domain.

The mind is easy for modern Western culture to compartmentalize into a neat category of understanding. The soul, not so much. The soul escapes quantification; the mind delights in it. The soul dissolves boundaries; the mind constructs them. The soul orients us toward the eternal; the mind toward the time-bound. For many people, the very mention of the soul is an unsettling proposition, for to acknowledge it means to acknowledge that life is more than a random conglomeration of particles floating through cold, infinite space. To acknowledge the soul is to acknowledge that in fact there is something *out there, down there, in there*, that escapes our understanding and control. To acknowledge the soul terrifies the ego.

The soul forms the foundation of my approach to psychedelic healing because the soul provokes our innate capacity for meaning-making: an introspective, solitary, yet socially entwined process that has its roots at the very beginnings of our species. Soul connects us to life, death, love, and loss, provoking and punctuating the very things that make us human. Always has. Always will.

Like vines threading their way through dense jungle canopy or mycelial networks enmeshing themselves across old-growth ecosystems, psychedelics and the soul are bound together in ways that trouble our understanding of what it means to be alive in a human body at this time on the planet. Taking the soul out of psychedelics by reducing them to molecules or psychological tools reveals both a poverty of the imagination and an inability to move beyond materialistic and economically driven models of healing that have proven themselves to be not only insufficient, but in many cases, unethical.

While the so-called psychedelic renaissance is just beginning, the roots of these liminal traditions of plant medicine and inner exploration thread their way down into the foundations of human cultures and their mythic traditions. As the fledgling field of modern psychedelic healing continues to spread its wings, unless we remember to look back toward the soul, toward more ancient ways of knowing, and toward the earth itself, we risk flying perilously close to the sun.

✳ ✳ ✳

At some point in many myths and folktales, a traveler arrives at a fateful crossroads. One road leads into the impending dark of the forest; the other back to the comforting lights of home. The first road is the path of initiation, transformation, and the mythic unknown. The second returns us to the comfortable life we've known before, and just more of the same.

All of us stand at this very crossroads. Collectively, our world faces multiple crises that are linked in inextricable ways. The most pressing of these is climate change, or the collapse of our planetary ecosystem due to centuries of colonial extraction. Nearly as urgent is the collapse of meaning, community, and rituals of belonging that permeate our daily lives. At its most basic level, we can understand this latter collapse as a crisis of *mental health*. Fueling both of these dilemmas are a capitalist economy and a materialist worldview that exile the soul.

PSYCHEDELICS AND THE SOUL

Depth psychology and psychedelics sit at the crossroads of these two modern emergencies: depth psychology because it offers a method of understanding the symbolic language of the soul as it is expressed through myth, dreams, and altered states of consciousness, and psychedelics because of their ability to reveal the soul itself.

Yet how can the evolving field of psychedelic healing possibly begin to address these overwhelming collective crises? What stories might aid us in our search for individual and collective healing at this precarious moment? And how does a practice of psychedelic healing converge with mythic wisdom into a coherent path?

Answering these questions requires a certain kind of recollection, a look back into wells of collective memory that the traditions of mythology, depth psychology, and Indigenous cultures all arise from.

On Myths and Fairytales

Once upon a time, our ancestors looked into the glimmering tapestry of nature and felt that the world was speaking to them. The hidden patterns of the stars, the ominous outline of a distant mountain, the snake-like flow of a river—all became gods and goddesses, mythic beings full of personality and meaning. No matter your recent heritage, this is a cultural and psychological fact.

According to mythologist Karl Kerenyi, "In mythology, we hear the world telling its own story to itself" (Radin, 1956, p. 175). Myths are expressions of the soul of the people and place from which they emerge. They do not "represent" aspects of a culture; instead, they constitute that culture's psychic and spiritual lifeblood. This lifeblood flows into a coherent cultural identity, weaving a landscape and a people into a single tapestry of meaning and belonging. In the modern world, we've come a long way from understanding what living in such a world might feel like.

As you read through this book and encounter the myths and folktales within, you may be tempted to interpret them. I, too, am tempted to analyze what these ancient tales might mean, but I do not pretend to fully understand them. Every time we interpret a story, we run the risk of reducing its vitality. Through analyzing a story, our ego seeks to colonize it. By way of supposedly understanding it, we declare that we "know what it means." When it comes to stories that emanate out of our decidedly undomesticated past, this is likely the last thing they want.

Instead, we must let these stories ripple through our emotional bodies like a stone dropped into a still, dark pond. The more we immerse ourselves in a story's imagery, the more purchase it has on our soul. To engage with myths in a meaningful way means that we bring as much of ourselves to the table as we can. This might look like identifying a particular moment or figure in the story that sticks with us long after we put the book down or leave the crackling fire where we first heard the tale. Something about that character or that image's symbolic resonance guides us toward the forest of our inner world.

Myths emerge from the liminal borderlands of consciousness, and they direct our attention back toward that place. We do not invent myths; we experience them—just like psychedelic encounters. Throughout these journeys, psychedelic or not, we can confront beings or forces that have the power to change us. Sometimes these are visually rich, intelligent, and frighteningly real. Other times, they might become an emotion that rattles our bones, leaving us in a place where words slip through our hands. In the realm of myth and non-ordinary states of consciousness, we confront powers far greater than ourselves. In the language of depth psychology, we call these experiences *archetypal*.

Archetypes

Myths are transmissions from the archetypal realm. The word *archetype* comes from the Greek word *archai*, meaning the basic elements out of which all experience is made—an idea that traces back to pre-Socratic

Greek philosophers, Plato, and the roots of Greek mythology itself. Carl Jung refined the term to refer to what he observed as universal patterns of experience that manifest throughout the human psyche.

Anything that resonates deep within our psychic magma contains an archetypal quality. So too does the natural world: images of the sacred mountain, the tree of life, and the mysterious forest, for instance, appear throughout countless religions and myths across the world. This book spirals through ten archetypal images and stories that emerge in the mythic realm, and explores how they can aid our understanding of psychedelic experiences.

Before we go any further, let's clarify some things about archetypes:

Archetypes are amoral. Morality is a subjective, human invention that aims to manage our societies and impulses. Archetypes, and the mythic world they inhabit, play by a very different set of rules. Many of the characters or events in the following stories might strike you as immoral, unjust, or inhumane—because they are. They do not conform to a twenty-first-century code of ethics or behavior. Even though some archetypal characters may embody moral ideals like justice, order, or peace—the ideal king or queen, for instance—they do so only because our culture has agreed so. Archetypes do not contain a morality unto themselves. Rather, they are vessels for whatever we collectively agree to fill them with. With this in mind, I invite you to suspend judgment as we walk through this very old terrain.

Archetypes are crystallizations of power. That power is mediated by the feelings that they evoke within us. Jung often defined an archetype as an image combined with an instinct or a strong feeling. Through this felt, emotional power, we are able to relate with these images and stories by experiencing our response to them. And that power can be overwhelming. Like a high mountain peak, an archetype is just as content to overwhelm you in an avalanche as it is to enlighten you on its summit. Like any force of nature, an archetype simply does what it does. How we relate with it determines how it will affect our life, for good or ill.

Archetypes are personal. When I first began studying depth psychology, I imagined archetypes as impersonal cosmic entities living "out there." They seemed ethereal, imaginary, and ultimately inaccessible to me. But the more I studied them, the more it became clear that we all encounter and can possess archetypal qualities. When we fall in love and are transfixed with a new partner, Eros and Aphrodite, gods of beauty and passion, are having their way with us. When someone is constantly on the move, changing life plans at a moment's notice, Coyote, Hermes, or any other traveling trickster is their copilot. When someone is struggling in the depths of alcohol and drug addiction, they are dancing with, and perhaps being danced upon, the great god Dionysus: spirit of ecstasy, fermentation, and divine intoxication. Some of these archetypal energies dwell in the spotlight of consciousness, while others are relegated to the *shadow* (a concept we'll discuss in detail in chapter 3).

Archetypes are collective. Archetypes form the building blocks of our shared cultural stories and beliefs. When our individual suffering is seen through an archetypal lens, we are able to widen our consciousness to encompass a perspective that weaves through time and space. This is not a means of escape, but rather a path of meaning-making. Because no matter what we're going through, myth helps us remember that it has all happened before.

Navigating the Myth World

Jung said, "Myths are original revelations of the pre-conscious psyche, involuntary statements about psychic happenings" (2014/1959, p. 154). The "pre-conscious psyche" is the realm of myth, dreams, and altered states, and it transcends rational understanding. It is a space not unlike the paradoxical terrain of quantum physics that science is now beginning to understand, confirming the ancient notion that there are domains of existence that do not play by the rules of rationality.

As we travel together through the stories and visions presented in this book, I offer you a few magic stones to keep in your pocket to help you find your way:

In the myth world, the usual rules of time and space don't apply. A year might unfold in a day, or a century in a month. Sometimes stories use symbolic numbers to express an undefined yet considerable length of time, like "101 days." That might be half a lifetime, give or take. We can see many parallels here to the way time works in altered states of consciousness. In my own psychedelic journeys, I can recall hours passing before me as if they were only moments, and moments that stretched out to feel like hours.

In myths, nothing occurs by accident. Every detail can contain profound symbolic value, and every image can become a crucible of meaning. Colors, objects, numbers, and animals are not inconsequential details meant simply to carry the hero from point A to B; they are intentional articulations of wisdom expressed through the story itself. Sometimes these details change between tellers or versions, but the point remains the same: every image matters.

Myths are alive. Take a step toward a story, and it will take a step toward you. In writing this book, I found the stories taking on lives of their own as I immersed myself in their rich inner worlds. As I researched obscure corners of ancient history, mythic genealogies, and anthropological exploration, I found that the stories themselves began to speak back to me through dreams and synchronistic encounters that stopped me in my tracks. The more I let the imagery of the story permeate my being, the more of itself it revealed to me. The myths began to *talk back*.

These stories have been with us for thousands of years. Is it so far-fetched to think that they might have a few thoughts of their own after all this time?

Some elements in a story must remain mysterious. Sometimes, parts of a story might not make sense. Remember that with myths, we are dealing with something very old that our modern minds might struggle to wrap themselves around. Sit with the discomfort of not knowing. To analyze every image, to extract every last morsel of the tale, runs the risk of interpreting it to death. It is my sincere hope to honor these stories as best I can. To do that, I must bow to the fact that the stories are living mysteries unto themselves. Myths have no author. They emerge from a place that humankind has always sought to explore and articulate, yet can never fully know.

Indigenous Traditions

The fields of psychedelics and depth psychology are indebted to Indigenous cultures in unfathomable ways. The fact that these cultures managed to keep their ancestral stories and ceremonial knowledge alive in the face of genocide and colonization is itself a miracle. These traditions and their living stewards deserve our respect, gratitude, and reciprocity. In studying and relating with Indigenous peoples, modern Western people might find something reflected back to them that, once upon a time, we could have recognized as an intact culture.

Indigenous cultures, teachings, and stories are woven throughout this book. As we embark on this journey together, I offer four points to keep in mind as I speak of Indigenous traditions, especially in the context of psychedelics and psychology:

Indigenous cultures are not a means to an end for the Western world to figure out its problems. Valuing Indigenous cultures simply for what they have to teach *us*, for what *we* have to gain from *them*, is yet another form of colonial extraction. This approach of siphoning Indigenous wisdom solely for the purposes of benefiting modern culture continues to marginalize these communities. Right relationship and informed, consensual reciprocity are two avenues that can help mitigate this subtle yet real dynamic. You can learn more about Indigenous reciprocity here: https://chacruna-iri.org/.

Indigenous peoples continue to exist as the most marginalized communities on the planet. Any discussion of Indigenous cultures that ignores the concrete, immediate issues facing these communities—namely, the ongoing march of the colonial machine in the guise of the fossil fuel industry and other mechanisms of extraction—is only telling half the story. Indigenous communities have always been, and still remain, the most vocal advocates against all forms of extractionist industries. Invoking the traditions of Indigenous peoples without also invoking their continued fight for political sovereignty, equal rights and access, and ecological and land-based justice ignores the reality of Indigenous life and struggles.

I cannot claim membership of any intact Indigenous or initiatory culture. Regrettably, my bar mitzvah did not suffice. Throughout this book, I will speak *of* many Indigenous traditions, but never *for* any of them. As much as possible, I will cite Indigenous authors and people, allowing them to speak for themselves by quoting and drawing upon their own work.

Many of the plant medicines mentioned throughout this book are at risk of extinction due to overharvesting, specifically the peyote cactus and the ayahuasca vine. All of the experiences mentioned throughout this book involving Indigenous plant medicine ceremonies were facilitated by trained Indigenous stewards of these traditions. Readers are encouraged to familiarize themselves with Indigenous-led conservation efforts to ensure the continual survival of these plant species.

The tradition that I can, without reservation, call my own is the tradition of depth psychology, which has also sought to integrate Indigenous perspectives and mythologies into its understanding of the psyche, ever since Carl Jung's momentous encounter with the Taos Pueblo people and a medicine man named Ochwiay Biano, or Mountain Lake. During his visit to their ancient adobe city, Jung found himself profoundly affected by the rich inner life and interconnected spirituality of the Pueblo people, seeing in them a reflection of all that white or European culture lost long ago. Reflecting on this encounter, Jung (1963) wrote:

> I felt rising within me like a shapeless mist something unknown and yet deeply familiar. And out of this mist, image upon image detached itself: first Roman legions smashing into the cities of Gaul. . . . I saw the Roman eagle on the North Sea and on the banks of the White Nile. Then I saw St. Augustine transmitting the Christian creed to the Britons on the tips of Roman lances, and Charlemagne's most glorious forced conversion of the heathen; then the pillaging and murdering bands of the Crusading armies. . . . Then followed Colombus, Cortes, and the other conquistadors who with fire, sword, torture, and Christianity came down upon even these remote pueblos dreaming peacefully in the sun, their Father (p. 248).

Depth Psychology

The soul and the psyche have always been the center point of interest, the heart of the labyrinth, which depth psychology coils itself around. Historically, *depth psychology* referred to any form of psychoanalytic work that focused on the unconscious. Today, the term is used as a shorthand for the various permutations of thought influenced by Carl Jung, the Swiss psychiatrist who helped shape psychology into the discipline we know today. While the mainstream psychological establishment has for many decades eschewed Jung's work, his legacy—which can include everything from the work of Joseph Campbell to archetypal astrology, teachings on the tarot, and Internal Family Systems therapy—continues to inform our culture perhaps more than that of any other figure in the history of psychology.

The history of modern psychedelic research is almost inseparable from the tradition of depth psychology. Stanislav Grof, Ralph Metzner, Terence McKenna, Timothy Leary, and many other early psychedelic researchers integrated depth psychology into their work, which others drew upon to inform newer perspectives like transpersonal psychology, ecopsychology, and somatic therapies. Due to cultural shifts in the twentieth century, including the war on drugs, current psychedelic research prioritizes quantitative and statistical analysis and often overlooks the subjective, emotional, and phenomenological aspects of these experiences. Just like human beings, no two psychedelic journeys are alike, so they resist a one-size-fits-all categorization. Instead, psychedelic experiences are reflections of the multifaceted, mysterious inner worlds of those who are brave enough to explore their hidden depths.

How to Use This Book

In the pages that follow, you will not find any ultimate blueprints, tips and tricks, or life hacks. What you will find are stories I've gathered from across our vast world, each illuminating some unique part of what it means to be human. Myths from ancient Ireland, Sumeria, Greece, Native America, and beyond will be our guides as we explore the archetypal realms that psychedelic medicines can escort us into and out of again. Don't take anything in here as doctrine or dogma. Rather, we are going to try to let the stories speak for themselves and see how the worlds of myth and psychedelics might converge in a meaningful way. The stories within these pages can offer meaning and direction and provide a mythic framework for navigating the vast realm of the soul.

Within these pages you will find stories that speak to the ubiquitous and troubling aspects of what it means to be a human being entwined within this living planet. Along the way, I will share lessons I've learned from time spent sitting in ceremonial huts filled with cedar smoke and eagle feathers, or encircled by the nighttime drone of jungle cicadas. I've also learned much from my work as a psychedelic therapist and guide working with many clients from diverse backgrounds. To the many brave souls I have been fortunate enough to work with: thank you for everything you have taught me.

Perhaps you will discover some perspectives and tools for the practice of psychedelic healing and integration and how to work with the archetypal threads woven throughout these experiences. For others, perhaps you will find these stories whispering to you through mist-filled trees, beckoning you to change your life.

This book is not a how-to guide, a personal journey, or an academic exploration. Rather, it is all of these—and none. My hunch is that it dwells more comfortably in the cracks between these disciplines. This book, like the many psychedelic medicines and archetypal beings that prowl through its pages, is a liminal creature. It smolders at the crossroads altar of Hermes, haggles with Baba Yaga, and gambles for cowrie shells with Eshu—trickster gods all, messengers between worlds who venture into and out of the mythic unknown, patron deities of the liminal traveler, soul guide, and psychonautic explorer. As you read this book, you too may find yourself betwixt and between realms as you behold these ancient stories weaving their way into the fabric of your being— stories that emerge directly from the luminescent cracks between nature and culture, mind and body, ego and soul.

I

The Well

The Unconscious, Symbolism, and the Mythic Unknown

Sing yourself to where the singing comes from.

—SEAMUS HEANEY

Connla's Well

*C*ome hazel, come yew, come hawthorne, come oak. Come stag, come swan, come raven, come wolf. Welcome, traveler. Warm your mist-chilled fingers around this campfire that never goes out, nestled between liche-nized stones. Sit down on the sheepskins, take a sip for those old ancestral bones, and pour a libation to the hungry earth beneath your feet. Listen now, for this story I'm about to tell you is more true than truth can tell, and older still.

There once was an ancient island. And before humans walked upon its churning shores, there lived another race of beings, versed in magic, whose days lingered on like lifetimes. The Tuatha de Danann, they were called. That was several worlds ago, and they are now gone. But it is said that they still live beneath the hills and stones scattered across the dew-soaked land, wandering through the hollow hills when the veil between the worlds grows thin. Some say *their deeds and exploits are inscribed into the very land itself: the land we know today as Ireland.*

In the days before days, one of their kin, a young woman with shining hair and moon-pale skin, found herself seeking the kind of knowledge that even in that ancient time was guarded by forces greater than we can understand. Sinann was her name, and while death would never haunt her, while she was beloved by all, there was a type of knowledge she craved that only the Otherworld could give.

Up within the hills amid the craggy stones, there was a well known to all as Connla's Well. Some say it was so deep that it was under the ocean itself. Others say this pool was a doorway between the realms, its waters going down to the Otherworld. Around Connla's Well grew nine hazel trees, whose ripe fruits would drop down into its shimmering waters. And within the water lived a salmon who would eat these sacred hazelnuts. But about the well swirled a dark magic, a mist that laid enchantment and protection around it. To be sure, this was a sacred place, guarded by powers that the Tuatha de Danann knew to honor and respect.

Despite all this, Sinann could not help but seek out this knowledge. She knew that if she could bring just a mouthful of that iridescent liquid to her lips, some wild intelligence would take root within her. Perhaps she sought mastery over the ecstatic arts of poetry and music, or longed for the wisdom to lead her people forward. Whatever the reason, Sinann knew that once the water touched her mouth, something would be different.

Ravens cawed and scattered as she entered the sacred hazel grove. Emanating from the well was a sound so full of mournful beauty that to hear just one note of it would devastate you in its grief. The bright maiden, peering into the water's depths, beheld the salmon swimming there, and rising up from the bottom of the pool she saw bubbles floating to the surface, enchanting her, lulling her deep into a dreamlike trance. It is said that these bubbles arose from the Otherworld itself and contained the very essence of that unseen realm's visionary power.

Closing her eyes, incanting a prayer in an ancient tongue that we now only know in our dreams, she took a breath, and drank.

Suddenly, all the knowledge of the world flooded into fair Sinann. Time bent itself backward until she saw its circular flow with no beginning and no end. Her senses stretched to encompass the hundreds of miles around her radiant body, intimately feeling the smooth stones, the wisps of lichen, the wise trees, and the vast ocean all in the same moment. Salmon poured from her eyes like tears of joy. Otters swirled out of her silken arms, dancing in the swift current that enveloped her body. Herons hatched from her head, spreading their elegant wings, carrying her sight from the deep waters all the way into the sunlit skies above.

Sinann began to dissolve, her body unfurling into a swift evergreen churn of life-giving waters. The girl died, but a river was born.

Some say the gods of the Otherworld became angry at her trespass, and they caused the waters of the well to drown fair Sinann and submerge her forever within its cold course to the sea—a lesson to not meddle with powers we don't understand.

But there are others who quietly claim that Sinann knew exactly what she had bargained for. Some say that this young maiden was a far more ancient goddess whose story is remembered by the land itself, told by the people in their ancient language around smoky peat fires down through the generations. To this day, the River Shannon in western Ireland runs its course from the green hills all the way to the Atlantic Ocean, bearing her name. For in her very dissolution lay the immortal wisdom she sought.

Drink one drop from the well, and your whole life can change.

Otherworld Wisdom

We begin with this simple tale from Ireland, which some speculate could be five thousand years old. A story I imagine my own Irish ancestors would have likely known well, it trickled down through the oral histories of an animistic, pre-Christian European culture, miraculously washing up on our modern shores in written texts several centuries ago despite nearly a millennium of English colonization.

The story of Connla's Well is a powerful example of what ancient myths can teach us about altered states of consciousness and psychedelic healing. Every time we work with psychedelics, examine our dreams, practice breath work, and even experience certain forms of psychotherapy, we are approaching the Great Well of the unconscious and entering the Otherworld of the mythic imagination.

Irish linguist and author Manchán Magan (2020) says:

> To fully appreciate this idea we need to understand that the Otherworld was more than an imaginary realm where ancient gods and heroes dwelt and feasted; it was an elusive and undefinable space that was as much connected to the subconscious or inner psyche of the individual and the group consciousness of the community as it was to magical gods, or the spirit of past ancestors, or the energetic resonances of the natural world. All these things come together in the Otherworld, just as they might in a dream, and place names became just another way to access them, like using sacred trees or rituals or charms. (p. 158)

Highlighting the prevalence of Otherworld awareness infused within the Irish language and landscape, Magan illustrates the connection between the Irish word for a physical place or locality (*ceantar*) and the word for its opposite, the Otherworld (*alltar*): "In the Irish mindset, the *ceantar* is closely shadowed by the *alltar*. They exist simultaneously, in all places, at all times. Our physical bodies occupy the *ceantar* but our minds can easily slip into the *alltar*" (p. 32). To the ancient Irish, and perhaps to all Indigenous, animistic peoples, the Otherworld dwelled just behind the surface of our own. One of the most reliable ways of accessing this parallel realm was through the sacred wells and other sites scattered across the landscape.

Wells are inherently introspective spaces, literally reflecting back our own image and beckoning us deeper into our internal world through their subtle invitation to fathom their waters. The Well is an image of deep but contained unconscious work, a boundaried yet immeasurable space that offers a distinct doorway for inner exploration. Across the world, springs and wells are often considered sacred places with healing powers. I recall sitting by many wells throughout my life—the headwaters of the Sacramento River at the foot of Mount Shasta, the boiling sulfuric pools at Breitenbush Hot Springs in Oregon, springs in Zimbabwe emitting a grandmotherly hum, sacred wells across Ireland—and feeling myself carried away into some vast, mysterious terrain both inside and outside myself that felt deeply familiar, yet decidedly unknown. If it's possible to feel both grief and joy, ease and edginess in the same moment, wells evoke this in me. Wells magnetize myths and people to them because they symbolize the doorway to the unconscious, the Otherworld, and the living earth.

If approached incorrectly, however, the Well can be overwhelming and dangerous. The dark, magical mist that encircles Connla's Well represents this potential peril and signals caution to those who would frivolously drink or disturb its waters. As with many sacred wells today across Ireland, there are appropriate ways to approach the Great Well of the unconscious—protocols and rituals that establish an atmosphere of reverence and respect that also serves to protect those who would venture within.

Let's also be clear about something: drinking from the Well can be a disruptive act. Otherworld wisdom is subversive. It turns our understanding of life on its head. We come away from our encounters with it bringing back new ideas about who we are, what our world is, and how we might change our course forever. This sort of wisdom challenges the established order of things. There is immense power here. It is no wonder that in the seventeenth century the colonial British banned the Irish from gathering at their holy wells. For as a great bard of the Irish tradition, Terence McKenna, famously said, "Psychedelics are illegal not because a loving government is concerned that you may jump out of a third-story window. Psychedelics are illegal because they dissolve opinion structures and culturally laid-down models of behavior and information processing. They open you up to the possibility that everything you know is wrong" (1987).

When we drink from the Well, everything we know can change. Yet knowledge without transformation is just information. The story of Connla's Well shows us that the wisdom we find at the bottom of the Well comes with a price. Sometimes the price is that we change how we live, break familial patterns, or release things we have tightly clung to when something deep within us knows we must let them go. It is not uncommon for people to emerge from psychedelic journeys with a conviction that they must change fundamental aspects of how they live. This is Otherworld wisdom speaking its cold, clear truth through those who drink from the Well.

The story ends with what some might see as a warning: Sinann drowns because of her transgressive thirst for self-knowledge. Though centuries of Catholic priests would have surely sunk their teeth into this as a cautionary tale, let's not forget that this is a pagan story, intimately connected to the land, cycles of life and death, and the unique spirit of a people and a place. In the West, modernity has brought us a long way from a realistic understanding of what such a culture might entail. But the myths remain. Like Ariadne's golden thread weaving its way through the labyrinth, myths are pathways of deep remembrance, leading us ultimately into a process that instigates individual healing and cultural repair. To see the conclusion of this tale simply as the consequence of overstepping our bounds ignores its deeper meaning.

The story of Sinann and Connla's Well is a story about transformation. Sinann doesn't end up with wealth or fame or a kingdom—conspicuously modern, and dare I say masculine, views of success and achievement. Rather, she gains a level of interrelatedness and kinship that is hard for our dualistic minds to even fathom. But the story says it clear as day: drink from the Well and discover what it means to be a living being connected to a living earth.

This sense of interconnection and unity is a foundational aspect of psychedelic experiences that could be considered "mystical" in nature. Emerging research shows us that psychedelic healing achieves its full potential of creating significant life transformations when people experience this mystical state of interconnectivity and oneness, which also serves to reframe our understanding of our relationship to ourselves, our communities, our planet, and the wider cosmos (Garcia-Romeu et al., 2015). Ego dissolution is a common term for this sort of experience. Sinann achieves not just a dissolution of her ego, but of her entire being, melting into the animate all that permeates our every breath. She is no longer an "I." She is water flowing into river, river rushing into ocean, ocean evaporating into cloud, cloud thundering into earth, absorbing into plant, metabolizing into animal, digesting into human, sung into song, and remembered into myth.

Sinann imbibes the wisdom of the Otherworld and finds herself connected to a vastness much greater than herself. The story tells us that when we dip into that mysterious terrain, we expand far beyond simple definitions of ourselves. This also occurs when we access the deep, uncharted regions of the psyche through psychedelic medicines and other avenues of accessing nonordinary states of consciousness. Depth psychology calls this realm the *collective unconscious*.

The Collective Unconscious

If dreams are the "royal road" to the unconscious, according to Freud, then psychedelics are the superhighway.

The collective unconscious is the Great Well of human experience that "contains the whole spiritual heritage of mankind's evolution, born anew in the brain structure of every individual" (Jung, 1959/1970, p. 158). Evoking the archetypal link between the unconscious and the element of water, Jung wrote that the unconscious can be understood as "something like an unceasing stream or perhaps ocean of images and figures which drift into consciousness in our dreams or in abnormal states of mind" (Jung, 2001, p. 191).

Depth psychology teaches that this is a different realm of the psyche from the personal unconscious. The personal unconscious contains all the unique aspects of our repressed personality: difficult memories, traumas, unexamined beliefs, and behaviors we're not even aware of. Within this region of the personal unconscious also lies the personal *shadow*. The shadow, according to Jung (2014), can be defined as "that hidden, repressed, for the most part inferior and guilt-laden personality whose ultimate ramifications reach back into the realm of our animal ancestors and so comprise the whole historical aspect of the unconscious" (p. 266). That's a complex way of saying that your shadow contains all the aspects of your personality that fail to neatly conform to your idea of who you are.

We can never predict what unconscious content will emerge when we're working with psychedelic medicines. That's because psychedelics don't cause *specific* effects, psychologically speaking. As Stanislav Grof puts it, psychedelics are *abreactives*, meaning that they bring to our conscious awareness whatever unconscious material has the most unconscious energy around it. Another term for this phenomenon is *nonspecific amplifier*, which highlights psychedelics' unpredictable effect on the unconscious, like the archetypal tricksters we will get to know in chapter 6.

The archetypes we'll explore throughout this book encompass many mythic themes I have frequently seen emerge from the unconscious through my work in psychedelic healing, but by no means do I present a definitive list. Like dreams, no two psychedelic experiences are the same—a river we can never set foot in twice. Each experience is a uniquely personal, emergent reflection staring back at you from within the Well's beckoning waters. The entire process of psychedelic healing—from preparation, to the journey, to integration—is essentially one long process of metabolizing the unconscious material that bubbles up from the Well.

Becoming fluent in the archetypal language of the deep psyche will inevitably require you to learn to speak two languages at once: keeping one foot grounded in the world of ego consciousness, professional ethics and practices, and objective reality, while also keeping another foot in the realm of symbol, metaphor, and the mythic unknown. Becoming literate in symbolic language takes practice and a dedication to your own inner work. Over the course of this chapter we will start learning to speak this language together.

But first, let's go back to the Well for another drink.

The Salmon of Knowledge

*D**eeds turned into history, history into folktales, folktales into leg- ends, and legends into myths. Centuries passed like the seasons; stones grew their rough, weathered skins; and forests shed their thousand leaves more times than time can tell. But the Well, the hazels, and the salmon all remained.*

Like most immortal things, stories of the Well filtered down through the generations. Hearing of Sinann's fate, the people developed a healthy fear of trifling in the ways of the Otherworld, which was becoming more and more the realm of the sidhe, or the fairy folk. People began to approach the Well with rituals and offerings of respect and gratitude, and ensured that they did not offend the invisible powers of the Otherworld and violate its ancient laws: Don't drink the water. Don't touch the hazels. And don't mess with the bubbles.

The salmon, though, was fair game.

Known as the Salmon of Knowledge, this magical fish swam calmly in the depths of the Well throughout the centuries, eating the hazelnuts that dropped from the silver branches of the nine sacred trees that surrounded it. It was said that anyone who ate of its speckled flesh would receive all knowledge of the past, present, and future and be blessed with a poetic vision that would, as the Irish say, light a fire in the head.

An old druid named Finnegas, whose sky-filled eyes had learned to read the land's stories and see them told in the milky river of stars above, decided to dedicate his life's last years in pursuit of this salmon. He made his way to the Well, and there he sat for seven long years, patiently waiting for the Salmon of Knowledge to bite the fishing line he held in the water, hoping it might bless him with its gift of poetic ecstasy.

On a day not unlike all the others, a young boy by the name of Finn Mac Cum huill (or Finn McCool, as they say now) wandered up to where Finnegas sat by the Well. Finn never knew his father, who had been killed before he was born. Finn's mother gave birth to him in secret, then quickly gave him to her sister and her druidic companion, Fiacra, who prophesied that one day Finn would grow up to be a great leader and warrior. Finnegas knew none of this when the lad wandered up the hill to the old druid's hut. And Finnegas, of course, was more than he appeared to be as well: not a washed-up old fisherman, but a bardic master, wise in the ways of owl-speech and raven-spell. In Finnegas, Finn found a man who could school him in the ways of the Otherworld through that old process called apprenticeship.

Perhaps it was through some luck the boy brought, but very soon after Finn's arrival old Finnegas felt a tug on the line—the first he'd felt in the seven years. To his amazement, he had hooked the salmon, and he gracefully pulled it out of the water. Smiling to himself in quiet amazement, Finnegas lit the fire, set up the cooking spit, and intoned the ancient words required for such a sacred occasion. As the fish slowly roasted, the old man tasked Finn with watching it cook as he stepped away to tend to some druidic business. Under no circumstances was Finn to eat—or even touch—the fish.

The salmon was cooked to perfection. Not wanting to burn his new teacher's long-sought prize, Finn went to remove it from the fire. Just as he was about to move the scintillating fish, a blister on its skin sizzled and popped, sending a splash of its hot juices onto Finn's thumb. Without thinking, Finn put the thumb in his mouth to ease the pain.

But one drop was all it took. (Some of us know what that's like.)

After Finnegas returned, young Finn wobbled back to his teacher and placed the fish delicately before him. The old poet looked into Finn's eyes, and there he saw the glimmer of the universe shining through his saucer-like pupils. Something deep within the boy had utterly changed. Finn was gone, gone beyond.

"Finn, my boy," Finnegas said, "are you certain you didn't eat from this fish?"

Almost in tears, Finn explained the sizzling blister on his thumb and how he put it in his mouth when he felt the burn. We don't know what occurred in the poet's mind right then. Yet perhaps all his years sitting patiently by the

Well had imparted some subtle wisdom that can only come from quiet soli-
tude. Taking a long, wistful breath, Finnegas knew that Finn now possessed the
knowledge of the salmon. Despite his seven years of effort, Finnegas accepted
that this knowledge was ultimately not for him—an old man with a life
well-lived—but for this bright young boy before him.

Finnegas took a deep inhale and breathed out the last of his smoldering
desire into the gathering dusk like sparks soaring into twilight. "So be it,"
he said. And for many years afterward, the old man instructed Finn in the
arts of ecstatic poetry, bardic wisdom, and mystical wit, giving him a way
to channel the overflowing wisdom of the Otherworld rather than drown in
it. Finn would go on to become one of the greatest heroes that Ireland had
ever known.

Cosmic Fisherman

Every time we venture out onto the dark ocean of mind on a psychedelic
voyage we are, as Terence McKenna said, like fishermen seeking to bring
back ideas that can somehow feed the village. There are ideas and energies down in that dark ocean that have the potential to transform our
lives—along with leviathans that might sink our boats, overwhelming
us with their unfathomable weight. We are also like salmon themselves,
who begin their life sheltered within tiny tributaries, then venture out
into the expansive ocean only to return to their precise place of origin,
utterly transformed, brimming with new life and stories of the Great
Beyond.

The story of the Salmon of Knowledge is an ancient tale that holds
countless layers of meaning. Yet before offering anything of my own, I
would ask you, reader: where do you find yourself in the story? What
moments are still reverberating through your heart's eye? Again, we
must be careful when seeking to interpret any myth, for they are beings
far older and wiser then we can begin to fathom. What I will share,

however, is how this story speaks to me and what I feel murmuring within myself when I sit with this myth and what it has to say about the Otherworld. Within this story, I hear three lessons that might teach us about working with psychedelic medicines to cast the lines of our psyche down into the Great Well of the unconscious.

First lesson: nothing about working with psychedelics and altered states of consciousness is a quick fix. There is no formula, no accelerated path, no shortcut for one's own inner work. A weekend workshop, or even a six-month training program, won't suffice; only time, and the embodied learning that comes with it, will do. Finnegas approaches the Well with a healthy reverence for its power. For seven years he waits, patiently honing his craft outside the pool, but with his awareness always connected to the unconscious depths. He maintains one foot in both worlds, embodying the balance required to artfully negotiate one's relationship to the upper world and the Otherworldly fish that swim below.

We can see the ancient Celtic horned god Cernunnos as one embodiment of this tension. Some long-forgotten strands may even link Cernunnos to Finnegas and Finn himself, as they are all associated with animals, the hunt, and the wild. The Gundestrup Cauldron, an iconic masterpiece of ancient Celtic metallurgy, depicts Cernunnos sitting in a cross-legged, meditative posture surrounded by animals, holding a snake in one hand and a traditional metal neck ring called a *torc* in the other. What meaning the Celts imbued within these images we can only guess. But from a symbolic perspective, the snake might represent the unconscious, embodying the unbridled forces of nature and the undulating chaos that continually eats and births itself anew. Sticking with this lens, the metal torc may be a symbol of grounding, restraint, boundaries, and ego consciousness. Cernunnos and his mythological descendant, Finnegas, are embodiments of the grounding and depth required of a skillful guide and ceremonial leader who calmly dwells at the crossroads of nature and culture, chaos and order, the unconscious and the ego. Mysteries within mysteries reside within this ancient horned god, his dense antlers branching far back into prehistoric memory. The Green Man, revered throughout old Britain and chiseled into many cathedral walls, is one incarnation of him. The enigmatic image known as "the Sorcerer," etched onto the walls of the Trois-Frères cave in France, is another, his piercing gaze staring back at us all the way from 13,000 BCE.

Second lesson: the story speaks to the necessity of mentorship as we fish in the dark waters of the psyche. Finnegas is an old, wise poet, and Finn still a young buck—enthusiastic, but unschooled in the ways of the Well. Through this relationship, Finn absorbs the salmon's knowledge almost by accident, just by being near the action. Finnegas inhabits the role of the archetypal mentor and recognizes immediately what needs to happen, and despite his personal desire, he performs the required rituals that life asks of him in that moment. And it is a two-way street, as Finnegas, while not the extravagant hero that Finn would become, retains the immortal role as his teacher.

For psychedelic facilitators, the importance of finding mentorship cannot be overstated. The elders of the psychedelic movement, well-seasoned psychedelic explorers and guides, as well as Indigenous elders maintaining their own cultural ways of prayer and ceremony, are vitally important lifelines for anyone seeking to apprentice themselves to this work. As a psychotherapist, I've had the honor of working with mentors who have been practicing in the field longer than I've been alive. I've also been privileged to know a variety of Indigenous elders and teachers who have served as invaluable models and guides on this path. (We will dive deeper into the role of elders and leadership in chapter 7.)

Third lesson: moments of illumination are unexpected. Finn doesn't grasp or eagerly devour the fish, desperate to possess its power. He is simply at work, serving his teacher, respectfully relating with powers that surround (but don't belong to) him. The gods of chance inhabit this critical juncture in the story. Trickster, who weaves his way between thresholds of consciousness leaving both disruption and renewal in his wake, pops the blister on the fish's skin at this precise moment. Some people call that luck, which is also the province of Trickster. We don't see him, but he's there. This is an Irish story, after all, where twists of fate are never far away. This moment is a reminder that we can never perfectly orchestrate transformation, and that it will rarely turn out the way we think. When working with psychedelics, we are obliged to always leave room for the unexpected, to be flexible and adapt to whatever emerges in the moment—just like dear Finnegas. (We will return to our friend Trickster later on.)

The Salmon of Knowledge is a story about apprenticeship, transformation, and mystical revelation, and we are only scratching its surface here. But it does reveal some core guidelines for working with psychedelic medicines that inform the foundation of this book's approach to psychedelic healing: Approach the Well with respect. Keep a foot in both worlds. Find a mentor. Stay grounded. And expect the unexpected.

The stories of Connla's Well and the Salmon of Knowledge speak to the power and wisdom that emerges from the Great Well of the Otherworld, or the collective unconscious. Such knowledge can open itself to us when we intentionally work with psychedelic medicines. This knowledge often takes the form of visions, images, bodily experiences, metaphors, and synchronicities that defy logic. Yet in order to fully understand and make sense of psychedelic experiences, we need to learn how to speak this language of imagery, archetypes, and symbols—the language of the psyche.

To do this, we will first explore the meaning of myths as they relate to both human culture and the psyche. Then we will learn to speak the symbolic language through which myth and the unconscious psyche communicate. Finally, we will explore five techniques for understanding psychedelic experiences through a mythopoetic lens.

Layers of Myth

On the most basic level, myths are stories passed down through time, within and sometimes between cultures, either through oral telling (the old way) or more recently through written texts. On another level, myths contain social and religious codes that keep alive a certain way of doing things—knowledge of the earth's cycles, the wisdom contained within specific places, or ritual customs and protocols—which, for Indigenous cultures, were not separate things. Taken together, this is the cloth that culture is made from. There is also ancient knowledge embedded in almost every myth. Sometimes this knowledge can be as practical as when to harvest certain crops or when certain animals migrate. Other times, though, myths contain teachings about navigating the vast terrain of the Otherworld, which is saturated in symbolic imagery, mysterious beings, and often, danger. Myths travel on the backs of wagons, sail across oceans, and become woven into the everyday fabric of a people and place. In the words of archetypal psychologist James Hillman, myths "never were, but always are" (Intellectual Deep Web, 2017).

This anthropological explanation of mythology is useful in understanding how cultures are shaped by the stories they tell themselves. Yet this is only one way of beholding these shaggy old tales that ultimately play by their own rules and refuse to conform to the rigid containers that we inevitably try to construct for them. But as every storyteller worth their salt will tell you, some stories are feral. Myths are living beings that dwell somewhere between the provocative moon-howl of the forest and the comforting hearth of home, often roosting in the nest of our minds.

This second layer of mythology invites you, the listener, to become a necessary participant in the story as it takes root inside you and finds its way to those delicate places within that long to be fed and felt with care. Myths can awaken us to the divine and troubling realities presently at play within our souls. Myths beckon us to get involved.

We can call this the *mythopoetic* layer of mythology—a way of looking at the world that sees story woven into the very ground upon which we walk. Sprouting from our footsteps like fruiting bodies of earthly wisdom, myths inhabit the intersection between our personal circumstances, the collective unconscious, and what cultural ecologist David Abram (1996) calls the *more-than-human world*.

A mythopoetic perspective helps connect our unique, individual story and all of its complexities to the archetypal Well of the collective unconscious, which is encoded into myth. We can define mythopoetics simply as "crafting a meaningful story." More precisely, mythopoetics is a way of perception that integrates the raw material of the human experience: our churning sea of emotions, the furrows of our senses, the luminescent web of our imagination.

The mythopoetic lens is the foundation of depth psychology, and perhaps every form of psychology. Freud's infamous exploration of the Oedipus myth and his conclusions regarding the nature of the unconscious, debatable as they were, was an act of deep mythopoetry that the modern European world had not seen the likes of since the Renaissance. "I am Oedipus," Freud once said, pointing to perhaps the most essential element of the mythopoetic perspective: an unflinching ability to look at one's self and see one's own reflection in a story.

The work of Carl Jung was for Western culture a rediscovery of some long-forgotten technology or art form that helped recontextualize these ancient tales as containers of profound psychological insight, whereas before they were seen only as archaic vestiges of so-called "primitive" cultures. Jung's method of teasing out deep thematic resonances between myths and the struggles he saw within his patients (and himself) helped establish psychoanalysis and the newborn field of psychology as a revolutionary form of healing—a modality of self-inquiry and inner work that lives delicately between the worlds of art and science.

The Language of the Psyche

Psyche speaks through images. Throughout this book, we will explore ways to see and work with the archetypal symbols that emerge from the unconscious in our work with psychedelic medicines. Ultimately, though, the meanings behind these images, stories, and experiences are crafted by their beholder. As a therapist and psychedelic guide, I can help people see the picture more clearly, but I don't determine what comes into the frame.

The mythopoetic perspective is about the ability to see more deeply into ourselves and the more-than-human-world, connecting our lived experience to the Great Well of archetypal images. Learning to speak this language asks us to negotiate the constant interplay between the amorphously subjective, poetic world of symbols and the gritty, emotional world of real human life. Like Finnegas, we keep one foot in each world, sitting firmly on the edge of the Well while another part of our awareness spirals beneath the water's surface, fishing for Otherworldly wisdom.

Thinking symbolically means trying to look at things "as if" they are, or might be, other than what they seem. We poke and prod with raven-beaked curiosity, sniffing out the unexpected, following the trail of some elusive creature burrowed beneath the fertile ground of the psyche. From a mythopoetic perspective, everything that emerges from the unconscious is an opportunity to make meaning, and none of it is taken for granted.

In our age of clinical certainty, it can be both challenging and refreshing to try to comfortably settle into this paradoxical realm of "both-and." Thinking symbolically requires us to get much more comfortable in the unknown. It is difficult, if not impossible, to reduce symbolic language into a bullet-point formula or blueprint. Such an approach would suffocate this highly emergent mode of perception. Instead of claiming with certainty that we know where we are going, we must instead allow ourselves to be led by the psyche's unfolding, speaking back to us through the symbols themselves. We must, in the words of James Hillman, "stick with the image," learning to listen to the psyche and to see as clearly as we can what it wishes to tell us. The next section offers a method for how we can begin to do this.

The Five Skills of Mythopoetic Integration

These five skills form the basis of what I call Mythopoetic Integration—a way of interpreting psychedelic experiences through an archetypal and mythological lens. This framework reflects how I intuitively began helping clients integrate their psychedelic experiences and how I continue to work today. But it is important to say again: this isn't something you do *to* people. Rather, it is a collaborative practice that simply asks us to stay open to what the psyche has to say and to be brave enough to listen.

The first two techniques are basic elements of psychotherapy and psychedelic integration that can help people feel comfortable opening up, telling their story, and inviting you into their inner world. These initial steps are about listening and creating safety. The last three techniques are grounded in Jungian psychology and offer different ways of working with symbolic imagery that arises in psychedelic journeys, dreams, and other altered states of consciousness. The goal of Mythopoetic Integration is to help you uncover personal and collective layers of meaning by exploring the archetypal aspects of psychedelic experiences. In my work with clients and in my own life, the mythopoetic lens has helped guide me toward a vast substratum of meaning and wisdom that resides within each of us—in the deep well of the soul.

1. Mythos (Story)

The soul lives in stories. Whatever shattering or blessing we may have received along the road of life constructs our personal mythos, our unique creation story. Every culture on earth has a creation myth that all other stories emanate from, and so do individuals. Healing can be seen as a process of revisiting the parts of our personal mythos that need tending and repair until we are able to heal larger stories than just our own.

Storytelling starts in the preparation stage of a psychedelic journey. What follows is not a comprehensive intake process, which ideally involves a much more in-depth conversation; rather, this is a loose array of information a practitioner should seek when helping someone preparing to drink from the Well:

▼ Your previous psychedelic experience: If this is your first journey, why now?

▼ Your intention for the journey

▼ Relevant, important moments from your life that led you here

▼ Your personal mythos and experience of childhood

▼ Significant mental health information, including any past diagnoses or episodes

- ▼ Family history and ancestry
- ▼ Lifestyle choices, social life, and consumption habits
- ▼ Relationship status and history
- ▼ Intersectional identities, such as socioeconomic, racial, cultural, sexuality, and gender-based contexts
- ▼ Significant traumas or core wounds
- ▼ Current life transitions or questions
- ▼ Current support network

In the integration phase after a psychedelic experience, the journey itself becomes the next story that, in the context of a formal psychedelic integration session between a client and a practitioner, is recalled in its entirety. This is the raw material that will inform the rest of the integration process:

- ▼ Begin with a chronological retelling of the experience.
- ▼ Describe the arc of the journey. Describe the beginning, middle, and end.
- ▼ Describe significant images, details, or insights they may have received.
- ▼ Describe how the journey relates to their intention.
- ▼ Describe how they are feeling, now that they have returned.

In the words of mythologist Martin Shaw, "Storytelling is a ritual enacted on the tongue" (2023). It is a vulnerable portal into someone's inner world that requires presence, attention, and compassion. Listen without judgment or needing to fix anything, and notice your own emotions that might arise. Listen with care and receive their story as if it were a priceless gift, because it is.

2. Pathos (Feeling)

No good story begins with "happily ever after." As Jung saw it, the psyche's innate desire to move toward wholeness begins with the sense that something in our life needs to change. Usually this is accompanied by some form of suffering or deep feeling.

Feeling makes things personal. Keeping feeling as the central thread woven throughout one's story ensures that the Mythopoetic Integration process remains relevant to the person in front of you. Especially when working with abstract, bizarre, or confusing psychedelic experiences, emotions are the bridge that connects the abstract to the personal. Even a lack of feeling offers plenty of information about the person sitting before you and where they are in their story.

Feeling keeps things grounded, ensuring that we remain tethered to our planet and our sense of self instead of drifting off into fantasy or avoidance. That drifting off is what's commonly called *spiritual bypassing:* an artful and imaginative way to avoid facing one's wounds, traumas, and shadow material. Mythopoetic Integration is not about connecting to fantasy, but to the real, messy struggles of being alive in a human body. It's usually not glamorous, and it's not meant to be. After all, the Greek word *pathos* means "suffering."

I also do my best to notice my own response to the feelings my client is sharing. Do they make me uncomfortable? Nervous? Delighted? Awed? Simply being aware of the emotions arising in yourself is a powerful aspect of this process.

3. Association (the Individual Unconscious)

Uncovering the personal associations with a particular image in an individual's unconscious psyche is a foundational element of psychoanalysis and depth psychology. Association connects us to the personal unconscious and helps us find unseen threads between one's lived experience and the Otherworld. When someone experiences a strong association with a particular image, there is always a backstory, a mythos, saturated in feeling.

Once I was sitting with a client emerging from a powerful psilocybin journey. He struggled to put the transcendent experience he had just undergone into words. I asked, "Is there any particular image that stands out to you?"

He replied, "I remember seeing this cave with a tiny opening, and inside was complete darkness. I couldn't see inside, but I just had this sense that something important was in there."

"Does anything come to mind when you think of caves? Do they mean anything to you?"

"You know," he said, "when I was a kid, I had a basement that was my happy place. I would spend almost all my time down there. Classic 1980s kid in a basement. I think back to that time in my life and can see how happy I was."

"What else does that vision of your childhood basement bring up for you?"

"I guess I always felt like that place was like a cave. You know, I can't shake this feeling that the cave I saw, that maybe that was me in there. But it felt so good. It felt so . . . special. Which would mean that . . . I'm special? That I have, I guess, a soul? And that inside my soul is, well, something good?"

I watched this man, who had spent years drinking excessively and hating himself, realize through delving into this symbol of the cave that he had an innate core of goodness and worth inside him. His revelation about the cave and his own soul marked a turning point in his healing process. He returned home with a new commitment to show up emotionally for his son, to stop his destructive drinking habits, and to no longer allow himself to engage in the vicious self-talk that had consumed him—all because of a few associations he was able to make between this mysterious cave and his personal story.

4. Amplification (the Collective Unconscious)

Thinking symbolically and seeing through a mythopoetic eye means developing an ability to perceive archetypal themes *behind* the image, story, or dynamic before us. It asks us to cultivate a familiarity with the world of myth and to develop our own relationship to mythic characters and themes so we can track archetypal motifs and connect them with the people in front of us.

Amplification, a depth psychological technique perfected by Jung and those who followed him, is a way of connecting associations from the personal unconscious with the collective unconscious. We amplify an image by playing with it, finding different angles from which to examine it, and curiously inspecting what it might contain. Anything can be material for amplification. Throughout this chapter, the symbols of the Well, the salmon, the fisherman, and the Wise Elder have led us toward greater understanding of the nature of the collective unconscious, interconnection, mentorship, and transformation. In fact, this whole book is a process of amplification, connecting unique personal stories to collective mythic themes.

Amplification offers avenues of meaning-making by helping us discover mythological elements that relate to our lived experience. For amplification to be meaningful, we must move through the previous three steps: mythos, pathos, and association. Only then can our psyche orient itself toward these larger archetypal themes.

However, this technique can become a way to spiritually bypass and avoid facing difficult emotions or telling harsh truths. It's much easier to get lost in the magical world of archetypes and bypass the personal. But done well, Mythopoetic Integration—and all forms of psychedelic healing—lead toward deeper feeling, not away from it. Skillful amplification supports us in this process and encourages us to go deep.

For example, here is a story I've heard in various forms from multiple people I've worked with, especially men:

"I never knew my father. I grew up in a household where I felt like I didn't belong, like I was on my own. I had to take care of myself from a very young age. In my psychedelic journey, I found myself out in this vast expanse, like a desert, completely alone. I didn't know where I was or who I was. I felt lost. Then I began to see something in the distance. This being approached me, like an old man or an animal, or somehow both, and began speaking to me, telling me things about myself and who I truly am. It felt incredibly important, and I remember the feeling, but not everything he said. When I came out of the journey, I felt this warmth in my heart, this strength that I haven't felt in a really long time. I felt like that being blessed me and saw me for who I truly am."

Using the Mythopoetic Integration process, after I explored this person's story of "feeling like they didn't belong" and "being on their own," I would create space for them to explore their emotions around this. How has this experience affected their life? How has it continued to inhabit their psyche and shaped their identity? After exploring these details, I would begin to look for their associations around the image itself—in this case, a wise being, spirit guide, or teacher figure. They might say something like:

"When I was in high school, I had this teacher who really took me under their wing. They supported me and really inspired me. I couldn't have made it through school without their help."

Or: "I've never had anyone I'd really consider a teacher or mentor. I always wished I had some wise person, like Obi-Wan Kenobi, or even just an older brother, to be there for me; but I haven't found them yet."

Here we have two avenues of personal associations with this symbol. It doesn't matter if there is a literal association—that is, an actual person from their life who matches this role. What matters is that we have a grasp of their emotional energy behind the image. Is it familiarity? Desire? Longing? Betrayal? These are the connections that will help in usefully amplifying this image and uncovering its mythological threads.

Then I would return to what feels like the emotional core of this experience: someone who never felt like they belonged finally encountering a being who saw them for who they truly are.

To me, this story resonates with the archetype of the Orphan—perhaps the most beloved character in all mythology—encountering what sounds like the archetype of the Mentor or the Wise Elder. This cherished figure appears throughout countless ancient myths and contemporary stories. In contemporary pop culture, Gandalf, the Fairy Godmother, and Yoda are just a few beloved examples. It is fitting that this person who, consciously or not, identifies with the Orphan would encounter an image that connects them to the archetype of the Mentor, which is exactly the healing energy that their psyche needs. In the Salmon of Knowledge, the Mentor is embodied by Finnegas, while Finn is essentially an orphan himself. It is a deep longing inside this person's soul that conjured the image of this mystical teacher, as the archetype exists both inside and outside of them. In many stories, an encounter with this sort of character signals the beginning of a much longer journey of transformation.

5. Personification (the Imaginal-Animistic Psyche)

It's not enough to simply *interpret* an image, extract our hit of personal inspiration, and move on with our lives. Mythopoetic Integration asks us to give psychic life to the symbol itself—what James Hillman called "personification." It is not enough just to think *about* an archetypal image. We must think *with* it—and sometimes *through* it—in order to fully receive whatever gifts it might want to share.

Hillman defined personification as "the spontaneous experiencing, envisioning and speaking of the configurations of existence as psychic presences" (1992, p. 12). Personifying, according to Hillman, clears the way for a mythic and ultimately more meaningful approach to life: "To enter myth we must personify; to personify carries us into myth. . . . To the mythic perspective the world appears personified, implying a passionate engagement with it" (p. 16). It is through personifying that mythology, archetypes, and psychedelic healing coalesce into a coherent vision, opening up new pathways for growth long after the journey ends.

Personification demands a change in worldview and understanding about what is *real*. "What is needed," wrote Hillman, "is a revisioning, a fundamental shift of perspective out of that soulless predicament we call modern consciousness" (1992, p. 3). This requires a foundational shift in perception that goes emphatically against the grain of Western philosophy and culture, orienting us instead toward what could be called the *imaginal-animistic* psyche.

To personify is to be in relationship. When we personify an image, we give it a level of psychic autonomy. We dialogue with it, exploring the unique scents, moods, and textures that this imaginal being might contain, warts and all. We continue to open ourselves up to the symbol, image, or story, allowing for new streams of information to pour forth from it. We must take the psyche at its word. This doesn't mean we must like, accept, or endorse all parts of it; it does mean, however, that we have to be open to what it might mean for us.

We can see personification as the quintessence of these previous four techniques. It is not a destination in itself, but rather a natural shift in understanding that emerges from working with psychedelics through a mythopoetic perspective. It is also the stage of Mythopoetic Integration that most easily translates into action.

Simply devoting more attention to the image itself through its recollection and creative expression is a good first step in personification. If this was your story, what would it be like to draw, paint, sculpt, dance, or otherwise invoke the archetypal Mentor (or Orphan) in your day-to-day life? Maybe you dialogue with it through journaling or other intuitive methods that utilize creative flow. Perhaps it deserves a place at the table somewhere in your tangible reality—a location in your home, on an altar, or a place somewhere in nature that you can visit.

Jungian psychology is full of ways of working with imaginal beings and the unconscious: active imagination, dream work, and sand tray therapy, among other methods. Other esoteric avenues accomplish the same thing through ritual, meditation, and prayer. Sometimes an archetypal image might enliven us with its energy and inspire us to take radical action in our lives. For instance, my client who witnessed the cave might create a space of his own where he can spend intentional time connecting with the innate core of goodness he encountered in his journey; or perhaps he might simply imagine himself inhabiting his own inner cave where his inner child dwells. For the client who encountered the Wise Elder, personification might direct their attention toward dialoguing with this imaginal being in a meditative state, thereby cultivating a relationship with it. Eventually, this being might become a familiar presence or "guide" they can reliably call upon for insight and wisdom. Personifying is how we ensure that the messages, symbols, and beings we encounter through psychedelic work have a place in our everyday life. Otherwise, they may sink back down to the bottom of the Well and be forgotten, or worse: they may transform into the very symptoms that we seek to heal in the first place.

❉ ❉ ❉

As we begin to drink from the Well, we too may find ourselves, like Sinann, dissolving into an unceasing flow of interconnection, or shocked into unexpected illumination like Finn. Both of these stories end with transformation, revealing a timeless mystery that ancient myths and psychedelic experiences invite us to embrace, and which our present-day planetary realities continually, and often painfully, beckon us to remember: that we are connected to all life, and all life is connected to us.

II

The Temple

Beyond Set and Setting

Heal yourself, with beautiful love and
always remember . . . you are the medicine.

—MARIA SABINA

Chavín de Huantar

*I*remember the carved primordial faces protruding from a mound of
stones so old it seemed like a heap of chthonic memory emerging from
the earth itself—contorted visages with fanged teeth and bulging eyes
beholding rare visions lost to modern life millennia ago. Not quite human,
but not fully animal.

I was introduced to the ancient Peruvian temple of Chavín de Huantar as an undergraduate anthropology student. While studying legendary
sites like Chaco Canyon, Tikal, and Teotihuacan, the unassuming ruins of
Chavín caught my attention above all else. I couldn't tell you why, but something in the way the old stones lay upon one another like a pile of bones pulsed
out a subterranean frequency that would one day call me into the temple's
inner depths.

Chavín de Huantar is one of the most fascinating archaeological sites in the world. A pre-Incan civilization that existed between roughly 1,200 and 200 BCE, Chavín had no military fortifications or standing army that we can find evidence of; yet the Chavín culture held sway over a massive territory in what is now Peru. That such an enduring civilization would rise without the aid of brute force seems difficult to conceive of today, but Chavín is one of those rare examples of human beings uniting behind something more significant, and more sacred, than military might alone.

It is an undisputed fact that Chavín was a ceremonial center—an ompha-los, *a "navel of the world"—known for its ritualistic use of psychedelic plant medicines. Considered the first major religious and pilgrimage center in South American history, Chavín boasts impressive frescoes depicting jaguar-fanged priests clutching the mescaline-containing* huachuma, *or San Pedro cactus, populating the temple courtyard. The carved "tenon" heads, which once adorned the high exterior walls of the temple, are said to depict the journey of transforming from human into something decidedly more than human.*

Another way to interpret these frightening heads is as a warning to all who would enter this place: do not fuck around here.

In 2013 I took a twelve-hour bus ride from Lima to Huaraz, a beautiful city located in Peru's Ancash region, a mist-filled terrain of glacial peaks and quiet mountain villages in the center of the Andean Cordillera. Two other young psychonautical seekers and I took another bus into the quiet hamlet of Chavín, nestled in a fertile valley sitting slightly above ten thousand feet. As we pulled into the town's bus station, a gentle hush settled upon us. I could feel this place calling me into a deeper form of reverence and reflection that my eager twentysomething psyche craved.

When I arrived in this small Peruvian town, all I had was a name: Martín, a man known by many as "the shaman of Chavín."

I walked up to the armed security guards at the gate to the national archaeological site and asked if they knew anyone by that name. Without missing a beat, the guard looked to his left, and from behind him stepped a smiling man who said without any pretense, "Yo soy Martín."

Martín and I had a brief, amiable discussion, and I explained in my most polite Spanish how I came across his name. I attempted to articulate how I had studied the temple of Chavín at university, and how I had felt immediately drawn to this valley ever since. "We are hoping to partake in a ceremony to connect to this place," I explained, trying my best to convey my intention to approach this medicine and this temple with respect. I wanted him to know that I had, in some sense, done my homework, and I wasn't just another gringo looking for a psychedelic ride. Yet in that same moment, I was struck by the weight of what I was so casually proposing: an afternoon sojourn into the heart of a primordial shamanic tradition with a man who, by all accounts, was one of only a handful of its living stewards left on the planet.

Part of me expected him to simply say no, which would have been more than fair. Across the world, towns just like Chavín have had to deal with the fallout of "shamanic tourism," their streets overrun with medicine-gobbling foreigners looking quite similar to myself and my travel companions. Huautla de Jiménez in Oaxaca, Mexico, the hometown of the renowned Mazatec curandera *Maria Sabina, was permanently altered after R. Gordon Wasson's infamous 1957* Life *magazine article catalyzed a mushroom cloud of interest and impact. Sabina's own life and family were the first casualties of this explosion. As a result of sharing the secrets of the* niños santos *(psilocybin mushrooms) with Wasson, her home was burned down, and her son was eventually murdered. She died penniless.*

Pisaq, in Peru's Sacred Valley, a gorgeous Quechua town renowned for its Incan ruins and abundant marketplace, now caters to spiritual travelers seeking every variety of neoshamanic activities, from rapé *tobacco snuff ceremonies to* kambo *toad venom detoxes. Lago Atitlan in the highlands of Guatemala—homeland of the Tzutujil Maya, and chrysalis for the potent work of writer and teacher Martín Prechtel—now features bamboo ecstatic dance floors and New Age cacao ceremonies that tower above the concrete pueblos and contaminated waters below. So no, I wouldn't have been surprised if Martín had shown me the way out.*

All of these colonial histories and present-day realities of spiritual extraction unfolded in my mind's eye as I spoke with Martín. I desperately wanted to show him that I was somehow different, to convey my respect for him and this ancient place that his family has called home for generations. At the same time, I was painfully aware of the paradox contained within this delicate moment.

After a brief contemplation, Martín calmly agreed to facilitate a huachuma ceremony for us. His offering was simple and direct, lacking any of the bells and whistles that accompany so many main-street shamans and expat "healers" who peddle their wares throughout Peru. No feathers, no white embroidered shirts, no retreat package upsell. There was something quietly reassuring about this. Martín had no need to prove anything to these wide-eyed gringos who were prepared to follow him into whatever shamanic realm he was about to open. I realized that because he truly didn't need anything from us, I felt safe with him.

Martín had a few short words with the guards, and then he bid us to follow him down to his house, located just a few blocks from the temple. Martín was born on the temple grounds, and his father was appointed the site's caretaker after a Stanford University research team completed excavations several decades ago. His family is indelibly linked to this temple, one of only several families and individuals connected by ancestral ties to a place as culturally significant as the Athenian Parthenon. Martín would be the first person I would drink this medicine with, which was (and still is) one of the greatest honors of my life.

We arrived at a house with white plaster walls, nondescript wooden doors, and a red tiled roof, nearly identical to every other house on the block. Martín directed us inside and led us down into the darkness of his basement. I became aware of the fact that, while I was about to embark on what felt like a significant, potentially terrifying ordeal, this was likely just business as usual for Martín. Like most traditional healers whom I've been fortunate to meet around the world, their ceremonies rarely look like a dramatic production; rather, they take the form of accessible, community-focused practices that occur in the basements and backyards of family homes. There is no need for a "retreat" in the Indigenous world, no conception of "getting away from it all," because the aim is to find and maintain a spiritual balance with all facets of life, including the unglamourous, monotonous demands of the everyday. There is no "away" in an animistic culture.

In the dim basement, small windows high up in the plaster wall admitted a shaft of overcast light from outside. I noticed bookshelves and glass cases full of stone objects in the back of the room. Several plastic chairs sat in a rough circle around a low table against the wall. He lit a candle, illuminating an impressive mesa, *or altar, that served as the focal point for this humble ceremony. Then he ignited a stick of palo santo, a beautifully scented Andean wood used to consecrate ritual space, wafting its smoke over everything.*

Through the curling, aromatic smoke and candlelight, my senses already awash in stimulation, I examined the mesa more closely. An open-jawed obsidian jaguar head gleamed with reflected flame. Owls with faces looking in four directions stood guard. Bottles of Agua de Florida (a distinctive perfume used across Latin America), stacks of palo santo, coca leaves, tobacco, and other sacred plants were delicately situated amid crystals and other objects that remained a mystery to me. Noticing my desire to anthropologically analyze this rapidly unfolding ritual, I realized that the most appropriate thing to do at this moment was to quietly surrender and simply witness Martín open this ceremonial doorway—a doorway that the four of us would soon be stepping through.

My awareness began to settle on one last thing amid the haze and scents. Two wide eyes, curving fangs, and a catlike nose emerged from a slab of green stone, staring straight at me from the middle of the altar: an ominous greeting from the deity of Chavín, who some say still lives in this valley. My heart started to pound as I felt its wild gaze fix upon me, hinting at some eerie, ancient power that I sensed I would be meeting soon enough. The immensity of what I had bargained for slowly began to sink in.

After a few moments of silence, Martín began to pray.

The Sacred and the Profane

Mircea Eliade, preeminent scholar of comparative religion, wrote extensively on the sacred and profane dimensions of human culture. According to Eliade, sacred space and time do not come into being as a result of following a religious formula or burning a certain amount of sage. The sacred can't be *willed* into being. It only reveals itself through *hierophany*, or sacred rupture, "the manifestation of something of a wholly different order, a reality that does not belong to our world" (Eliade, 1957, p. 11).

The word *profane* comes from the Latin *pro fanum*, meaning "outside the temple," clearly directing our awareness to the relationship between sacredness and the space it occupies. Sacred space and time involves an inherent element of crossing thresholds—of entering, occupying, and then leaving this reified space. In the world of psychotherapy, we often call this the container: an intentional, ritualized space where people can safely bare their souls. Jung wrote about the *temenos*, a Greek word meaning an enclosure within a temple, or a ritual vessel that holds something sacred, which he used as a metaphor for therapy. Within sacred space there is an inherent element of containment, boundaries, and protection.

While Eliade described at length what constitutes sacred space and time, citing many examples across human cultures, his assessment of the modern world's relationship to the sacred is perhaps the most striking: "It should be said at once that the completely profane world, the wholly desacralized cosmos, is a recent discovery in the history of the human spirit" (1957, p. 13). Historically and culturally speaking, the modern West's understanding of space and time, especially concerning the sacred (or lack thereof), is the exception, not the rule.

However, according to Eliade, there has always been, and always will be, an innate desire that wells up in the psyche to seek out "the sacred," even if our buttoned-down egos fail to understand it as such. Eliade says, "To whatever degree he may have desacralized the world, the man who has made his choice in favor of a profane life never succeeds in completely doing away with religious behavior. . . . Even the most desacralized existence still preserves traces of a religious valorization of the world" (1957, p. 23).

Perhaps most important for our current era's crisis of mental health, Eliade claimed that when people begin to live in an entirely "desacralized cosmos . . . there is no longer any world, there are only fragments of a shattered universe, an amorphous mass consisting of an infinite number of more or less neutral places in which man moves, governed and driven by the obligations of an existence incorporated into an industrial society" (1957, pp. 23–24). Such a world now seems all too familiar. I feel myself within it when I'm drifting through fluorescent grocery stores, observing a colorful selection of "festive" produce that comes from monoculture farms located a continent away. The Halloween pumpkin before me reveals itself as a hollow symbol, an emotional illusion meant to conjure the idea that through purchasing this, I will somehow become spiritually reconnected to my place and my time, thereby realigning to larger cosmic cycles of growth and decay that were the function of seasonal festivals in many animistic, earth-based cultures. The pulse of solstices and harmony of equinoxes is all eclipsed by the mechanistic grind of consumerism, the "amorphous mass" of terminally neutral space and time of the "desacralized cosmos."

But it's not the pumpkin that we want. It's the feeling of being reconnected to something eternal. Often, when people seek psychedelic medicines or ceremonies, what they really seek is a return to that ritualized, mythic lens of perception that we know in the ancestral canyons of our bloodstream. Deep down, the medicine we actually need is to return to something that our souls might recognize as "home." At the soul level, human beings need to feel connected to sacred time and space.

Creating sacred space and time is an act of mythopoetic orientation. Mythically speaking, humans have used rituals and ceremonies to evoke the original creation myths of the tribe or people in the *time before time*, thereby reestablishing the link between the mythic past and the eternal present. Stepping into this space was and is an act of psychic revitalization that feeds the souls of individuals and the culture itself. Sacred space, therefore, speaks directly to the roots of Western culture that long to drink from the waters of mythic and communal ritual.

Finding Mythic Ground

The first step in this process of mythopoetic orientation involves turning toward our inner mythic ground and examining where we are coming from. On the most immediate level, your current mythic ground might be a fresh heartbreak, a traumatic past, or a fork in the road of your life. Personally, my mythic ground increasingly orients around facing grief related to the tattered state of my culture (if we can call it that). Along with this comes a prayer for loving, healthy relationships, clean food and water, family, deep remembrance, ancestral reconnection, and cultural healing. Becoming intimately familiar with the contours and chasms of your own mythic landscape is the first step in orienting toward anything that might be considered "sacred" for most modern Western people.

One's mythic ground is not entirely internal and psychological, either. Many Indigenous cultures have preserved, in the face of immense violence, elements of their own mythic landscape that they encode into the literal landscape around them. Australian Aboriginal peoples have their own complex mythological system of *songlines* that connect their totemic and tribal identities to particular "Dreamings" that live within sacred places tied to the land itself. A water hole, when seen through the lens of a Dreaming, is no longer a small desert pool but a wellspring of spiritual power and identity that might be the literal birthplace of an Aboriginal person's soul, and the soul of their clan.

Before entering sacred space and time, one must first orient to one's own mythic ground. This can be as literal, psychological, or spiritual as you want, but make no mistake: approaching psychedelic medicines from a disoriented place will only result in further disorientation down the line. (We will return to this issue in the "Skills" section at the end of this chapter.)

⚒ ⚒ ⚒

I raised the cup to my lips and gulped down the murky green liquid as fast as I could.

The tendrils of its vegetal scent wind their way into my nose, filling my brain with a sensation both earthly and alien, like rancid aloe vera with a mean aftertaste that makes my skin crawl. After a few minutes of smoke-filled silence, Martín blows out the candles. It's time to go.

Emerging back into the light, we return to the temple grounds. The machine gun–wielding guards step unquestioningly out of our way as Martín guides us through the gated entrance. We walk to the river at the far end of the site, sit down in a grove of eucalyptus trees, and watch the current roll by. This is the same river that the ancient citizens of Chavín redirected to flow beneath the temple, creating a cacophonous growling sound that would reverberate throughout their mescaline-infused skulls: the roar of the jaguar.

After an hour or so, the medicine's accelerating hum begins to saturate my body. I feel a sickening saliva fill my mouth as my heart rate increases. I know what's coming. Awkwardly lurching toward a tree several feet away, I feel myself get kicked in the stomach as a frothy green liquid erupts out of my mouth. *Huachuma* is not a purgative like ayahuasca, but as with many other psychedelic plant medicines, its effects can become so powerful that the body simply recoils in terror. After enough silence, Martín graciously offers me another dose poured into a thin plastic cup, which I begrudgingly accept. This time the medicine lands gently in my stomach, already awash in bitter cactus-juice.

Soon, time begins to have more in common with the crystalline flow of the river than with the angular numerals on my watch, swirling and drifting until I lose track of it entirely. Gentle trees and old-growth *huachuma* cacti perched upon the opposite bank waft back and forth with a languid knowing, blissfully waving their verdant appendages in my direction. Slowly, the natural world begins to wink and nod like I've just been let in on some cosmic secret, confirming something that my rational mind can still barely articulate. It is a slippery sort of knowing, more of a feeling than a thought, and intimately connected to the place I find myself in. I sit and ponder this until time itself slips through my awareness. But now it's time to get up and slowly make our way toward the temple itself.

Chavín de Huantar is no Machu Picchu. There are no grand vistas celebrating the glory of the once-mighty Inca, no New Age theories of Lemurian quartz temples or UFO portals. No hordes of shutter-snapping tourists queuing and jostling for the exact same picture. Chavín is not Instagrammable, and I hope it always remains that way.

And yet, in writing these words, perhaps I am spelling the same doom for this town that Wasson spelled for Huautla de Jiménez decades ago. In the ten years since I visited Chavín, I was shocked to learn from a cactus-cultivator friend that a magnificent cathedral-like stand of old growth *huachuma* I visited was reduced to a meager stump, a casualty of overharvesting and psychedelic tourism. Despite my best efforts, here I am, a privileged gringo who arrived unannounced in a small mountain pueblo, searching for some shamanic secret that I imagined would be provided by an Indigenous person whom I had only just met. The irony is not lost on me in the slightest.

And yet, this birthplace of Andean cosmology and civilization still sits quietly in its mountain valley, biding its time. There are no theatrics here, but three thousand years ago it was the beating heart of a powerful shamanic culture that spanned some of the world's highest mountains, resonating out a primordial call from its secluded den that reached from the Pacific Ocean to the Amazon. In every regard, this temple is oriented not toward the flight of spirit, but the descent of soul. What Chavín lacks in grandeur, it makes up for in depth.

And descend I shall—but first I must climb. As I walk up the steps at the entrance to the temple, Martín points out the serpents carved into the green stones beneath my feet. For the people of Chavín and their cultural descendants such as the Inca, the serpent symbolized the underworld, which all signs indicate I will soon be entering.

Just beneath the temple exist layers of labyrinthine chambers and passageways that are still revealing their secrets. Human remains have been found in the lower levels of the temple, along with a plethora of animal bones and ritual artifacts, including a trove of ornately carved conch shell trumpets, or *pututus*. The innermost levels of Chavín's labyrinth are still being excavated, shedding literal light on just how old—and just how important—this temple truly is to the global legacy of psychedelic plant medicine (Valdez, 2022).

At the top of the steps I reach a ceremonial platform—a flat, elevated surface not quite on top of the temple, but inset into its stones, surrounded by three walls. To my left and my right are two small passageways that open into sheer darkness. Silently, with a stern look on his increasingly condor-like face, Martín gestures toward the door on the left. A chill washes over me as I think, *Am I actually going down there?* No directions. No instructions. Just an ominous portal into the abyss. Heart pounding and head aswirl with mescalinated perception, I bow my head, take a breath, and enter.

Invoking Sacred Space

In the many permutations of New Age or neoshamanic spirituality I've encountered, there is a pervasive desire to invoke the sacred. Most of the time, this fails miserably. Awkwardly forcing participants to hold hands, fumbling out some vaguely Indigenous chant, and wafting aromatic smoke up the nostrils of unwitting participants is all designed to approximate some amorphous notion of what "sacred space" might look like to a culture that thoroughly lost sight of it millenia ago. Sure, we might play along, desperate in our hunger for a life more infused with meaning; but deep down, we know that something is painfully absent.

Creating a sacred or intentional space is crucial to effecting meaningful and transformative psychedelic healing. Most existing literature on psychedelic healing describes this principle as *set and setting,* a term popularized by Timothy Leary that is now a foundational concept in psychedelic therapy. *Set* corresponds to one's inner mindset, their psychological and emotional situation at the time, while *setting* applies to the physical surroundings where the experience will take place: the people, the location, even the lighting and atmosphere of the room where one embarks on their journey.

Yet there is much more going on than these two words fully encapsulate, both in the deep psyche within participants and in the intersubjective space between participants and facilitators. Many of the people I've worked with as a psychedelic therapist have never experienced sacred or intentional space outside of a graduation or a church. To assume that we would all be sitting in lotus position chanting *om* by the end of the retreat would be a fantasy (although stranger things have occurred). But no matter their background, people can feel what it is to be in a safe, well-held, and intentional space, even if they don't consciously understand it.

Creating intentional space is an art that has everything to do with the presence of the person holding it and almost nothing to do with the bells and whistles that merely adorn it.

As I descend the stairs into the labyrinth, dimly lit by a feeble strand of lights bolted to the stone ceiling, I am struck by a flash of kaleidoscopic intensity, as if the *huachuma* coursing through my blood instantly recognizes this subterranean realm and surges to its full potential. At the bottom, I encounter an eerie crossroads: three more corridors leading deeper into the bowels of the temple, one left, one right, and one straight ahead up a flight of stairs. I choose (or rather *huachuma* chooses) to go up the central path, until I am traveling down a series of contorting passageways with no discernible pattern or logic. Right, right, left, right—corners give way to even more unsettling intersections and hallways as I become even more lost in this nether realm. Suddenly, I find myself in a small, dead-end chamber where I have no choice but to sit down and take a breath.

My mind is reeling from the disorientation of so many identical passages and turns. The pulse of *huachuma* feels as if it has been directing me this whole time. How far have I ventured into this spidery labyrinth? How do I even begin to get out? Such questions only enhance the sensation of being deep within this underground space. A thought occurs that this labyrinth is most likely designed for the dissolution of such answers. Instead of thinking about how to get out, the only option is to go even further within.

My eyes are closed. Minutes go by. Or hours. I'm not sure which. The energy of this space is palpably heavy, the weight of thousands of stones and years surrounding my vibrating body. Then I notice a perfect square hole in the stone wall, about a foot on each side. Upon peering into the eerie window I meet a void of utter darkness, a blackness that unfurls into even more unending blackness, a hall of dark-matter mirrors reflecting itself into an impenetrable infinity. The hairs on the back of my neck stand to attention as some rational part of my brain heads for the hills.

Nietzsche said that if you gaze into the abyss long enough, it will gaze back. This abyss, however, takes no time at all in staring right back into the core of my being. It dawns on me that while inside this temple, every possible avenue for sensory input from outside is ruthlessly shut down by the weight of its impenetrable containment. There is no sound, no wind, no connection whatsoever to the outside world. There is only a three-thousand-year-old silence that creeps its way slowly into my bones. Within the temple, all frames of reference dissolve until I am off the map entirely. This is not accidental.

Eyes still closed inside the chamber, I wonder how many generations of people have sat here before me. I imagine them fasting for days on end, deeply disoriented, their psyches utterly dissolved by a steady intake of *huachuma* and the DMT-containing *wilca* snuff. What ordeals and visions greeted the young initiates of Chavín as they steeped themselves within this fertile darkness?

Approaching the Numinous

When I entered the temple of Chavín, I came face to face with a force that Jung and others called the *numinous*. The numinous is an ineffable and all-encompassing power. It is not a thing, but a quality that certain objects, beings, or experiences possess (or seem to possess). Archetypes are numinous, along with anything that the psyche might register on a fundamental level as sacred or transcendent. Encounters with love, birth, and death are three reliable avenues toward numinosity that any person might experience.

Jung writes, "Numinosity . . . is wholly outside conscious volition, for it transports the subject into a state of rapture, which is a state of will-less surrender" (1959/1970, p. 186). In the face of the numinous, the ego surrenders (willingly or not) whatever scraps of power it so tightly clings to. A complete reorientation of the psyche occurs in presence of the numinous—a tectonic shift in priorities, understandings, values, and belief systems. (Some call this a "mystical" or "peak" experience, which we'll discuss more in chapter 8.)

Eliade described encounters with the numinous as "something 'wholly other' . . . something basically and totally different. It is like nothing human or cosmic; confronted with it, man senses his profound nothingness, feels that he is only a creature, or, in the words in which Abraham addressed the Lord, is 'but dust and ashes'" (1957, pp. 9–10).

While this all might sound nice on paper, encounters with numinosity can be shattering. They can leave us decimated by their power, initiated into some profound mystery we might spend decades trying to comprehend and integrate into our lives. Anytime the psyche confronts something numinous, the experience challenges the ego's grasp on reality and provokes a mythic reorientation on a fundamental level. This can also be terrifying, and so we must approach such experiences with caution.

There is a reason that frightening imagery of monsters and demons decorates temples and sacred places the world over. Gargoyles perch atop Gothic cathedrals. Fanged dragons flow down the steps of Thai Buddhist temples. Skull-belted deities dancing amid wrathful flames adorn Vajrayana monasteries. In every sacred tradition on earth, frightening images live right next to the sacred. And for good reason. This juxtaposition reminds us of the inherent duality of the universe, the darkness contained within the light (and vice versa), an interweaving that plays itself out inside the heart of every human being. Like the carved tenon heads that once encircled the temple of Chavín, these beings act as symbolic messengers to the psyche, serving as a warning that if you enter this space, you better be ready.

Fear is the correct response when approaching both the numinous and the psychedelic medicines that can reliably evoke it within us. When I'm working with someone approaching a psychedelic session, if I don't detect a trace of fear, a hint of anxiety, or at least some serious reverence, that's a sign that something might be off. There is little room for being cavalier with this work. Fear has its place. And yet, fear is not a problem to solve, but an experience to relate with. In every ceremony or psychedelic journey I have personally embarked upon, fear has always been present. For a good long moment before consuming the medicine, I tremble, and I pray to the old gods and the new that I make it out of this one alive. I remember this when sitting with clients who are utterly terrified. How much space can we make in our own lives for fear? I would say that only through facing fear ourselves can we adequately support people preparing to walk through their own valley of the shadow of death.

✳ ✳ ✳

Emerging from the labyrinth beneath Chavín, I surface into the light under a crisp blue sky. Words fail as I struggle to meet Martín's eye. I breathe in the clear mountain air, filling lungs that felt like they had just been a hundred feet below water. Martín only offers a silent gesture directing me toward the second passageway across the platform, another door leading into unknown blackness. I already know something about this temple, and I have a guess regarding what I am about to face next.

I descend the dark, narrow stairway as the second passageway makes a sudden ninety-degree turn to the left before opening into a long, tapering tunnel with a strange orange glow in the distance. As my eyes adjust to the darkness, I begin to discern a set of Otherworldly features gazing back at me, evoking an emotional cocktail of awe and terror that I have never felt before or since.

Placing one foot tentatively in front of the other, I make my way down the increasingly confined walkway, coming closer to the orange glow. Finally I face the towering presence residing at the inner sanctum of this temple: the Lanzón.

To describe the Lanzón by using empirical facts—like its imposing height of fifteen feet and its solid granite composition—fails to do justice to the actual reality of the being living at the heart of Chavín. A massive stone carved in the likeness of a fearsome earth-god, its presence alone was designed to be evocative and frightening. And it still is. Lit from below with gold and orange light as if by flame, its features become vividly amplified and emotionally jarring, aided by my altered psyche. As I gaze into its wide eyes peering down at me, taking in its gnashing fangs, serpentine hair, and intricate, swirling patterns, something within me becomes slowly eviscerated, and I am reduced to an awe-filled puddle of insignificance. Sitting at the foot of this ancient god, *huachuma* pulsating through my blood, I feel small, plainly confronted with my powerlessness against the wild forces of the cosmos and the natural world that emanate from this fiercely impartial, frighteningly wise, utterly primordial being. I feel an overwhelming truth begin to take root in my mind, a truth that Indigenous cultures like those from Chavín have always known, and something we are now painfully confronting in our modern era: Nature doesn't serve us. Doesn't even care about us. Nature doesn't need us at all. We, on the other hand, serve nature, humbly and on our knees, eyes wide open, as we are put in our place before numinous powers far greater than we could ever comprehend.

Skills

Finding Your Mythic Ground (Preparation)

In 2016, while working as a study-abroad guide, I spent a month visiting several Maori communities on the North and South Islands of New Zealand. While there, I learned about a Maori custom called a *pepeha* or *mihimihi*, in which a person introduces themselves by referencing the landscape of their home. By ritualistically invoking the mountains, rivers, and oceans where they come from, Maori people offer both a physical place to situate themselves in and a spiritual location that connects them to the larger mythic landscape of their island nation. For the Maori, as with many Indigenous cultures, the physical landscape of their homeland creates a mythic ground that is saturated with ancestral and spiritual meaning. For those of us not immersed in an intact Indigenous culture, we likely need to excavate many layers deeper, both inside and outside ourselves, to find this mythic ground of the soul. In doing so, we discover the deeper context of our lives and circumstances, the unique creation story of our family and upbringing, and the larger cultural narratives that inform additional layers of our identity. In preparing to venture into the numinous inner realm, we must ask ourselves, "Who am I, and where do I come from?"

Preparing for a psychedelic journey requires taking the time to ready one's psyche to submerge into a realm that does indeed belong to a "wholly different order." Outward preparation might take the form of creating certain boundaries around one's time and accessibility and limiting the omnipresent need to be productive. It might also involve changing certain habits, especially around the consumption of alcohol, certain foods, and forms of media.

Inwardly, preparation might look like allowing your unconscious psyche time to unfurl. Recording your dreams, journaling, making art, and other creative work can be powerful ways to access the unconscious. I find walks through the forest to be incredibly helpful.

Within this process, there must be intentional space for grief and pain. There must also be space for joy and hope. A foundational element of psychedelic healing involves being able to artfully navigate both of these mythic territories of the soul.

Opening and Creating Intentional Space

There are many ways to open the doorway to intentional or sacred space. One might lead a guided meditation, instigate a contemplative activity such as art or journaling, or offer a song, prayer or invocation. Many Indigenous traditions invoke the four or seven directions, use smoke from sacred plants to cleanse the space, or ritualistically smoke or offer tobacco. Opening intentional space can be elaborate or simple. What's important is that it is done with sincerity, mindfulness, and attention to the needs of the participants, the space, and the medicine itself. Often, less is more.

One of my favorite ways of invoking intentional space is to read a poem. I do this for two reasons. The first is to honor my elders from the mythopoetic tradition, poets and troubadours whose words grace many pages of this book. The second is because poetry opens the door to the inner world, which is also the world of the soul. To collectively enter or even glimpse this inner realm is an act of creating community. A group of people who peer into their own internal world together, who collectively touch or wonder about the nature of their souls, are cultivating community whether they know it or not.

Using Aromatic Smoke

Using the smoke of certain aromatic plants like sage, cedar, mugwort, or *palo santo*—smudging, as it's called by most North American Native peoples—can be a powerful way to invoke intentional or sacred space. Yet before we go any further, let's talk about some caution where smudging is concerned.

I never impose this practice on someone, and I do my best to discuss it with folks to see if it will actually benefit them or not. In many of the psychedelic-adjacent circles I've run in—festivals, yoga classes, kava bars, you name it—smudging is relatively commonplace. Perhaps you run in some of these circles yourself. Yet many of my clients were unfamiliar with this practice, and in some cases they were uncomfortable with it. Some people simply don't like smoke. While I personally adore smudging, I approach it with caution for several reasons.

Smudging is a cultural practice used by many Indigenous traditions across the world. When done poorly, smudging can easily become a cringe, mock-Indigenous performance. That said, there is archeological and historical evidence suggesting that burning aromatic plants was done across the ancient world, from Europe to Asia to Africa and beyond. No one owns this practice, though it is most often associated with Native American cultures. Working with aromatic plant smoke can be adapted to fit a particular bioregion, depending on which plants are local and abundant in that region. For instance, where I live in Oregon, cedar grows prolifically, while white sage does not.

Lastly, just because *you think you should* is not a good enough reason to smudge. Creating a contrived facade of "sacred space" might turn out to be worse than creating no space at all. Again, space is created by the presence of the one holding it, not all the fancy tools.

Creating a Safe Container

This topic is worthy of an entire book in itself. All protocols, rules, and agreements within a psychedelic healing container should be in the interest of establishing safety and peace of mind for participants and facilitators. Otherwise, you might be in for more of an ego trip, rather than the other kind.

Here are a few simple guidelines for establishing safety in psychedelic healing.

Informed Consent

All participants should be as informed as possible about what medicine they are taking, their dose, and where the medicine comes from. They should be informed about what to expect during the journey, how to ask for help if and when things get difficult, and the type of help they can expect to receive. Someone cannot truly give consent if they are already in an altered state of consciousness.

Touch

Many traditions and healing modalities use therapeutic touch. Boundaries around touch in psychedelic healing are more amorphous than in traditional psychotherapy; therefore, they require even more discussion and nuanced forms of consent. Especially when working with people who have a history of sexual abuse, it is crucial to discuss therapeutic touch in depth, well before anyone takes psychedelics.

I like to discuss with clients why therapeutic touch in psychedelic work can be effective, and to let them know that they will *always* have the ability to withdraw that consent. Before touching anyone who is in a psychedelic state, I take every measure necessary to ascertain their level of genuine consent. One does not need to look very hard to discover a shadowy vault of abuse that well-trained and formerly highly regarded practitioners have committed within psychedelic spaces.

I always defer to the acronym WAIT (Why Am I Touching/Talking?) and take a moment to check in with myself and my own energy before touching or even approaching someone who is in a psychedelic state.

Group Agreements and Protocols

Psychedelics can often inspire people to play out younger, rebellious, or unintegrated parts of their psyche or to dissolve all constructs of acceptable social norms altogether. This isn't inherently bad, and it can actually result in a powerful healing process when artfully held. Yet this can also pose a problem if a person is at risk of compromising their own safety or the safety of others. Here are two simple group protocols I use that can help minimize the potential for this:

▼ **Respect the space of others.** Do not speak to, touch, or disturb other participants until the session is complete and there is mutual agreement regarding interaction.

▼ **Stay in the circle.** This applies whether you're in an actual circle or simply a predefined space or property. You don't want someone wandering off into an old-growth forest on eight grams of mushrooms during a thunderstorm.

Agreements and protocols in psychedelic spaces are vital to establishing trust and safety between participants and practitioners. Basic agreements around group-discussion formats are also essential to holding emotionally safe integration circles.

The Way of Council, developed by Jack Zimmerman and Gigi Coyle (2009), is a simple method of group discussion that I have employed for years. It abides by four easy guidelines, which you can adapt as you see fit to facilitate open, powerful sharing within groups:

▼ Listen from the Heart (Openness)

▼ Speak from the Heart (Authenticity)

▼ Be Lean of Speech (Brevity)

▼ Speak from the Moment (Spontaneity)

Lastly, I add confidentiality to this list. What happens inside sacred space stays there. This simple framework of group agreements and integration circle etiquette has given me a solid foundation for doing group psychedelic work, which continues to be some of the most rewarding work I have ever done.

Nondogmatic Approach

No psychedelic facilitator worth their salt will dictate the meaning of someone else's experience. It is one thing to offer perspectives informed by your training or tradition. It is another thing entirely to tell someone what their experience means and what they should or should not do with their lives. Beware the "guru complex." (We'll speak more about leadership in chapter 7.)

Suggestibility

A client once told me a story about his experience at a posh, well-known ayahuasca retreat in Costa Rica. After two ceremonies, a "facilitator" brought him into a room and sat him down with a staff member who pitched him on a $14,000 "stem cell treatment package." These "facilitators" turned out to be more like salespeople designed to enroll participants into their several-thousand-dollar coaching program. He described the manipulative tactics these people used on his already fragile psyche, trying to subtly shame him for not "showing up for his healing," all the while preying on him while he was in an incredibly vulnerable state.

Not only are these sorts of practices highly unethical; they are also morally bankrupt, manipulative, and straight-up shadowy. These tactics play on the heightened suggestibility and openness that psychedelics can evoke in people, and they have no place in ethical psychedelic work. I've had people offer me thousands of dollars in investment funding after I helped facilitate a psychedelic retreat that changed their life. But because of their highly suggestible state, it felt unethical to even entertain such an offer. I am also extremely cautious about offering advice or guidance that might severely destabilize the lives of the people I work with.

Marginality and Diversity

Another topic worthy of an entire book; indeed, several have been written on this very subject, such as *Psychedelic Justice: Toward a Diverse and Equitable Psychedelic Culture* and *Queering Psychedelics: From Oppression to Liberation in Psychedelic Medicine*. I have seen firsthand the immense potential for healing that can occur when a safe, intentional space is made for people specifically from marginalized backgrounds.

Psychedelics do not reside in a compartmentalized realm conveniently separate from people's identities and collective histories. The basic cornerstones of creating safety for all people involve making space for this fact; being able to comfortably presence differences; examining one's own biases; and most basic, yet most important, of all, listening—and all of this is especially true for those from marginalized communities. Lastly, make space for all of this, but do not lose sight of the *person* before you.

Confidentiality

Confidentiality is a basic component of psychotherapy, a principle that bears repeating here. Who you work with, the content of their experiences, and whatever occurs during the work itself should be held in confidence. While there are nuances to this, as there are in traditional therapy, the reason for this confidentiality is to create a greater layer of safety and protection for everyone involved.

Closing Intentional Space and Ending Well

The door flap opens as steam-soaked prayers swirl out into an expansive sky. A frog croaks in the Amazonian night as a *curandero* lights a solitary candle. Ceremonial embers flicker as bleary-eyed people shuffle out of a tipi into the cold morning air. Gratitude is given, praises spoken, the spirits gently sent back to their homes nestled somewhere between stone and stars. People embrace and smile. Some cry.

Just like stories, ceremonies possess three parts: opening, middle, and close. Closing intentional space is just as important as any other aspect of the experience. A clear ending, however it may look, helps signify to the psyche (and the spirits) that we are no longer in the presence of the numinous, that we are emerging from whatever Other-worldly realm we may have entered, and that we have survived the encounter.

This ending might unfold through the sharing of simple foods, lighting a candle, playing soft or celebratory music, and generally creating a space for minds and bodies to relax. The Native American Church has the beautiful tradition of not only bringing into the tipi the consecrated foods of corn, buffalo, and berries after the sun rises, but of also throwing a larger feast later that day that the whole community is invited to join. There is an element of communal celebration and nourishment here, showing a way to build genuine culture around healing.

I've also been in ceremonies where things didn't end well. Instead, they just lingered on until wilting into an ambiguous, gaping space that people had to climb their own way out of. I left feeling raw and adrift, and it took me about a week to fully feel grounded again. The existential psychotherapist Irvin Yalom once said, "Never take away anything if you have nothing better to offer" (2012, p. 165). Decimating someone's ego only to let them crawl back to solid ground is not healing. Shattering the psyche does no good if you cannot provide the support necessary to aid in its reconstitution into wholeness. Offering no avenues of meaning-making for someone whose world just turned inside out is not only care-less; it is dangerous, opening the door for even more confusion and a potential retraumatization.

A psychedelic journey that does not "end well" can still hold the promise of greater healing down the line, assuming that people can receive enough integration and support. But sometimes we are simply a frayed rope by the end of things. In these cases, assuming that the session or ceremony actually unfolded in a safe and well-held container, we must trust that something in the psyche needs to let itself unravel and dissolve, and that both the psyche's inner healing intelligence and the medicine itself are moving us, step by step, toward something important that, in time, will make sense. Just because we didn't get what we wanted doesn't mean it wasn't what we needed—a lesson I've sat with many times myself.

✳ ✳ ✳

To this day, Chavín de Huantar remains a mystery within a mystery. Failing to mention the site's other enigmatic features—the way its unique construction amplifies sound to echo from inside the temple out into the ceremonial courtyard; the ornate conch shell trumpets and subterranean waterways that conjured vibrations we can only dream of; the use of the powerful DMT-containing wilca snuff; the masterful Raimondi Stela, a stone carving depicting one of the oldest versions of Wiracocha, the pan-Andean "staff god," wielding two brilliant *huachuma* cacti—would do a disservice to the full magnitude of this profound, ancient place.

It is unlikely that Steven Spielberg knew the significance of this site when he placed one of Chavín's iconic tenon heads in the opening scene of *Raiders of the Lost Ark*, but something about it clearly caught his attention. The parallels are not lost on me either: yet another white American in a long line of explorers and thieves seeking some secret contained within that vast continent to the south.

Yet unlike Indiana Jones, wielding a whip and a gun to secure his golden treasure, I bow my head to the inexplicable powers I found within the walls of Chavín, respect and reverence my only prize as I emerge back into the light, humbly shaken, breathlessly changed, surrendering to the great gods that dwell within.

III

The Underworld

Shadow, Grief, and the Descent to Soul

Mankind owns four things
That are no good at sea:
Rudder, anchor, oars,
And the fear of going down.

—ANTONIO MACHADO

Inanna's Descent to the Underworld

The Sumerian myth of Inanna is the oldest written story of an underworld journey we have glimpsed through the tattered veil of time. Deciphered from a collection of ancient cuneiform tablets found in modern-day Iraq (named after Inanna's sacred city, Uruk) and finally translated in its entirety by Samuel Noah Kramer in 1944, it is one of the most recent myths to reemerge into our collective psyche. Widely studied in Jungian circles as a gateway to understanding the archetypal feminine, we can also see Inanna's descent as a mythic guide for navigating the underworld journey that psychedelics inevitably invite us to surrender to.

The myth begins:

From the Great Above she opened her ear to the Great Below.
From the Great Above the goddess opened her ear to the Great Below.
From the Great Above Inanna opened her ear to the Great Below. . . .
Inanna abandoned heaven and earth to descend to the underworld.
She abandoned her office of holy priestess to descend to the underworld. . . .
She gathered together the seven me *[sacred powers].*
She took them into her hands.
With the me *in her possession, she prepared herself.*
(Wolkstein & Kramer, 1983, pp. 52–53)

Why would such a well-loved deity sacrifice so much adoration from her earthly domain? Why do any of us give up the comforts of the known to descend into the realm of the deep psyche, when we could stay blissfully on the surface?

Any turn inward always involves some kind of sacrifice. The roots of the word *sacrifice* come from the Latin *sacre* and *ficére,* meaning "to make sacred." We cannot approach the sacred without giving something up. In preparing to embark on a psychedelic journey, whether through changes in diet or behavior or simply by accepting the quiet humility that comes with sitting vulnerably in a circle of others, we too abandon our temples of comfort and ease.

Inanna is called down to the depths. Like a deer subtly shifting its attention toward a snapping branch, Inanna's "ear"—which, in ancient Sumerian, was the same word for "wisdom"—turns in the direction of the underworld. Something in her knows it's time. Nearly everyone I've worked with as a psychedelic therapist felt "called" in some way to venture into their inner depths; or else their life had become so untenable, their habits and relationships so unsustainable, that they were pushed there. As Jungian analyst James Hollis says, "Where we do not go willingly, sooner or later we will be dragged" (1996, p. 15).

Truly, why do any of us consciously choose to undertake an experience that may, by all accounts, be physically and emotionally exhausting, punctuated by nausea, or simply terrifying?

Within each of us exists an archetypal desire to know ourselves. Every person who approaches psychedelic medicine does so for their own unique reasons, but for the vast majority of people, those reasons can be distilled to some deep knowing that beckoned them toward the Great Below. For many I've worked with, their suffering became a persistent call that led them through the labyrinth of treatments the psychiatric establishment constantly hurls at its patients, with an arsenal of medications, electroconvulsive therapy, and transcranial magnetic stimulation being the most common methods today. Before that, it was lobotomies.

Instead of focusing on symptoms, psychedelics and depth psychology direct us toward the root causes of our suffering—roots we can often find only by trudging through the brackish waters of the soul. Like it or not, we cannot ignore this calling for long. When the ego can no longer hear the messages rising up from the soul, then we are firmly in the territory of despair, addiction, hopelessness, and for some, death.

The call to know oneself is a voice that begins as a whisper, but if left unheeded, it grows into a scream.

CASE STUDY: *Veronique*

(Note: In this case study and all others that follow, all clients' names have been changed.)

On the last retreat I led during my time working in Jamaica, a tiny owl of a French woman approached me the first night, just after our welcome dinner. "Just so you know," she smiled, "if this doesn't work, I'm going to kill myself."

Veronique was in her late sixties, and after she had led a full and colorful life as an opera singer and artist, she found herself swallowed by a vicious depression that left her physically and emotionally incapacitated. In fact, her sister, who was joining her in Jamaica, had to push her through the airport in a wheelchair to get her on the plane. Veronique had not sung opera, or done anything creative at all, in years.

During our sharing circles, Veronique could barely get through a sentence without breaking down in tears. Her heart had been broken by an unrequited love affair decades ago that she had never gotten over, and she had let most of her relationships fade away except for her sister. She had little hope of ever getting over the severe depression that had come to haunt her life.

On her first dose of psilocybin, Veronique just cried, wailing for hours, awash in her pain. Afterward, puffy-eyed and teary, she confided in me that she wasn't sure this was going to work out for her. She didn't know what the experience had done for her, and in fact she felt even more of her pain than before. I did my best to comfort her, and I shared about the hundreds of people I had seen transform through working with psychedelics. We also discussed how psilocybin can open the gates of the unconscious and that perhaps the only way out of her depression was to go *through* it, feeling the depths of her emotions more fully now than ever before. Despite her conviction of being hopelessly depressed, I didn't believe she was a lost cause, and I made sure she knew that. She felt even more exhausted than usual that night and couldn't even bring herself to eat.

On her second dose, Veronique began to wail once again as a tidal wave of sadness and pain welled up within her. I sat down next to her mat beneath the green leaves of a mango tree, silently witnessing her pain. After some time, she removed her eye mask and headphones, her tear-filled eyes blinking as my form came into focus. This time on a substantially larger dose of psilocybin, she sat up and stared into my eyes as hers flooded with tears. I could tell that most of her psyche was immersed in something vast, completely removed from normative consciousness.

I breathed deeply, and Veronique followed my lead. Some underground rhythm started pulsing through her body, rocking her as she breathed. I mirrored her movements and breath and continued looking into her eyes. "You're doing so great," I said. "Let it out."

Slowly, a different emotion crept across her face that I hadn't yet seen her express: rage. Eyes narrowing, this petite woman suddenly roared before me, letting out a hurricane of repressed anger that simmered beneath her otherwise delicate exterior. She was on fire, eyes aflame with some unspeakable anger, screaming into my face like a demon. All her years of suffering, all the years lost to depression, all her grief, surged from her diminutive frame in an unstoppable torrent. I felt her scream pass through me, releasing into the hot sun above.

Panting, exhausted, awash with incalculable emotions, Veronique collapsed and looked up at me with the faint trace of what could have been a smile. For the rest of that journey, she lay there, utterly still, at rest.

As the week progressed, I began to see more and more life pulse through Veronique. She became more animated in our conversation, lively, opinionated, intensely interested, and sassy. At one point I told her, "Veronique, this is not how a depressed person behaves." Her last psilocybin journey was again filled with tears, though notably more contained and private, less explosive and interpersonal. Tears of quiet grief. Making peace.

On the last day of our retreat in our final integration circle, Veronique did something that none of us expected, least of all her. "I haven't done this in years," she said, "but I want to offer this to you all. To say thank you." Taking a breath, she rose out of her chair, her small frame suddenly statuesque before us, and began to sing.

The Gates of Grief

Inanna prepared to enter the underworld by adorning herself with seven sacred powers, known as the *me* in ancient Sumerian: a sacred crown upon her head, a necklace of the finest lapis, a double strand of beads falling over her chest, a sacred breastplate of protection, a golden ring around her wrist, a lapis measuring rod held in her hand, and a royal robe wrapped around her luminous form.

Before entering the land of death, Inanna instructed her loyal priestess, Ninshubur, on what to do if she does not return after three days:

> *"Ninshubur, my constant support . . .*
> *Who gives me wise counsel,*
> *My warrior who fights by my side,*
> *I am descending to the* kur, *to the underworld.*
> *If I do not return,*
> *Set up a lament for me by the ruins.*
> *Beat the drum for me in the assembly places.*
> *Circle the houses of the gods.*
> *Tear at your eyes, at your mouth, at your thighs.*
> *Dress yourself in a single garment like a beggar."*
> (Wolkstein & Kramer, 1983, p. 53)

Inanna told Ninshubur, "Seek aid from Father Enlil. Seek aid from Father Nanna. If your pleas should at last come to naught, find Father Enki, God of Wisdom. He alone possesses the water of life and knows its secrets. He will know what to do."

Inanna approached the looming gates of the underworld. Before her, a black gate blocked her way. But she would not be deterred. Inanna pounded on the gate, demanding admission.

> *"Open the door, gatekeeper!*
> *Open the door, Neti!*
> *I alone would enter!"*
> (Wolkstein & Kramer, 1983, p. 55)

A dry voice slithered down the walls of the underworld, like coarse sand blowing in from the desert. Neti, gatekeeper of the underworld, rasped:

"Who are you?"
She answered:
"I am Inanna, Queen of Heaven,
On my way to the East."
Neti said:
"If you are truly Inanna, Queen of Heaven,
On your way to the East,
Why has your heart led you on the road
From which no traveler returns?"
Inanna, starry Queen of heaven, answered with full voice:
"Because . . . of my older sister, Erishkigal,
Her husband, Gugalanna, the Bull of Heaven, has died.
I have come to witness the funeral rites.
Let the beer of his funeral rites be poured into the cup.
Let it be done."
    (Wolkstein & Kramer, 1983, p. 55)

Like so many of us, Inanna finds her way to the doors of the underworld by way of grief. Yet many causes and methods besides grief can compel such a journey. As Sylvia Brinton Perera, Jungian analyst and author of *Descent to the Goddess: A Way of Initiation for Women*, said: "All descents provide entry into different levels of consciousness and can enhance life creatively. All of them imply suffering. All of them can serve as initiations. Meditation and dreaming and active imagination are modes of descent. So too are depressions, anxiety attacks, and experiences with hallucinogenic drugs" (1981, p. 50).

Psychedelics can often catalyze ecstatic experiences that lift us into expansive heights and reveal spiritual insights. These revitalizing and deeply necessary experiences can conjure the renewing energies of childlike play and joy. Such moments are blessings, and we should count ourselves lucky when they occur. I've known some people who seem to always have a fantastic time on psychedelics, basking in universal one-ness and love without a care in the world. If only we could all be so fortunate. There's nothing wrong with this. But Inanna takes us on an entirely different sort of journey. (We will revisit the ecstatic side of the psychedelic experience later, in chapter 8.)

For many, myself included, psychedelic journeys most often take the form of ritualized opportunities to descend into the dark, unknown, or fearful places within us that the psyche recognizes as connected to the archetypal underworld. Countless myths tell us that there is an initia-tory potency or power we can only find in descent and darkness. Deep within we can encounter a chthonic fertility that modern Western cul-ture has manically organized itself around *not* feeling, not relating to, and not knowing, no matter the cost. We will do almost anything to avoid going, or even glancing, *down there*. Yet inevitably, at some point in our lives, the call to the Great Below perks our ear.

Depth psychology teaches us that like the elements of fire and air, the spirit moves up and out. The soul, however, moves down and in, bringing us into the waters of the unconscious and the terrain of the hungry earth. Soul orients us toward darkness, grief, body, shadow, and death. Culturally speaking, the West has had two thousand years of *up* and *out*, fixing our gaze toward the transcendent stars or a heavenly savior, all the while neglecting the divine being right beneath our feet.

Psychedelics help shake us out of the trance states we might routinely find ourselves in, opening the doorway to face painful emotions, memo-ries, or thought forms that we've been dragging along with us, sometimes for years. I've seen people have full-fledged conversations with departed loved ones, forgive their deceased parents, and mourn the loss of relation-ships that ended decades ago. I've seen rough-skinned, two-hundred-pound Australian police officers grieve their abusive childhoods and watched war veterans cry their first tears since coming home.

Beneath these layers of personal grief exists even deeper strata of collective suffering. Ancestral traumas like slavery, the Holocaust, forced relocation, and other forms of genocide may well emerge through the psychedelic experience. The planetary ecocide occurring daily throughout the world evokes a layer of collective grief that is almost impossible to feel in our daily lives without being crushed by its weight. Centuries of oppression and subjugation of women, and the poison of racism, still churn just beneath the surface of seemingly advanced and "progressive" communities.

In the fields of psychology and psychedelics there currently exists a fixation on "day world" solutions: superficial advances that purport to be oriented toward "healing" but that ignore the collective wounds of the soul. The clinical obsession with measuring incremental increases in "mental health" and "symptom reduction," while turning a blind eye toward systemic health and cultural repair, is one example. When we start to see psychedelics as "medications" rather than "medicines," we can be certain that we've forgotten the soul.

Ketamine clinics shoot people full of this powerful disassociative, only to boot them back into their lives with no integration or support. In New Age circles there is an extreme emphasis on *ascension* and *downloads*, which can become a merry-go-round of escapism that continually allows participants to bypass the difficult work that can only happen in the archetypal underworld. Pharmaceutical companies seeking to remove the "trip" from psychedelic medicines—confining them to the sterilizing world of clinical quantification and bureaucratic domestication through their overregulation and control—attempt to master the underworld by synthesizing it to death.

Yet myth teaches us that such strategies never work out as planned because the underworld plays by its own rules.

James Hillman wrote, "Our civilization, with its heroic monuments, tributes to victory over death, ennobles the Herculean ego, who does not know how to behave in the underworld" (1979, p. 110). To enter into the underworld requires a different approach from what serves us up above. Inanna, Osiris, Persephone, Eshu, Hermes, Coyote, Maui, Quetzalcoatl, and other gods and goddesses of underworld descent show us how it's done.

"So it matters very much the way we descend," says Hillman (1979, p. 112). "Ulysses and Aeneas . . . go down to *learn* from the underworld which re-visions their life in the upper world. Hercules, however, goes down to *take*, and he continues with the muscular reactions of the upper world, *testing* each phantom for its reality." We cannot fight and win in this domain, according to the myth. When we enter this realm, we must surrender to some things we might never understand and are ultimately defeated by. "The villain in the underworld is the heroic ego, not Hades," Hillman reminds us (p. 113).

To work with psychedelics at a time like this is strange. Yet I can't help but feel like these earthbound medicines are returning to the world stage at the precise moment when they are needed most, when the gates of the underworld seem to be bursting open all around us. The word *pandemonium*, intimately linked to the word *pandemic*, can be translated as "many demons loosed upon the world." Is it any wonder that these death-eating, soul-revealing substances are reemerging onto the world stage at this precise time in history? Tell me: from where do demons come?

The Bull of Heaven

Gugalanna, the Bull of Heaven, husband to Inanna's sister Erishkigal, the queen of the underworld, was slain by no less than Gilgamesh himself, conquering hero of Sumerian legend. The Epic of Gilgamesh, considered the oldest written myth in recorded history, is intimately linked with Inanna (in some tales, Gilgamesh and Inanna are even siblings). In the epic, Gilgamesh spurns Inanna's sexual and marital advances. As a consequence, Inanna sets loose the Bull of Heaven, a massive beast that threatened to destroy Uruk—the city ruled by Gilgamesh, yet curiously dedicated to Inanna. The first of his heroic exploits is to kill the Bull of Heaven, disobeying the will of the gods, thereby setting himself apart from all other mortals and the gods themselves.

Gilgamesh's victory over the Bull of Heaven echoes another tale of sacrificial bulls: the Greek myth of Theseus and the Minotaur. This story unfolds on the island of Crete, birthplace of the Minoan culture, a proto-Greek civilization widely regarded as the last European matriarchy before its invasion by the Mycenaean warriors from mainland Greece who came to dominate much of the northern Mediterranean.

The Minoans also venerated the sacred bull, their art depicting festivals where people jumped over their curved backs, and featuring women wearing ornate clothing we would now consider revealing. The bull's crescent-shaped horns represent the ever-changing aspect of the moon, the cycles of nature, and the archetypal feminine. The killing of the sacred bull in both Greek and Sumerian mythology could be seen, according to many scholars, as a mythologized depiction of the diminishment of matriarchal culture, speaking to a pivotal moment that changed the West, and therefore the world, forever (Eisler, 1988; Graves, 1960).

In the not-so-distant past, American hunters were paid a government bounty to shoot from trains at the herds of buffalo they passed on freshly laid railroad tracks dissecting the Great Plains. In photos of this time, buffalo skulls, stacked up by the hundreds, tower above a few proud men who appear as children in the shadow of their genocidal trophy. The sacrifice of bulls, it seems, is not something exclusive to the mythic past, but continues frighteningly into the present. Today, every giant old-growth tree that falls to earth, every animal that fades into the abyss of extinction, is a Bull of Heaven sacrificed at the altar of the conquering hero.

The Seven Gates

When we left her, Inanna was standing at the gates of the underworld, demanding that its guardian, Neti, allow her entrance.

With yellow eyes and rotting skin, Neti gurgled, "Well then. Stay here, Inanna. I will speak with my queen. I will tell her all you have said."

Neti slinked through the cold palace of death, through dusty passageways and haunting chambers, all the way to the desolate throne of Queen Erishkigal.

"My queen, there is a girl outside your gates. She says she is your sister, Inanna. She banged on your gates. She shouted at your walls, demanding admittance to your queendom of death.

Erishkigal, languishing on her throne of bones, smiled wryly in the flickering torchlight. Like a lioness licking her chops before a kill, she bit her lip in vicious anticipation.

"Neti, my sweet, listen here.
Bolt the seven gates to the underworld.
Then, one by one, open each gate a crack.
Let Inanna enter.
As she enters, remove her royal garments.
Let the holy priestess of heaven enter bowed low."
    (Wolkstein & Kramer, 1983, p. 57)

Neti returned to the gate. The cold scrape of stone rumbled out beneath Inanna's feet as the first gate of the underworld cracked open before her. Ghoulish whispers filled her ears. Invisible hands caressed her gilded body, beckoning her into the darkness before her. As she stepped over the threshold, Inanna felt her crown blown off by a ghostly wind.

"What is this?" she demanded.
"Quiet, Inanna, the ways of the underworld are perfect.
They must not be questioned."
    (Wolkstein & Kramer, 1983, pp. 57–58)

Once more, the rumbling of stone. And once more, Inanna felt the icy breath of the underworld wrap itself around her. As she entered the second gate, her lapis necklace dropped bead by bead from her neck, the blue stones shattering on the floor.

"What is this?" she demanded again.
Neti replied, "Quiet, Inanna, the ways of the underworld are perfect.
They must not be questioned."
    (Wolkstein & Kramer, 1983, p. 58)

As she entered the third gate, Inanna's sacred breastplate dissolved, drifting away like desert sand as she felt herself even more exposed to the yawning void.

76

"What is this?" she said.
"Quiet, Inanna, the ways of the underworld are perfect.
They must not be questioned."
    (Wolkstein & Kramer, 1983, p. 58)

On this went, seven times, each gate requiring that one of Inanna's sacred adornments be removed. Finally, Inanna entered the underworld: bowed, stripped, and naked.

Seven gates barred Inanna's entrance to the underworld. Seven layers of her earthly identity had to be shed as she passed through each successive threshold. Seven temples the goddess abandoned before she began her journey. There are countless layers of symbolism here, most of which still lie with the Sumerians in their ancient tombs.

The number seven, which occurs throughout this myth and in myths across the world, is often imbued with mystical meaning. In the language of the Akkadians, who shared many cultural elements with their southern neighbors the Sumerians, the number seven literally translates as "wholeness" (Wolkstein & Kramer, 1983, p. 158). We can conceive of these seven gates in any way we like. Myths are good like that. The chakra system from the yogic traditions also contains seven "wheels" that correspond to different areas of our body, symbolizing different energetic qualities. This is but one way of thinking about the seven gates. Regardless of how we interpret the number, the fact remains: everything we have accumulated or gained in the upper world becomes ashes when we walk through these gates.

Inanna's disrobing is a ritual of release. Learning how to let go, and helping others feel safe enough to do the same, is one of the most important elements in psychedelic healing and facilitation. In the underworld, Inanna is progressively stripped of her seven sacred adornments— vestiges of her upper-world identity. Similarly, working with psychedelics can require us to be "stripped" of our familiar comforts and stories.

Neti instructs Inanna not to question the rites of her descent. Her complete surrender is required if she is to enter the underworld. No more clinging to adornments, outward adoration, prestige, wealth, notoriety, and comfort. There is a certain logic here, or even a natural law. Perera writes that Inanna's passage through the gates "suggests a need to be utterly exposed, undefended, open to having one's soul be searched by the eye of death, the dark eye of the Self.... This, the myth tells us, is part of the law of the underworld: those who descend must disrobe" (1981, pp. 59–60).

The Shadow Sister

Inanna staggered through the ghostly halls of the *kur*, arms clutched tightly to her chest. With each step the rough stones scraped away her skin until a trail of blood marked her footsteps. Entering a vast chamber, Inanna finally made her way to Erishkigal's inner sanctum. Piles of bones adorned her hall. The torch flames felt cold.

> *Naked and bowed low, Inanna entered the throne room.*
> *Erishkigal rose from her throne.*
> *Inanna started toward the throne.*
> *The Annuna, the judges of the underworld, surrounded her.*
> *They passed judgment against her.*
> *Then Erishkigal fastened on Inanna the eye of death.*
> *She spoke against her the word of wrath.*
> *She uttered against her the cry of guilt.*
> *She struck her.*
> *Inanna was turned into a corpse,*
> *A piece of rotting meat,*
> *And was hung from a hook on the wall.*
>   (Wolkstein & Kramer, 1983, p. 60)

Finally, Inanna is stripped bare, revealed in her naked vulnerability to the dark queen below. Erishkigal is Inanna's shadow sister, her dark twin, her terrifying opposite. She embodies what Jung would call Inanna's shadow. In beholding Erishkigal, Inanna beholds the unknown parts of herself.

Erishkigal was once a primordial grain goddess called Ninlil, wife to the great sky god Enlil. But Enlil violated and raped Ninlil repeatedly.

As punishment, the gods sent Enlil to the underworld. Yet Ninlil followed him, and in the darkness she slowly became the one known as Erishkigal, "the Lady of the Great Below." Trauma is infused into Erishkigal's story, a theme we will revisit in chapter 5.

Inanna and Erishkigal represent—and perhaps first established—a reflective pattern represented by other goddess pairs throughout world mythologies. "Athena and Medusa; heavenly Aphrodite and Uranian Aphrodite, the eldest of the fates; Mother Kali and devouring Kali-Durga; the light and dark side of the moon" are all embodiments of this natural dynamic, according to Perera (1981, p. 44). Persephone and Demeter, Greek goddesses of descent and fertility, are also mythic representations of the same primordial duality, the same dance of birth and death, growth and decay, shining light and deepest darkness.

Facing Erishkigal is the epitome of facing one's shadow. We've already heard Jung's definition of the shadow in chapter 1. Jungian analyst June Singer further described the shadow as a "splinter personality . . . [that contains] all of those uncivilized desires and emotions that are incompatible with social standards" (1994, p. 165). The shadow is where the psyche places all that we repress, all that does not conform to our ego's idea of who we are and can be, which Jung called the *persona*.

Confronting one's shadow is no easy task. According to Jung this endeavor presents "a moral problem that challenges the whole ego-personality, for no one can become conscious of the shadow without considerable moral effort. To become conscious of it involves recognizing the dark aspects of the personality as present and real. This act is the essential condition for self-knowledge, and therefore, as a rule, meets with considerable resistance" (1959/2014, p. 8).

The shadow is a place, not a thing. It is morally ambiguous, even though it may be filled with morally reprehensible things. It is simply the part of ourselves that we cannot see, that we have chosen to deny or repress for the sake of social cohesion, familial expectation, and outward acceptance. It is the dark side of the persona's moon. All of us have a shadow. Believing that you are the exception to this rule is perhaps the darkest shadow of all.

Psychedelics present us countless opportunities to meaningfully engage with the shadow. Any time we create space for our deepest and most vulnerable selves, any time that we open ourselves to an encounter with soul, we make space for the shadow to present itself. As an "essential condition for self-knowledge," according to Jung, shadow work is something that all human beings must engage in at one point or another if they wish to live an examined and soulful life. Otherwise we are merely strengthening the ego.

Especially when money, sex, and power are involved, we can be sure that the shadow lurks nearby. In her book *The Ethics of Caring* (2017), author Kylea Taylor identifies these three domains as primary "centers" of vulnerability for those of us in the helping professions. This is because these three areas often hold the highest concentration of our shadow material and are therefore more subject to our unconscious. We don't have to think hard to recall situations where money, sex, or power led to the downfall of some teacher or leader previously held in high esteem.

This is difficult territory. Genuine shadow work is not something fit for social media. It doesn't happen in a yoga studio. There is nothing pretty or glamorous about it. And despite the renewed popularity of the term in recent years, "shadow work" is the last thing any reasonable person would ever want to engage in. Only when we are caught in Erishkigal's piercing gaze after descending to our most vulnerable depths can we have any chance of truly meeting the shadow.

When we feel the "eye of death" upon us, we are both perceiving and being perceived by an immense force that emanates from the natural world and transcends the human psyche. "Like the eyes in the skulls around the house of the Russian nature goddess and witch, Baba Yaga," writes Perera, "they perceive with an objectivity like that of nature itself and our dreams, boring into the soul to find the naked truth, to see reality beneath all its myriad forms and the illusions and defenses it displays" (1981, p. 32).

Erishkigal's gaze confronts us with ourselves. Looking deeper, we come face to face with the inevitability of death, the fragility of life, and the preciousness of the fleeting moment as we feel our animal bodies pulsate with this delicate breath of life. We know, or our souls know, that someday we too will join in this great dance, dissolving back into the earth as the forest floor consumes the decaying body of a fox. One day, we too must surrender to the perfection of the underworld.

The Inner Judge

Moments before Inanna confronts Erishkigal, she is swarmed by the seven Anunna (or Anunnaki), terrifying beings that render their harsh judgment of Inanna, condemning her to death. They embody the archetypal image of the underworld judge present in many world mythologies. One example is the jackal-headed Egyptian god Anubis, both the guide of departed souls and their judge, who weighs the heart of the deceased against a feather from Ma'at, the winged goddess of truth. Only if one had "lived in truth," so to speak, were they allowed entrance into the afterlife. For just beside Anubis lurks the monster Ammut, patiently waiting to devour the souls of those who betrayed their own inner knowing.

One of my favorite stories of underworld judgment comes from an Abenaki legend from the northeastern United States. The Abenaki say that when you die, you will come to a bridge, and on that bridge you will meet all the dogs you knew in life. If you were kind to them, they will greet you as a friend and walk across with you. But if you were cruel to them in life, then you will never cross that bridge.

The Anunna are not kind to Inanna. They shout at her, shame her, and heap guilt upon her. Have we not parts of ourselves that do the same? While facilitating psychedelic journeys, I've often heard people shame themselves for "doing it wrong" or self-flagellate for their past mistakes or poor choices. Usually, we are our own worst judge. The Anunna embody all of these self-loathing voices that can pour into one's awareness during a psychedelic descent to soul.

Another common moment when the inner judge might take control is when people are returning to normative consciousness. When the effects of the medicine begin to wear off, these self-critical voices rush back into the fray, establishing their dominance. This type of backlash can be common with people who are suffering from extreme depression, anxiety, or posttraumatic stress disorder (PTSD), as these "underworld judges" are the ones whose voices scream the loudest. When we are plagued by a constant stream of negative self-talk, poor self-esteem, shame, or disgust, we can be sure that the Anunna are in control, not us.

Living under the Anunna's regime becomes a "living hell." Psychologically, such voices are called *symptoms,* which mainstream psychology cast as enemies to conquer. Yet depth psychology teaches us that symptoms, and the suffering they cause, actually point us in the direction of the soul.

Initiation and the Hook

Three days and three nights passed as Inanna hung on the hook, turning into a corpse. Slowly, as decay and rot begin consuming her, Inanna seemed to merge with Erishkigal, thus stepping fully into her queendom of death. Archetypally speaking, we are now in the realm of initiation, the liminal space where one thing becomes another, realities converge and intertwine, and the logic of "both-and" surpasses that of "either-or."

Initiation is an archetypal framework we find in many coming-of-age rituals practiced throughout the world by nearly every Indigenous or earth-based culture we know of. Yet at some point in history, the Western world lost (or more likely destroyed) these rites. In fact, Mircea Eliade described this conspicuous lack of initiation as a foundational aspect of modernity: "It has often been said that one of the characteristics of the modern world is the disappearance of any meaningful rites of initiation. Modern man's originality, his newness in comparison with traditional societies, lies precisely in his determination to regard himself as a purely historical being, in his wish to live in a basically desacralized cosmos" (1995, p. 17). By doing away with initiatory rites, according to Eliade, modern Western culture also did away with a framework that reliably provided access to the realm of the sacred and therefore the soul.

Academically speaking, initiation consists of three major phases: separating from the known world; immersion into *liminal* space, often culminating in some ordeal, trial, or wound; and returning to the community, recognized as a changed being.

Initiation presents us with five distinct qualities, which we will revisit in the "Qualities of Initiation" section at the end of the chapter.

Pleas to the Patriarchy

After three days and three nights of hanging on the hook, Inanna's loyal servant Ninshubur followed the goddess's instructions precisely. She lamented for her in the abandoned temples. She beat the drum for her in the sanctuaries. She cut her own eyes and slashed her own body and face. She clothed herself in dirty garments. Then she set out to the house of the gods, seeking their aid.

First Ninshubur pleaded with Father Enlil:

"O Father Enlil, do not let your daughter
Be put to death in the underworld.
Do not let your bright silver
Be covered with the dust of the underworld.
Do not let your precious lapis
Be broken into stone for the stoneworker.
Do not let your fragrant boxwood
Be cut into wood for the woodworker.
Do not let the holy priestess of heaven
Be put to death in the underworld."
    (Wolkstein & Kramer, 1983, p. 61)

Enlil's voice thundered in reply:

"Inanna craved the Great Below.
She who received the me of the underworld does not return.
She who goes to the Dark City stays there."
  (Wolkstein & Kramer, 1983, p. 61)

Father Enlil would not help.

If there are any heroics present in this myth, Ninshubur exhibits them most of all. Inanna's priestess embodies the warrior in all of us willing to fight tooth and nail to make it through the darkness of the underworld. She is the part of us that picks ourselves up after the hardest night of our life, determined that we see the light of day. In psychedelic healing, Ninshubur represents the part of us still able to maintain some distant tether to upperworld consciousness, the part that still knows our zip code while reality disintegrates. "Psychologically," Perera says, "she seems to embody that small part of us that stays above the ground while the soul descends" (1981, p. 44).

This is an interesting moment in the story, as we see these powerful male gods turn away from their kin in her deepest moment of need. Enlil, Inanna's grandfather, is a sky god, an old, wrathful deity known to have caused the great flood that wiped out entire civilizations as told in the Old Testament, the Epic of Gilgamesh, and many world mythologies. Enlil is like the Judean Yahweh or the Greek Zeus: bearded, muscular, and angry. He probably doesn't care about your feelings.

The medicine of the expansive sky, of wind and thunder, and of far-seeing visions that bring our gaze up and out simply won't do in the land of the dead. Enlil is the archetypal patriarch, the masculine sky king who illuminates with lightning clarity, piercing through the darkness. He is powerful, to be sure. Yet that sort of power doesn't work in the underworld. After all, how much power does a sky god really have underground?

Next, Ninshubur visited Father Nanna, the moon god, who would seem the obvious candidate to support Inanna. Yet Nanna refused as well, parroting the words of Enlil.

A deeper look into the power of Nanna reveals that he too lacks the gifts that could aid Inanna. As a moon god, Nanna is more related to the archetypal feminine, the ebb and flow of the tides, and earth's slow rotation through the cosmos. Nanna's power also relates directly to the human intellect, specifically to time, numbers, counting, and calculated knowledge, which the Sumerians and other ancient civilizations spent immense amounts of time perfecting.

But Inanna has traveled to the realm of the soul, which is symbolically connected to the deep earth. While the moon is intimately linked to the earth, it still resides in the sky. If we examine the moon and her cycles through an overtly intellectual lens, compulsively counting and predicting the peaks and valleys of her fullness, always optimizing and aiming to maximize our yield, we are attempting to fit the untamed wilds of the soul into a prison cell built of the mind.

The current fixation on pushing psychedelics into the overly clinical and material-reductionistic framework of the medical model is yet another example of attempting to cram nature into a box. In the underworld, linear time does not exist. In my experience quantitative methodologies of healing ultimately don't work with psychedelics. Research offers a necessary lens to prove the efficacy of these medicines after centuries of stigma. But it doesn't paint a complete picture. Clinging to what we *know*, to the ego's understanding of who we are and how things are, is the antithesis of the underworld journey. We might as well stay home.

Frequently in my work as a psychedelic therapist I've found myself explaining to people why controlling every element of the journey or documenting each new realization in a sleek app might not really be in their best interest. It's reasonable to want to know what one is in for before taking the plunge. But for many people who identify as "type-A" (a curiously prolific personality in the modern West), the last thing they need is more technology, more incessant quantifying, more controlled objectivity. There are no apps for the underworld.

There's a reason that so many Indigenous traditions rely on the most basic elements of life in their ceremonies: fire, water, earth, and air. The soul understands these things and the messages they carry. Even if the intellect is left grasping at straws, something in the body or spirit is cleansed or renewed. We cannot *science* our way through a descent to soul.

At last, Ninshubur visited Enki, Inanna's uncle, god of plants of the flowing waters of life. One last time, Ninshubur made her impassioned plea. Father Enki answered with a voice like a roaring river:

> *"What has happened?*
> *What has my daughter done?*
> *Inanna! Queen of All the Lands! Holy Priestess of Heaven!*
> *What has happened?*
> *I am troubled. I am grieved."*
>   (Wolkstein & Kramer, 1983, p. 63)

Then Enki scraped out some dirt from beneath his fingernails and created two strange creatures: the *kurgarra* and the *galatur*, androgynous, infernal beings he would send to Inanna's aid. To the *kurgarra* he gave the food of life; to the *galatur*, the water of life.

Finally, Ninshubur's pleas are answered. Enki is a male fertility god who implicitly understands the ebb and flow of life and death. The ancient Sumerians occupied the heart of what is now called the Fertile Crescent, that swath of land set perfectly between the Tigris and Euphrates Rivers. Much like the ancient Egyptians, the Sumerians were utterly dependent on the seasonal floods of these rivers, which they personified in the god Enki. Unlike the wrathful Enlil or the impersonal, calculating Nanna, Enki's power tangibly benefits the preservation of life and culture through the moist nourishment that allows grain and other life-giving plants to grow. Of the three gods whom Ninshubur confronts, Enki's power is closest to the earth, closest to the muddy, pedestrian matters of human life. Closest to the underworld itself.

Enki is also associated with mischief, knowledge, crafting, and culture, and is connected to the Greek god Hermes, or Mercury, the guide of souls, whose tricks we will encounter more of in chapter 6.

Feeding the Demons

To his creations, Enki gave the following instructions:

"Go to the underworld, enter the door like flies.
Ereshkigal, the queen of the underworld, is moaning
With the cries of a woman about to give birth.
No linen is spread over her body.
Her breasts are uncovered.
Her hair swirls about her head like leeks.
When she cries, 'Oh! Oh! My inside!'
Cry also, 'Oh! Oh! Your inside!'
When she cries, 'Oh! Oh! My outside!'
Cry also, 'Oh! Oh! Your outside!'
The queen will be pleased.
She will offer you a gift.
Ask her only for the corpse that hangs from the hook on the wall.
One of you will sprinkle the food of life on it.
The other will sprinkle the water of life.
Inanna will arise."
  (Wolkstein & Kramer, 1983, p. 64)

Enki knows something about the Great Below and its grieving Queen. Unlike most hero myths, where the masculine savior vanquishes the monster through a test of domination, the myth of Inanna reveals an alternative and essentially feminine way of facing the darkest parts of the psyche.

Enki's instructions to "enter the door like flies" offers another lesson in underworld etiquette: approach the gates slowly, and with humility. Something I've occasionally experienced with people working with psychedelics is a desire to push their limits until the liminal gates are blasted off the hinges. At best, the results are disorienting and difficult to integrate. At worst, they are terrifying and traumatic. This is the heroic ego banging on the gates of the Great Below, seeking to conquer the underworld rather than relate to it, as Hillman discussed above.

When Enki's creatures enter the underworld, Erishkigal, terrifying as she may be, is utterly vulnerable. She is lying like "a woman about to give birth": "Ereshkigal, the dark side of Inanna, went into labor and needed to be reborn. It was this labor or 'call' that Inanna had heard from the Great Above" (Wolkstein & Kramer, 1983, p. 160). From a mythopoetic perspective, we could say that the depression or grief that draws us down into the underworld is calling to us because some part of us needs to die and be reborn as well.

If this was a hero story, this vulnerable moment would be the time to vanquish the monster once and for all. But it's not. Instead, Enki advises something that is miraculously unexpected: he instructs his creatures to *comfort* Ereshkigal. They mirror back and validate all the pain she feels in an act of mythic therapy. When confronting our own dark other, and when accompanying others as they do the same, we have much to learn from the gentleness and compassion exemplified by Enki's creations.

The Tibetan Buddhist practice called *feeding your demons*, traditionally known as *chöd*, consists of facing one's suffering, or "demons," and integrating them into full consciousness. Developed in the eleventh century by a rare female Tibetan tantric master named Machig Labdron, *chöd*—popularized by Lama Tsultrim Allione in her book *Feeding your Demons: Ancient Wisdom for Resolving Inner Conflict* (2008)—is described as "cutting through" the illusions of ego by imaginatively dismembering the self.

The essence of the practice consists of making contact with our inner "demons," personifying them, and asking what they want until we are finally able to understand and ultimately satiate their longings. Similar to elements of Internal Family Systems and Gestalt therapy, as well as shamanic traditions from around the world, the practice of feeding your demons shows us that when we approach the darkest parts of our psyche with care, we may come to see them as misunderstood elements of ourselves—exiled deities that have been long neglected and cast into the shadow, our personal underworld.

When confronting our inner demons, the ancient words of Machig Labdrön offer a guiding light as we traverse this winding, sometimes treacherous, but always rewarding path:

With a loving mind, cherish more than a child
The hostile gods and demons of apparent existence,
And tenderly surround yourself with them.
    (Rotterdam, 2021)

The creatures did exactly as Enki instructed. Ereshkigal stopped and looked at them. We can only imagine the surprise on her face.
    She asked:

"Who are you,
Moaning-groaning-sighing with me?
If you are gods, I will bless you.
If you are mortals, I will give you a gift.
I will give you the water-gift, the river in its fullness."

The *kurgarra* and *galatur* answered:

"We do not wish it."
    (Wolkstein & Kramer, 1983, p. 66)

On this went, as the queen of the underworld offered Enki's creatures gifts of eternal life and wealth. They refused, until Ereshkigal gave them Inanna's lifeless corpse.

The kurgarra sprinkled the food of life on the corpse.
The galatur sprinkled the water of life on the corpse.
Inanna arose.
    (Wolkstein & Kramer, 1983, p. 67)

Chthonic Knowing

Perera says, "Often when the moment of return comes, you do not even know it. We may simply feel befuddled and dizzy like an infant, new before life" (1981, p. 78). As Inanna moved upward, toward the glimmering light above, she felt cold hands wrap themselves around her again. The Anunna swarmed her once more, holding her down in the depths, whispering frigid judgements in her ear as she ascended toward the distant brightness:

"No one ascends from the underworld unmarked.
If Inanna wishes to return from the underworld,
She must provide someone in her place."
　　(Wolkstein & Kramer, 1983, p. 68)

This was the bargain.

The seven gates of the underworld groaned open once more. As Inanna made her way back to the light, an entourage of demons, or *galla*, encircled her from all sides, accompanying the queen of heaven into the world above.

The galla were demons who know no food, who know no drink,
Who eat no offerings, who drink no libations,
Who accept no gifts.
They enjoy no lovemaking.
They have no sweet children to kiss.
They tear the wife from the husband's arms,
They tear the child from the father's knees,
They steal the bride from her marriage home.
　　(Wolkstein & Kramer, 1983, p. 68)

At last, Inanna emerged out of the underworld depths—but the laws of the underworld are clear: you can't get something for nothing. There is always some form of exchange when dealing with powers greater than ourselves.

Mircea Eliade says a core activity of shamans is bargaining with the spirits of the upper or lower worlds to support the well-being of the human community. As ecstatic intermediaries, shamans understand the dynamic cycles of give and take that constantly require negotiation between the human world of culture and the natural world of spirits. This is the oldest—and perhaps the only—reason for descending to the underworld: to serve the life of those above.

Bargaining is also considered one of the five stages of grief, according to psychiatrist and grief-work pioneer Elisabeth Kübler-Ross (2014). As anyone who has faced serious loss will know, there comes a time when you find yourself attempting to make a deal with the unseen forces that have orchestrated the unthinkable. These imagined bargains, spoken to the darkness, to the silent trees, to howling of the wind, are ultimately addressed to the underworld. When we find ourselves brooding over these doomed bargains late into the night, we too are like Inanna, opening our ears to the Great Below, pleading with Ereshkigal herself.

Just as Inanna was about to make her glorious ascent, the Anunna, the underworld judges, rushed back onto the scene, issuing their demand for a replacement. Psychologically, the Anunna might embody patterns of self-sabotage, trauma cycles, and shame that often keep people from enacting positive changes in their life. They are the whirlpool of self-destruction. These forces require something to take their place if they are ever going to change.

Finally, Inanna emerges from the underworld, flanked by demons. The word *galla* is connected to our word *ghoul*, which comes from the Arabic *ghul* or *ghala*, which means "to seize." They hold onto things, grasping them with their ghostly hands. Sometimes what is seized is a person's innocence, naivety, or aspects of their persona or story that are no longer true. When she ascends, Inanna is no longer a virginal goddess but a fierce queen who has faced her shadow, returning with a newfound power. Some encounters with the underworld take away pieces of ourselves that we will never recover. "No one ascends from the underworld unmarked." This is the second part of the bargain: once we've set even a single foot in the underworld, some part of us must remain there.

After a stint in the Great Below, there are things that trail behind us like moonlit shadows. When someone says they "have demons," they are referring to the parts of themselves that are connected to the underworld. In the right container or culture, we can transform these demons into sources of power, or *medicine*, as many Native American traditions say. Like a war veteran who has endured his or her own form of underworld initiation, these demons leave people forever changed. Sometimes their weight can be crushing, turning into PTSD and various forms of addiction. Initiation shares many borders with trauma and can contain elements that the psyche can interpret as traumatic. Yet when held in the right context, demons that might otherwise haunt our dreams can turn into sources of profound strength.

The lessons of the underworld stay with us long after we emerge. It is the look in the eye of someone who has *been there* and *seen things*. It is the way someone carries themselves, an invisible gravity that gives a solidity to their being. It is a clarity of voice and tone that does not mince words or speak lightly. This type of chthonic knowing cannot be bought.

"Chthonic," meaning from beneath the earth, within the earth, also refers to the underworld. The word itself beckons us to get our shit together. This is not the forgiving Earth Mother Gaia, providing us yet another delightful meal to eat at the harvest celebration. No, this is the earth that eats you. And even though the chthonic underworld is the land of the dead, it is very much alive.

Like anyone undergoing a harrowing psychedelic journey, dealing with death and loss, or contemplating their own mortality, Inanna might come out alive, but she won't come out the same.

As soon as she emerged from the underworld gates, Inanna's loyal servant Ninshubur threw herself at her feet, weeping. Ninshubur was covered in dust and wearing filthy rags, signifying her mourning for the goddess. Inanna knew that Ninshubur had done everything asked of her and had performed all of the necessary rites of grief.

The next part of our story follows as one would expect: Inanna reclaimed all of her earthly domains that she abandoned at the beginning. Everywhere the goddess traveled, she observed her subjects mourning her death.

That is, until she arrived home. Her husband, Dumuzi, god of shepherds and livestock, lounged on Inanna's throne, beautifully dressed in the finest garments. As his teeth plucked one last grape dangling from the hand of a servant girl, we can only imagine the expression on his face as he saw Inanna return.

Inanna fastened on Dumuzi the eye of death.
She spoke against him the word of wrath.
She uttered against him the cry of guilt:
"Take him! Take Dumuzi away!"
   (Wolkstein & Kramer, 1983, p. 71)

The demons seized Dumuzi then and there, kicked over his churns of milk, and tore away his shepherd's flute. The party was over. Inanna, furious with rage, ordered the demons to take her husband back down to the Great Below.

After experiencing the queendom of death, Inanna now embodies those frightening qualities of her dark sister Ereshkigal. From a Jungian perspective, we could say that she has successfully integrated her shadow aspects by way of her descent. On another level, we could simply say that she no longer has time for Dumuzi's bullshit. The people I've known who have spent the most time in the underworld—veterans, divorcees, artists, and true healers—share this quality. And yet Dumuzi is Inanna's mirror, her lover and consort. It makes sense that he too must learn to face his own darkness.

Perera links Dumuzi to the "dying shepherd king, a prefiguration of Abel and Christ" (1981, p. 81). Western culture has kept many threads to Dumuzi through other masculine gods that die and are reborn. What makes the myth of Inanna so unique is that both the feminine and the masculine must descend to the underworld. Both must face their inner darkness, and both must transform if life is to go on. Apparently the Sumerians knew a thing or two about couples therapy as well.

But Dumuzi flees, appealing to the sun god Utu to protect him. Utu turns Dumuzi into a snake so that he might slither out of the hands of the terrifying *galla*. Then the texts recount Dumuzi's "dream," a long saga of his attempted escape that culminates in Dumuzi begging his sister, Geshtinanna, to accompany him into the underworld and share his burden. Geshtinanna, whom we can see as a Persephone-like fertility goddess, agrees. Sadly, the two never meet again.

> *Inanna and Geshtinanna went to the edges of the steppe.*
> *They found Dumuzi weeping.*
> *Inanna took Dumuzi by the hand and said:*
> *"You will go to the underworld*
> *Half the year.*
> *Your sister, since she has asked,*
> *Will go the other half.*
> *On the day you are called,*
> *That day you will be taken.*
> *On the day Geshtinanna is called,*
> *That day you will be set free."*
>   (Wolkstein & Kramer, 1983, p. 89)

Geshtinanna, whose name means "vine of heaven," embodies "the force of the autumn-harvested grape and of its spring-fermented wine, just as Dumuzi personifies spring-harvested grain and its fermented beer" (Perera, 1981, p. 90). Perera says, "Every new crop of the vine must descend for fermentation into the underworld and come up transformed as the fruit also of underworld transformation. . . . Forerunner of Dionysus [Greek god of wine and ecstasy], Gesthinanna points us towards a new kind of individuation ego: one that celebrates and acquiesces in the transformation process of life and death; one that embodies an ever-changing balance between transpersonal and personal; one that dares to encounter the shadows in the underworld and to return to life" (1981, p. 93).

Finally, the myth concludes:

> *Inanna placed Dumuzi in the hands of the eternal.*
> *Holy Ereshkigal! Great is your renown!*
> *Holy Erishkigal! Sweet is your praise!*
>   (Wolkstein & Kramer, 1983, p. 89)

I once heard a Native American Church ceremonialist, or "road man," joke, "Why do we eat peyote? For the berries in the morning." And he wasn't lying. Despite all evidence to the contrary, there is an undeniable sweetness that can await us on the other side of the descent, if we can make it all the way out.

Every time we humbly accept a cup of blackest ayahuasca, the "vine of the soul" in the Quechua language, something in the dregs of our psyche bows to the power of Ereshkigal. Mushrooms literally feed on death and help compost the parts of our psyches that so badly need to be returned to the earth. Ergot, the fungal source of LSD, also abides by this mycelial cycle of life via decay. Dimethyltryptamine, or DMT, famously known as the "spirit molecule," is said to surge through the brains of every human being at the time of birth and death (Strassman, 2000).

The notion that psychedelics place our psyches in direct conversation with the underworld is a hard pill to swallow. But for those who have tasted the wine of the underworld and emerged into the light of day, there is often a newfound sweetness to life that before was inaccessible or invisible. Loss has a way of lifting the veil of our consciousness so that life's true preciousness becomes a gift within the ashes. The closer death comes to our doorstep, literally and metaphorically, the more our soul requires us to orient toward the eternal. Psychedelics can escort us, either gently or briskly, to the underworld's gates. How we choose to walk through the threshold, however, is ultimately up to us.

Qualities of Initiation

There are no skills for navigating the underworld. The very notion that there might be a set of tools to "hack" this transformative realm is an expression of the ego's desire to control it. Like Hillman said above, that's Hercules behavior, and it simply doesn't work down there. So I won't pretend to offer anything of the sort. But in some myths, the heroine or hero who ventures into the Great Below is given a few pieces of wisdom, maybe a magical item or two, that might aid them in their journey. The underworld is a place of initiation and change. Sometimes we arrive there without even knowing it. Below are five qualities of the underworld, emotional or phenomenological signposts that might help you gain your footing, should you find yourself wandering Erishkigal's halls. May they help you chart the depths.

Paradox

Did Inanna know what she was in for when she knocked on the underworld's gates? Do any of us truly know what we are in for when we imbibe a psychedelic or enter an altered state? I think not. And yet, something within us compels us to make the journey.

The underworld is a place where nothing makes sense, where reality is turned on its head, and where we are confronted with seemingly impossible things. If you've ever found yourself in the midst of an intense psychedelic experience, wondering if you're ever going to make it out, and contemplating the possibility of a life of hopeless insanity, then congratulations: you've touched the initiatory realm.

Paradox is a quality of initiation because it locates us in the liminal space between opposites. Becoming acquainted with liminality helps us become more accustomed to sitting in paradox and embracing the inexplicable complexities of human existence. As we do so, we cultivate emotional and psychological flexibility and resilience. Only by going down to the underworld is Inanna able to ascend into her fully realized form as the queen of heaven.

Death

The underworld is the realm of the dead. Initiation cannot occur without the death of something. From an anthropological perspective, initiation serves as the death of the dependent, naive child-self, and the birth of the responsible, mature adult, capable of being a reliable member of their community. But something has to die in order for something else to be born.

To embrace a soulful and mythopoetic approach to psychedelic healing means to embrace its connection to the realm of death. Like a vision fast or any other initiatory endeavor, psychedelic work can be seen as a death practice, meaning that we are confronted with not only the inevitability of physical death, but an experience that the psyche interprets as deathlike. It's well known that someone may become convinced that they're dying as a psychedelic surges into their bloodstream. At such a time, something deep within the psyche recognizes that it is about to enter the archetypal underworld. There is an esoteric truth contained within this myth, and all myths of descent and rebirth: that only through letting ourselves (or a part of ourselves) die can we experience new life.

Catharsis and Suffering

Inanna hanging on the hook is the apex of her descent, the crux of her initiation, her ecstatic undoing. While catharsis isn't a gauge of how valuable or meaningful a psychedelic experience is, it can often be the pivotal moment in someone's healing process.

From the Greek *katharos*, meaning to purify or purge, catharsis is an experience that can be necessary to move through to thoroughly process an emotion or aspect of suffering. With ayahuasca and other plant medicines, purging or vomiting can be a cathartic moment that can feel like a literal cleansing, as the purge itself carries away lingering psychospiritual residue that is no longer welcome in our bodies. Tears, tremors, and all manner of bodily processes can be avenues of catharsis in psychedelic space. We'll come back to that in the next chapter.

Inanna on the hook is an image of profound, cathartic surrender. In kink and BDSM communities—a subcultural underworld that exists in after-hours clubs and dimly lit "dungeons"—people engage in all manner of ritualized restraint and often pain aimed at inducing a state of transcendent catharsis through submission. Shibari, the Japanese art of rope bondage, often culminates with the submitting party being strung up and hung in midair, suspended by the very ropes that intricately constrict their bodies. In the world of extreme body modification, people suspend themselves from hooks that pierce their backs. These are modern expressions of practices that date back thousands of years, all the way from ancient India to the *okipah* ceremony of the Mandan tribe, where young warriors were suspended from the longhouse rafters until they fell (Marshall, 2012). Similarly, Christ hanging on the cross is the apex moment in Christianity. Something that the ego might normally abhor, the soul, when in the underworld, adores.

Because Inanna is the goddess of fertility, creation, and death, her descent feeds not just the human community, but the earth itself. Perera links Inanna as a feminine precursor to Christ and Odin, two other hanging gods, yet she also notes their differences: "Not for humankind's sins did Inanna sacrifice herself, but for earth's need for life and renewal. She is concerned more with life than with good and evil. Nonetheless, her descent and return provide a model for our own psychological-spiritual journeys" (1981, p. 21).

Within many myths and religions, ritualized suspension can be seen as an apex moment deserving of the highest ceremony. Odin hung on Yggdrasil, the world tree, for nine days and nights in order to gain the wisdom of the runes and of all existence. The Lakota people still practice a form of ritual suspension in the Sun Dance ceremony, where men insert hooks into their chest that connect to the ceremonial tree arbor at the center of the dance ground. For four days they dance without food and water, and finally they pull against the tree until their flesh is ripped free, blood splattering onto the bone-dry earth. Another Sun Dance rite requires some men to drag buffalo skulls across the ground, attached to them through hooks inserted into their backs, when they are carrying the burden of others. Even the Jewish practice of *tefillin*—ritually binding one's arm and head during prayer—could perhaps recall these more intensive expressions of ritualized restraint.

Transformation

The underworld is a transformative space we're meant to move through, but not to stay in. When we're constantly going from from one ceremony to the next, consuming peak experience after peak experience, we actually limit the possibility of real transformation. There is a necessary ripening and crystallization that allow transformation to become real and manifest in everyday life. In the psychedelic context, this is the role of integration.

Yet it is possible to get stuck in the cycle of initiation, never quite making it out, forever magnetized back into the liminal underworld. Houselessness, a widespread crisis across the United States and other modern nations, is a reminder of the underworld all around us. Although a mythopoetic lens cannot provide a universal explanation for this extremely complex issue, this perspective does ask us to consider the possibility that many living on the streets may actually be stuck in an initiatory cycle, unable to reach the final phase of completion and return. Addiction itself is a liminal cycle wherein one can never fully realize the fruits of initiatory experiences.

Experiences like addiction or getting stuck in an initiatory cycle are known as *liminoid* rather than liminal, characterized by an inability to progress beyond the cathartic moment. Instead of ritualistically visiting the underworld and then emerging as a transformed being, the liminoid experience leaves us forever uprooted, forever nowhere, forever oriented toward the Great Below. This is the definition of a "living hell."

Once again, the importance of integration in psychedelic work cannot be overstated. If a facilitator is unable or unwilling to hold someone on the other side of an initiatory journey, to walk with them all the way through the liminal realm, and to catch them on the other side, then they are themselves unprepared, and perhaps require more time down in the darkness.

The Earth That Eats You

In the modern West, we are allergic to grief. Most of us immersed in this culture attempt to fight off the underworld with a heroic zeal that usually results in even greater suffering. Our aversion to grief and loss seems to only create more of it. A person's grief can motivate their own destruction. The grief of entire nations and peoples can be displaced onto marginalized communities they seek to dominate, onto the global

South through unchecked extraction, and onto the planet through ecological destruction. All of it a cycle of unprocessed grief.

So I wonder: how would our culture be different if we made a place at our table for this ghostly visitor? If only we could enlist some part of ourselves to venture closer toward the River Styx, going against our stronger impulses. What dockside tales from the Great Beyond might Charon, the boatman, share with us if we kindly offer him a drink to warm his bones against the cold?

We are living through a time of collective trauma. The word *trauma* has a long pedigree, starting with Greek and Latin and going all the way back to the Proto-Indo-European word *tere*, which means to twist, rub, pierce, or grind. All these words suggest space being created within or through something. *Tere* implies some kind of opening, much like a wound—the literal, medical definition of trauma. The questions then arise: What exactly is being opened, and where does the wound lead?

By now, you may well have guessed the answer.

The king of the underworld in Greek mythology was Hades, shadow brother to Zeus. A far cry from the Christian image of Satan, Hades was known as a gracious host for the dead. It was said that once in his kingdom, no soul ever wanted to leave because they couldn't part with his intelligence and generosity.

Perhaps we are long past due to get acquainted with this old god, regardless of whichever cultural mask they wear around the world. Perhaps we owe these underworld deities a debt that long ago modern culture convinced itself it doesn't have to pay, despite the unprecedented amount of death now occurring across the planet—human and otherwise.

The ancient ones knew that each of us owes a debt to life. They knew that a person or a society who denies this debt denies life itself. Is it any wonder that Hades was also known as "the wealthy one"? Now he is sitting at our table. We've had our banquet, our centuries of plundering fruit and grain from his cornucopia. He will try his best to remind us politely, first with a tap on the shoulder, then a tragic loss, then a new extinction, then a global pandemic. But the fact remains: it is time to pay up.

Just how one begins to account for this debt is an inquiry that can span a lifetime. Many Indigenous cultures place profound emphasis on giving back to the earth and offering hard-won praises for simply being kept alive. If, in the words of Martín Prechtel, grief is praise, then perhaps what the underworld wants most of all is the salt from our tears and the songs of our praises sung during our brief time on this glistening planet.

Whatever area of your life has been reduced to rubble holds immeasurable value. I don't blame you for not believing me. But I'd wager that if you lie down there next to the fire and sleep in a bed of ashes for a while, you will discover something precious. Sacred, even.

There's one last thing: whatever gold you find down there in the underworld, you must give it away.

Life does not expand by keeping gifts to oneself, even if you received them during intensely private moments of loss. Hoarding the gift and locking away your suffering is dragon behavior, and we all know how that ends. The gift lies in the giving, not in the thing itself. Someone, somewhere, desperately needs the very thing that was wrought from your unique journey of suffering. The treasure we pick up in our bleary-eyed scrounging around in the dust of the underworld has in it something our souls sorely need. Something the living world needs.

So give away the gold. Even if you give it to the mountain winds, to the churning oceans, to the sleeping soil, to the hungry fire, don't for a minute fool yourself into believing that you gave it to no one. For even more burdensome than grief is our obligation to transform it into something imbued with so much life, so much praise, so much gold, that the echoes of its hallowed sound can be heard by those listening, far below.

IV

The Serpent

Psychedelic Somatics and Shedding Your Skin

*There is more wisdom in your body
than in your deepest philosophy.*

—NIETZSCHE

The Lindworm

*I*nside you and outside you there is a forest, where trillium flowers sprout *from every step. Within this forest there was a kingdom. And within this kingdom there was a castle, and within this castle there lived a king and queen. They were kind and generous, loved by their people. But they had a problem: they could not conceive a child.*

One day, overcome with angst, the queen was wandering in the castle gardens. Then, near the edge of the garden, close to the old forest, an old woman emerged. The tiny babushka smiled at the queen. Craning her neck with barn-owl curiosity, she croaked, "You have a problem, my child?"

Only slightly surprised by the appearance of the old woman, the queen shared the weight on her heart. "Well, the king and I long for a child, but try as we might no child comes."

The old woman nodded as if she had heard this story a thousand times. "Ah, yes. There is a simple solution, my dear. Do exactly as I say, no more, no less. Tonight, go home and take a bath. Before you lay with your husband, place the bathwater in a small basin beneath your bed. Make love to him like you mean it. The next morning, take the basin out into the garden, and empty the water. After three days, you will see two flowers: one white, one red. Eat the white flower, my girl. But under no circumstances eat the red. Do as I say, and you will have your child."

The queen thanked the old woman. That night the queen did exactly as the old woman said. The next morning, she emptied the basin into the garden, praying for a child.

After three days, the queen went into the garden. To her amazement, she found two flowers growing there: one white, one red.

Nobody knows the secret spark of desire that guided the queen's hand, or what carnelian passions danced before her eyes. All we know is this: as the queen knelt down to pluck the white flower, she found herself reaching for the alluring pulse of the red. And just like that, it was done.

As if waking from a dream, the queen shook her head, realizing what had happened. Blushing and a bit frantic, she plucked the white flower and ate it too, chewing quickly, praying that the old woman's spell would still work.

Well, some new fire kindled within the queen, and within days she could feel the stirrings of life blossoming inside her. After nine sweet months, the queen was ready to give birth. Finally, huffing and puffing up the spiral stairs, the midwife (who looked not unlike the old woman from the forest) arrived in the queen's tower as a storm outside ravished the windows.

But as the queen gave birth, something unexpected occurred. The first thing to come out was not a baby, but a small, black snake, which the locals called a worm. *The midwife, who had seen a thing or two in her time, thought to her-self,* Well, let's just throw this out, then. No one needs to know. *And she flicked the worm out the tower window into the raging night.*

The next thing to emerge from between the queen's legs was a beautiful blue-eyed boy. The queen melted with love for the child, and the king shed tears of joy when he came into the room. The kingdom rejoiced, gifts were sent from across the land, and the royal couple couldn't have been happier.

For a time . . .

The boy grew to become a bright young man, and according to the custom, it was finally time for him to find a wife. Donning his shiniest armor and mounting his whitest horse, the young prince set off to visit the neighboring kingdoms and galloped down the road. His entire life seemed to be perfectly unfolding before him.

Finally he came to a crossroads. Before he could choose which road to take, though, he saw a massive black snake slithering out of the forest. The snake raised its scaled head and said with a sharp hiss, "Me first, brother! Me firsssst!"

The prince's whole body shuddered. Wheeling his horse around, he galloped in the opposite direction. But at every crossroads he came to, he encountered the black snake, who hissed, "Me first, brother! Me firsssst!" Three times this occurred, until the prince turned his horse back home.

The next morning, still shaken from the encounter, he approached the king and queen and told them the story. The prince needed answers. "Was there anything strange about my birth?" he asked. "Any snake-like older brothers I should be aware of?"

The king and the queen sipped their tea in quiet bewilderment. Eventually they decided to summon the old midwife, who seemed not to have aged a day in nearly twenty years. They asked her if, during the prince's birth, she had noticed anything a little . . . strange.

"No no no," she said. "I recall nothing of the sort . . . Well, now that you mention it, there was maybe a small black snake that came out of her majesty which I threw out the window. But other than that, no! Completely normal!"

The prince, the king, and the queen all looked at each other, and a pregnant silence fell upon the room.

The king, who had only grown gentler and wiser in his years, finally spoke up. "We cannot let this creature continue like this. And if it is truly our son, we cannot send hunters to kill it. Send out the musicians and poets of the court. We will enchant this serpent home with music and lure him back into the castle walls to keep the people safe."

If only all kings could be so wise.

Soon, a place was made in the castle big enough for the massive serpent. Slowly but surely, the magic woven by the king's artisans enticed the beast toward the castle. Heaving and hissing, the massive serpent squeezed itself through the castle doors that cracked around its iron-hard scales. Finally it slunk down to the dungeon, where they had prepared a room filled with straw—a nice little lair, all his own. The proverbial parents' basement.

Swallows fluttered away from the castle. The deer scampered off into the forest as the serpent growled its menacing call from the castle's depths: "Me firsssst!"

Messengers were dispatched to all the nearby kingdoms with offers of marriage for the king and queen's eldest son. A valuable proposition indeed. But the devil is in the details, as they say, and in this case one very large detail had been left out. He looked good on paper, at least.

Pretty soon, a princess arrived from a nearby kingdom. Fires were lit, trumpets blared, and the young girl was lavished with the finest wine from the oldest corner of the cellar. Tomorrow they'd hold a feast to honor her wedding day. First, though, she needed to actually meet the prince. "Right this way," the king's servant winced, leading her down toward the lair, unable to meet her eye.

When the door closed behind her, the girl turned and saw a slithering black presence unfurl itself around her. Before she knew what was happening, she was gone. Slurp. Crunch.

The gruesome nature of the king and queen's situation began to settle upon them. The next day a new maiden arrived. Cue the trumpets and feast. Again, the following day, only a pile of clothes remained. But the serpent was growing bigger by the day.

Things went on like this long enough that the local lords began to figure out that something sinister was occurring within the castle walls. Whispers shared over pints of black ale in smoky taverns spoke of something evil lurking beneath the castle. A dark cloud settled upon the castle ramparts like a fog of quiet suffering.

Desperate to resolve the situation, the king finally sent his messenger to a poor shepherd who lived in a hut in the kingdom's woods. By now even the shepherd knew of the situation occurring down in the dungeon. The shepherd had no wife, and only his daughter to keep him company; so after summoning all his courage, he refused the messenger. But something in the girl knew she needed to go. Against her father's wishes, she accepted the invitation, for reasons she could not explain. Something in us always knows when we need to do such things.

The shepherd was beside himself with grief. The girl began walking in the woods to try to make sense of the terrifying situation she had just committed to. One day while in the forest, anxiously anticipating her impending nuptials, she turned on a bend in the path, and out of the hummocks of moss and tufts of lichen stepped an old woman.

The old woman asked, "What troubles you, child?"

The girl explained the situation as tears poured from her eyes.

"Listen to me, my darling," said the old woman. "Brave you were to accept the proposal. Yet wiser still you would be to listen to my instructions: ask the king for a year and a day to prepare for the wedding. During that time, sew yourself twelve shifts of the purest white linen, paying special attention to the embroidery around the heart. Then, make sure that two baths are prepared for your wedding night—one of ashes and water, and one of milk. When the snake asks you to remove your gown, ask him to remove a layer of scales. And once all is said and done, you must hold the creature in your arms. And don't forget a sponge and scrub brush. You'll need it!" she cackled, slipping back into the murky forest.

So for a year and a day, the girl spent her days sewing the nightshirts and embroidering them with red and white flowers—the designs of her village— around the heart.

After a year and a day, it was time. The girl arrived at the castle, bedecked in twelve beautifully embroidered gowns, one atop the other. By this point, the servants had grown weary of the whole charade, and what was once a feast was *now a humble last meal. She was given the last drops from the castle's remaining bottles of mead before being led down the damp, winding stairwell to the serpent's lair.*

As the heavy door groaned shut, she peered into an impenetrable darkness. The blackness seemed to move before her. Feeling the cold scales of a tail encircle her, she looked up to see the eyes of the massive snake staring into her own.

"Shed a shift, fair maiden" the serpent hissed.

The girl did, and then replied, "Slough a skin, dear prince."

The serpent was shocked. No one had ever spoken to him like this before. Usually these nights involved a lot more screaming and terror. Hissing, but appreciating a little sass and variety, the serpent did what she asked. But he did not anticipate the excruciating pain that removing the scales would involve.

"Shed a shift, fair maiden" he hissed again, a little more pain in his voice.

"Slough a skin, dear prince," she said.

Again, the girl slid out of one of her nightgowns, and the serpent removed a layer of scales, roaring with pain, revealing the raw skin below. This went on ten more times until the serpent became a raw, bloody mess, writhing with a level of pain he'd never experienced before. At that moment, the girl knew exactly what to do. She grabbed the steel-toothed scrub brush, dipped it in the bath of ashes, and began to scrub the lindworm's raw flesh. The creature howled in desperation, pleading for her to stop. Up above, the servants exchanged worried glances, fearing the worst.

After hours of scrubbing, her hands now bloody, she had reduced the serpent to a shivering heap of tender flesh. With the last of her strength, the girl picked up the creature, wrapping its bloody form in her arms, and with one final heave she dropped him into the bath of milk. Exhausted, she collapsed on the floor and fell asleep.

In the morning, the soft light of dawn shone through the one tiny window high up on the dungeon wall. The whole room became slowly illuminated in a gentle glow. Stirring and standing, the girl cautiously approached the milk bath.

Lying before her was not a snake, not a monster, not a blob of ugly flesh, but a man who had spent his entire life cloaked in a skin of black scales, a person who had been cast into the darkness so long ago.

He looked at her, she looked at him, and wildflowers bloomed across the meadows of their hearts.

When morning came, the king and queen couldn't believe their eyes. Tears of joy flowed down their faces as they met their eldest son in his true form for the first time. Not one but two weddings were in order, for the younger prince finally did find himself a wife in a distant kingdom (after much clarification). A sensuous feast was thrown, and the castle once again was bathed in warmth and radiance. Swallows returned to their nests beneath the castle eaves, white-tailed deer grazed in the fields beyond, and somewhere out in the forest an old woman sat near a smoky fire and chuckled to herself with a snort.

"Kids these days."

The Barren Kingdom

Our story, a tale from old Scandinavia, begins with a barren kingdom. In myths and fairy tales, a barren kingdom is often a sign of staleness, cold remoteness, and the absence of warm-blooded vitality. In psychological terms, this might look like depression, resentment, or a chronic state of disembodiment and anxiety. On some level we have become disconnected from ourselves. Some spark or wonder that once animated our lives has blown away in the wind. We find ourselves sitting alone in a tiny apartment one night listening to the rain, wondering what the hell happened.

The king and queen seem nice enough. They're nice people who hold nice dinner parties for their nice friends. Americans are great at this sort of niceness. But are they truly alive? The story tells us that they've lost sight of their inner animals, some primal luster that courses through the veins of vibrant individuals and cultures. In the old stories, a barren kingdom is usually a situation that requires some journey outward into the wild unknown to help revitalize it. The medicine for this moment can only come from beyond the groomed palace grounds, beyond the realm of rationality entirely. Here be dragons. As well as wise old women, apparently.

Following the old woman's advice, the queen makes love with the king after placing a bowl of bathwater beneath their bed. Some luscious sympathetic magic is at work here. After the queen pours it out onto the earth, onto the primordial body, two flowers appear, one red, one white—colors that animate the very cells of our bloodstream. Some hot-blooded spell is clearly at play.

We can only guess why the queen ate the red flower. Perhaps something dark and instinctive writhing within her compelled her hand to reach out, pick it, and shove it into her mouth. Her intuitive guidance toward the red flower is a moment of sacred transgression, an acting out of the bodily desire that lives within all of us. Many of us, at least in Western culture, often keep this pulsating force firmly at bay. Despite whatever social advances seem to have occurred in recent decades, our bodies tend to remain locked storehouses for the emotions and instincts we still outwardly shun. Our society demands that we cram these feelings back down into our carnal depths, where they coil up like forgotten snakes. But against our best efforts, they emerge, rules be damned. Haven't we all had those moments when the lights turn on or the sun rises and we silently ask ourselves, "Why the hell did I do that?" That's when we know we've eaten the red flower.

In the story, the midwife throws the black snake out the castle window into the night, only for the prince to encountered it later. What a potent metaphor for how we cast out our own trauma, grief, and pain into the dark night of our bodies, only for them to resurface years later as autoimmune disorders, chronic fatigue, or mysterious ailments. Sooner or later, the dark serpent living within us must be dealt with. We must find a way to court this horrific thing back into the contained boundaries of our own psychic castle and make a place for it to finally come home.

Thankfully, the king in our story is wise enough to employ art as a means of drawing this feral power back within the confines of the castle walls. While this story certainly has its fair share of darkness, we see that beauty and art have a necessary place in the healing process. A wise leader always makes room for beauty. Even when it means we must dine with serpents.

Snakes, Sins, and Symptoms

For thousands of years, the serpent has been the storehouse for Western culture's collective shadow.

In "The Lindworm," we see with piercing clarity that when the undesirable and shameful elements of our lives get cast out into the darkness of the psyche and repressed into the body, they only grow to become even greater sources of suffering. In the language of medicine and psychology, we call these phenomena *symptoms*. The Greek root word *sympiptein* means "to befall, happen; coincide" or to "fall together." These meanings immediately direct our attention downward, falling into the body, the soul, and the earth. We can see symptoms as underworld messengers that demand our descent, painfully requiring us to reorient and sometimes fall down toward our troublesome bodies and the worlds contained within.

When we leave our symptoms out in the wilderness of the psyche, repressed into our bodies and unconscious, they can become behemoths who rear their heads at important junctures in our lives. They become the fearsome black snake stopping the young prince on his path to happiness. Many people I've worked with ignored their symptoms for so long that they grew into frightening creatures that threatened to consume their entire life. For many of these people, psychedelics were their last stop.

Just like in the story, until we deal with the roots of our symptoms, we will find no peace. It is no coincidence that the serpent, an animal who spends most of its life span with its belly locked in intimate embrace with the earth, so often represents archetypal impulses that Western culture collectively represses. The serpent is an ancient symbol of the earth, the body, and the shadow—what Jungian analyst Joan Chodorow called the "unholy trinity." For centuries, feeling connected to one's corporeal form and experiencing the red-blooded desires that emerge unbidden from the body was akin to an allegiance to the devil. For within the body lived the primordial serpent who misled Adam and bewitched Eve, which Christianity saw as evidence of humanity's innate sinfulness.

Yet in the pre-Christian world, serpents were almost universally regarded as beings embodying immense power. Serpents were linked to the vital, unstoppable forces of the earth itself, encapsulating the dual-sided nature of creation and destruction with equal capacity to nurture and devour. Ancient peoples saw the shedding of the serpent's skin as a profound symbol of rebirth, encapsulating the cycles of birth and death that are inescapable in nature and in everyday human life. The serpent and all its chthonic power posed a threat to religious powers that sought to disconnect people from the earth and their own inner agency, so they turned it into the devil.

The ouroboros, an ancient image of a snake eating its own tail, can be loosely traced to ancient Egypt, and it resonates outward across millennia. Jörmungandr, the world serpent of ancient Scandinavia, was said to encircle the earth. Plato, in his *Timaeus* dialogue, uses the image of the ouroboros to describe the nature of the universe and the cyclical pattern of life and death that animates the living world. Later, the alchemical tradition employed the image of the ouroboros to again symbolize this cosmic principle, weaving a thread from Plato and the early esoteric schools of Egypt and Greece through the Middle Ages and into our present day.

In other parts of the world, serpents retained their archetypal power until the crucifix arrived there. Coatlicue, the primordial earth goddess of Nahuatl-speaking peoples like the Aztecs and Mexicas, was depicted with a face of two serpent heads facing each other, a skirt made of snakes (the literal meaning of her name), and a necklace of human hands, hearts, and skulls. She is the personification of the feminine earth mother who nourishes all and devours all. Damballa, one of the most important *loas*, or spirits, in Haitian Vodou, was seen as a giant snake, and the dances meant to invoke him involved devotees embracing a black or white snake as they writhed to the pulse of polyrhythmic drumming long into the night.

In the Amazon, where there is a palpable sense that every square inch of the forest wants to eat you, many Indigenous cosmologies speak of the great anaconda that encircles the world. The work of ethnobotanist Richard Evans Shultes delved deep into the vast cultural world of several related tribes of the Colombian Amazon who collectively called themselves "the people of the anaconda," connecting their totemic identity to this mythic being.

Asian mythologies, particularly those that draw upon the Hindu tradition, are saturated with serpents: Shiva wears a serpent around his neck, and Vishnu blissfully sleeps on Shesha, the cosmic serpent that encapsulates the universe (not unlike Plato's vision). It is said that even when the world is destroyed, Shesha, the divine creative essence of eternity, will remain, and so the world will begin again. In yogic traditions, the link between the serpent and the body is preserved in the concept of *kundalini*—the coiled serpent of energy that embodies an ecstatic, feminine form of primordial energy, or *shakti*, that lives at the base of your spine. It is said that when *kundalini* uncoils herself and travels up the spine—whether as the result of yogic practices, or a spontaneous occurrence, or perhaps when aided by psychedelic medicines—spiritual awakening occurs.

The archetypal serpent that dwells deep within the body and the earth has old wisdom to share with us as it slowly unfurls its all-encompassing form. Our bodies want to feel its primal intelligence, to writhe and swoon to the heavy pulse of its root-chakra rhythm. And yet, according to Joshua Schrei, mythologist and host of *The Emerald* podcast, "Sometimes embodiment means being torn apart" (Schrei, 2022).

Shedding Your Skin:
How Psychedelics Work with the Body

Just like in the "The Lindworm," psychedelic healing can be a painstaking process, requiring us to uncover the many layers of armor and protection that take root within our body and psyche. Simply by living in a human body, we don these hard scales to protect us from being utterly incapacitated by the swelling tides of life. Yet through the undulating waves of our body's sensate intelligence, psychedelic medicines can help us slowly chip away at whatever paves over our soft mammalian skin. By the end of our story, the once-fearsome black snake is reduced to a tender blob, utterly exposed, with a receptive nervous system and an open heart, feeling everything.

While research is slowly catching up to measure how psychedelic medicines operate within our physiologies and neural networks, our current scientific understanding of how psychedelics work with the body reveals only a small part of the picture. The varieties of somatic and bodily experiences that psychedelics can evoke are diverse, dramatic, and simply weird. Despite our evolving understanding of psychedelics from a biomedical perspective, many aspects of how these medicines work in the body still remain a mystery.

CASE STUDY: *Carolina*

Carolina was a young entrepreneur who was dealing with a life-changing onslaught of autoimmune issues, extreme dietary sensitivity, anaphylactic allergies, and other unique health challenges. Many times in her life she had found herself bedridden, body shutting down, unable to function. Understandably, she was terrified of putting a strange mushroom into her already fragile body.

But like the shepherd's daughter in "The Lindworm," Carolina knew what she had to do. A tropical storm was brooding over the usually pristine Caribbean horizon. As the rain began to gently sprinkle, I sat with her as nausea flooded through her body and awareness, brought on by the powerful mushrooms she had just taken. I brought her outside onto the grass as I witnessed her become even more physically uncomfortable. I sensed that she would likely need to purge or at least move the energy surging through her, and hoped that the earth would help her do this. Soon she was on hands and knees, rocking back and forth, breathing deeply, fingers dug into rich Jamaica soil. Thunder crashed over the once-placid sea as the skies broke open and a torrent of rain pummeled us. She was struggling. I couldn't tell you why, but I placed my right hand on her back, directly behind her heart. At that moment she began to cry, sobbing from a place deep within. I felt a cloak of gravity settle upon us as her body writhed in a cat-cow yoga posture.

After about fifteen minutes, mud streaked and soaking, we moved back inside. She crawled into the fetal position, and I placed my hand once again on her back. Her mumbled words evoked confusing scenes from her childhood, the remaining shreds of her cognitive ego just barely capable of processing.

"Wait . . . what? Why? I don't understand . . ." She began to paint a troubling picture of memories she had repressed for most of her life. This went on for at least several more hours as she grappled with what the mushrooms were showing her. Over the course of her three psilocybin journeys, Carolina uncovered several instances of sexual trauma that, until that point, she was unaware of.

She continued rocking back and forth as I saw her moving the stuck energy of trauma through her body. With snakelike undulations of her spine, she heaved and trembled with sobs. Carolina continued somatically releasing energy and emotions that her mind had buried deep in her body for years. After what must have been hours, she eventually slumped toward me, resting in exhaustion. For as long as my knees could take it, I held her in silence.

This was a massive experience, and one that required extensive integration and ongoing care. Yet over the course of our week together, Carolina found that she could begin to trust her seemingly problematic skin-suit once more.

She told me, "I thought for so long that my body was unsafe, and that the earth was unsafe. But nothing could be further from the truth. Because of this experience I learned that I can trust my body, and that I can trust the earth."

Our bodies know, regardless of what our minds think.

Heaviness and Lethargy

Predictably, the onset of many psychedelic journeys involves a sensation of heaviness settling over the body. The internal world of our organs and bodily systems might feel like they are suddenly working overtime or are shocked by the outlandish brew or plant it has now been tasked with assimilating. This can be a terrifying experience.

On one level, this is the body metabolizing and absorbing the medicine and adjusting to its effects. On another level, we can see this heaviness as an invitation to deepen into the labyrinth of our bodies as we slowly begin to peel away the first layer of scales. The truth is that the sooner we can surrender to the fact that we must shed our skin and allow our bodies to do as they see fit, the sooner this sensation passes.

Tremors

People can also experience inexplicable shaking during a psychedelic journey. Legs, hands, and sometimes the whole body may surge with convulsions that have no apparent explanation. I've seen a man go through what looked like high-voltage electric shocks that would animate and contort his whole body. The tremors continued for about twenty-four hours after this particular experience, making it difficult for him to even lift a fork to his mouth. Eventually, they subsided.

While I've heard some medical professionals speak about tremors being an indication of possible psychedelic "serotonin syndrome," especially for the tryptamine-based psychedelics like psilocybin and ayahuasca, the jury is still out. Tremors are a great example of the circuitous, unpredictable way that psychedelic medicines can work with the body. There is no clear biomedical understanding of why they occur, despite many theories. In my experience, tremors are rarely an accidental overload of neurotransmitters or a medical mishap, though I am clearly not a doctor and can only speak from my experience.

Nausea

Another predictable aspect of working with psychedelics, especially plant medicines like psilocybin, ayahuasca, and mescaline-containing cactus, is nausea. It is tempting to view nausea solely as a physical issue resulting from either an overly ambitious breakfast or merely a clash of unfamiliar alkaloids absorbing into your belly and bloodstream. While nausea of course can result from these variables (maybe forgo the bacon and eggs next time), it may also have nothing to do with them.

Feeling sick to our stomach can both bring up our repressed material and be a result of it. Like circling the drain, nausea can often be a signal from our body that we are getting closer to important emotional material that our conscious mind is likely unaware of. It might literally be something we simply cannot "stomach" any longer, a thought we dare not think, or a hidden emotional depth that we have gained heroic mastery over by stuffing it down into the caverns of our psyche in our daily life.

Nausea itself is not a problem to be solved, but an experience to be worked through. Becoming overly fixated on dispelling or ridding ourselves or our clients of the nausea, while an understandable intention, should not eclipse the emotional and psychic content that may also be wanting to be expressed and felt. More often than not, nausea is a sign that something within us needs to be purged.

Purging

As a child, I was terrified of vomiting. This fear persisted into my midtwenties, right until I began my relationship with ayahuasca. Over time, the tell-tale signs that a purge was coming—rapid heartbeat, increased salivation, extreme nausea—became such a reliable element of my journeys that my only choice was to make peace with this visceral mechanism of the human body. Now I welcome the purge when I feel it emanating from below. *Viva la purga.*

Especially with plant medicines like ayahuasca, huachuma, peyote, and even psilocybin, purging is a way that the body releases psychic energy. One explanation is that increased serotonin activity can cause nausea and vomiting, especially with the gut producing 95 percent of this important neurotransmitter. Every shamanic tradition I have encountered, however, would say that much more is going on when we purge.

CASE STUDY: *Bill*

Bill was a Vietnam veteran with a severely traumatic childhood who had never seen a therapist or talked with anyone about his inner life. He purged dramatically every single time he took psilocybin. Like many people of his generation, Bill had constructed an entire personality and lifestyle around repressing emotions into his body, never sharing his experiences of war or as a young runaway from an abusive household.

His first dose was an excruciating journey of stomach pain and heavy blackness, which in his mind he chalked up as a meaningless descent into agony. Yet midway through his second dose two days later, on an idyllic Jamaican morning, I finally heard a wail emerge from the depths of his being as he shed tears that had not left his body since he himself had left Vietnam. Then the purging started.

Bill began to realize that the more he cried, the better his stomach felt. The more he opened up and shared emotionally in our integration circle, the more his body began to relax. And while his stomach pain increased over the course of the retreat, I shared with him that after five decades of repressed traumas and emotions, he was just now opening the manhole cover of his psyche. It was only natural that his body would bear the brunt of fifty years of this rigid, masculine repression. I could also see that this concept—that the body is actually much more than a sack of meat, but rather a vessel of our psychic and emotional selves—was something he had never entertained and would have a hard time accepting. "Now," I told him as I bid him farewell in the Montego Bay airport, "the real work begins."

Over time, we peel away our layers of scales, often with great effort and suffering, until our raw interior is revealed. Yet just like in the story, the more hardened layers we remove, the more we venture closer to our own hearts, which we must also tend to and adorn with embroidered flowers.

Archetypal Somatics

The story of "The Lindworm" takes us through the process of ritual preparation—eating the two flowers, the bathwater beneath the bed, embroidering the 12 nightgowns—and down into the depths of the soul where we finally meet the black snake lurking within. If we are every character in the story, just as we are every character in a dream, then we are both the girl and the snake. Two parts of ourselves—our resistant, armored, and defensive side, and our small yet shockingly brave inner child—meet in an alchemical encounter that leaves both of them changed.

Removing our scales can be a rough ride. Sometimes this starts within a romantic relationship, where we are asked to open our hearts to an uncomfortable degree of vulnerability. Perhaps it starts through psychotherapy, or through psychedelic exploration. Even after we go through the excruciating process of removing these embodied layers of pain or grief or trauma, we are left like the creature in the story: tender, raw, and vulnerable. And that's not the end of it.

The girl had to prepare two baths: one of lye—ashes and water, symbolically and literally a source of cleansing and purification—and one of milk, a symbol of purity, nourishment, and the resourced body. Both baths require the lindworm's full immersion and surrender. Both baths require him to die to his old self—the scaled serpent—and be reborn as a real human being.

Myths of the dying or devoured god exist all over the earth, with the one about the Jewish carpenter being only the most recent. Along with this dying comes elaborate depictions of the ways in which the god is dissolved, tortured, or torn apart. Yet there is much more going on here than our ancient infatuation with gore. Is it a coincidence that people in the depths of a psychedelic journey often report experiencing these same archetypal motifs of their bodies being deconstructed or destroyed? Of course, we could simply take the reductionist road and explain these experiences away as visual depictions of "ego dissolution." But a mythopoetic lens has much more to say about this archetypal process that occurs throughout the ancient world.

There is one mythological figure who might aid us in understanding the archetypal juncture of mind and body. Xochipilli, the Nahuatl god of entheogenic plants and divine intoxication—whose body is literally adorned with a plethora of psychoactive plants like *ololiúqui* (morning glory flowers), *teonanácatl* (psilocybin mushrooms), and tobacco, among others—is a patron deity of the psychedelic body. This god is immortalized in a famous statue held at the Museo Nacional de Antropología in Mexico City. Ralph Metzner describes the statue thus: "This is a depiction of a man in ecstatic trance. His feet are crossed, toes curled, hands held lightly above the knees at the level of the heart. All around the base of the figurine as well as on his body are images of various flowers.... This deity is a kind of Mesoamerican Dionysus, a god of rapture and inebriation" (2005, p. 15). By adorning his body with psychoactive plants, perhaps the Aztecs were communicating that Xochipilli is literally infused with their intoxicating power, and that when we consume those plants, we are consuming the god himself, whom we personally commune with as he takes up residence inside our own flesh and blood. After all, the Nahuatl word for psychedelic fungi, *teonanácatl*, literally translates to "flesh of the gods." The Greeks viewed Dionysus in the same way, as do billions of Catholics who regularly consume their god through the Eucharist. It's a strange thought, but some gods want to be devoured.

Xochipilli, whose name means "prince of flowers," is the embodiment of the fluid, somatic connection many of us have likely felt on the dance floor, captured by musical rapture, perhaps a bit altered ourselves. R. Gordon Wasson writes that Xochipilli is "the god of youth, of light, of the dance and music and games, of poetry and art; the Child God, the god of the rising sun, of summer and warmth, of flowers and butterflies, of the 'Tree-in-Flower' that the Nahuatl poets frequently invoke of the inebriation mushrooms" (1980, p. 59). Another translation of his name reads as "flower child," as if the god himself conjured the sexual and consciousness revolution of the 1960s. It is fitting that in "The Lindworm," the catalyst for the entire story is the consumption of two flowers, each of which has resounding implications for the queen's body. Each time we imbibe a psychedelic medicine, we too are plucking one of these sacred flowers, perhaps red, or white, or an iridescent shade our eyes have never glimpsed before.

There is an undeniable archetypal element to psychedelic experiences wherein we feel like we are being devoured. The myths teach us that there is always some greater reason for a god or person being torn apart. It is not death for death's sake, but death in service to something greater, as we saw in the previous chapter.

What is born through its own destruction? What animal body might we awaken into after we're devoured? What seeds might sprout from our decomposing psyche? What strange elixir is being distilled through the arcane dissolution of the ego and all it knows?

Dismemberment, Dissolution, and Devouring

A red sun rises over the shimmering desert, black waters of the Nile turning lapis blue in the dawn light. Papyrus reeds sway in the morning breeze, still cool before the onslaught of the punishing Egyptian sun. Ibis birds pick their breakfasts from the muddy banks next to languid clans of crocodiles, their scaled backs unchanged since the beginning of time.

The story of Osiris—the mummified king of the Egyptian underworld—is a story about being torn apart. Osiris' brother, Set, killed him and scattered his body across the land. Isis, beloved goddess of the ancient world, bride and sister of Osiris, sets out on a quest to reunite his dismembered body and reanimate him into an eternal afterlife, presiding over the kingdom of the dead. Every year, when the seasonal Nile floods brought new life to the parched Egyptian landscape, Osiris was awakened into new life again, his green body becoming the verdant crops that would nourish an entire civilization.

Of the many gods who are dissolved only to be reborn, perhaps none is more famous than Dionysus, the Greek god of wine, fermentation, and ecstasy. His body was trampled each year with the grapes that contained his sleeping spirit, waiting to rise again through their mysterious transformation into intoxicating wine. His followers, groups of women known as the *maenads*, were said to roam the countryside in an intoxicated frenzy, copulating and dancing and destroying as they went. Eventually, the cult of Dionysus (or Bacchus, as he was known in Rome) became so widespread and powerful (and perhaps revolutionary), that the Roman Emperor Augustus outlawed its existence in CE 14, fearing its subversive potency.

In myths from across the world, gods are dismembered and devoured in order to create new life. The ancient Maya saw the creation of corn, their sacred food that nourished all life, as resulting directly from the death of Hun-Hunahpu, or First Father, as told in the *Popol Vuh*. The ancient Norse, Greeks, Hindus, and many other cultures believed in a primordial being whose body became the earth and the cosmos after it was cleaved to pieces, usually by its misbehaving children. And in many Indigenous cultures across the world, stories of a young shaman's visionary dismemberment, surgery, or rebirth becomes the initiation into their spiritual vocation. When seen through a mythopoetic lens, *ego death* means that not just our psyches but our entire bodies are surrendered to the devouring jaws of a force much larger than ourselves. And just like in the stories, we will emerge renewed, shedding our skin like the great cosmic serpent that is continually being born anew.

Skills

Preparing the Body

Our bodies are the vehicles through which psychedelic medicines flow. An ill-prepared body can result in an ill-fated experience. With every psychedelic medicine there is an initial onset period that can often be difficult, like a plane climbing altitude and going through turbulence. The better we can prepare our bodies, the less turbulence we can expect.

Here are some basic suggestions:

- ▼ Limit food intake in the hours leading up to a psychedelic experience. I personally fast, and I suggest that my clients don't eat for at least four hours prior to a session if possible. Some Indigenous traditions are strict in this regard, some less so.
- ▼ Avoid alcohol for at least three days before and after a journey. A week is even better.
- ▼ Eat simple, healthy foods twenty-four hours before.
- ▼ Avoid red meat for one to three days prior.

The Shipibo ayahuasca tradition places extreme emphasis on the *dieta* process, which involves severe restrictions regarding food and behavior. This ancient method of preparation does many things, but it especially serves to calm and prepare the body to process the powerful ayahuasca brew. We will revisit this tradition more in later chapters; however, it is worth saying that the calmer and healthier the body, the higher the likelihood you'll have an easy ride.

Breathing

Breath conducts the body's symphony. Our inhalations and exhalations offer the best mechanism for regulating our heart rate, blood oxygen, nervous system, and thoughts. "Keep breathing" may be the simplest and most useful phrase in all of psychedelic facilitation. The breath clears the way for the body to relax and open. Just like meditation, returning to the breath helps clear the mind and creates space for the body to speak.

Midwifing the Purge

Once again, nausea is not a problem to solve, but an experience to move through, and there are ways to "midwife" the purge, to be with it, guide it, and help it on its way.

A simple method I've used with many clients is to help them get on their hands and knees and slowly rock back and forth, breathing deeply, like in Carolina's story above. The idea here is to move deeper into the body and lean into the nausea. More often than not, moving toward that discomfort helps send it on its way.

That said, I only intervene when a client is having a difficult time moving it on their own or seems stuck. I don't try to force anything to happen here. As one *ayahuasquero* told me, "if it comes, it comes."

Therapeutic Touch

Done well and with intention, therapeutic touch can be grounding, calming, supportive, and encouraging. However, this is an extremely nuanced facilitation technique that is far better learned in person, and it requires more than I can offer here.

Water

I've heard some Indigenous healers refer to water as the original medicine. In Native American Church ceremonies, water is a luxury that is prayed over at midnight and dawn, and then it is shared around the tipi to mark the blessing of the day and the completion of a hard night around the fire. When working with ayahuasca, drinking excessive amounts of water is usually avoided during the ceremony as it doesn't mix with the bitter medicine.

Water is symbolically and literally linked to cleansing and renewal. Even a simple dab of cool liquid on the forehead can be a powerful moment of redirection and relief. During my time facilitating retreats in Jamaica while working under the Caribbean sun, when people would find themselves frantically disoriented or lost, cool water was a trusted companion to help shift someone's inner state. There's nothing quite like a good psychedelic hose-down.

Water can serve as a powerful tool for shifting energy, marking the end of a ceremony, and connecting our liquid-filled bodies to the source of all life.

Warmth

Never underestimate the power of a well-timed blanket. Many people report getting cold during psychedelic journeys. Just as the wood beams of a house contract and expand with the seasons, warmth is essential to aid our body in unfurling. Gravity blankets are also fantastic tools in psychedelic facilitation, providing both warmth and a heavy, grounding layer that is supremely comforting. Imbibing a psychedelic medicine around a warm fire is an experience perhaps as old as time, and something all the more important in an age of increasing clinical coldness.

Food

Eating simple, nourishing foods after a psychedelic journey helps the body ground and come back to the earth. Chocolate and fruit can be revelatory after any journey, and a good soup can do wonders to soothe the soul. After traversing the cosmos or descending to the underworld, the simple things that remind us of our animal bodies can bring unfathomable comfort.

Go slow. Just because your mind feels "done" doesn't mean your body is. Take little bites. Savor it. Appreciate this moment. This is also a good moment to observe your own patterns of consumption.

In the Native American Church, the sacred foods of corn, meat, and berries are ritualistically shared around the tipi at the close of the ceremony. Anyone who's been through a grueling, all-night peyote ceremony will confess that they've never tasted better berries in their life.

※ ※ ※

Nature is constantly devouring and being devoured. Dandelions scatter their puffed, seeded bodies upon the spring wind. Cherry blossoms burst forth into pink efflorescent beauty, only for their delicate petals to crumple down to the earth. The returning salmon, fat from years of ocean living, almost home in fertile culmination, is snatched by the bear who eats his catch at the base of old cedars, fertilizing ancient roots.

Every deer hunted, every apple plucked, every chicken raised for slaughter, plays a fateful role in this endless play of devouring and dissolution. And so do you.

It's a hard sell, being devoured. Not very marketable. And yet it is a fact, encoded into nature and enshrined in myth. Somewhere in our bodies we know this. Psychedelics show us this while bringing our bodies with them into their undulating dance. Layer by layer, we peel back the armor around our hearts, the electric fences that bind our nervous systems, the calcified patterns of self-effacing thoughts that restrict our ability to dream and blossom. We scrub and chip away until, like the lindworm, we are immersed in the purifying waters of life, waking up to the pristine light of dawn.

V

The Monstrous

Trauma, Exiles, and the Wound That Heals

There is a reason, after all, that some people wish to colonize the moon, and others dance before it as an ancient friend.

—JAMES BALDWIN

The Myth of Medusa

*L*ong ago, before the hymns of Homer graced the minds of men, eons before the clash of spears at Troy and the famous deeds of Heracles, there lived three sisters: Stheno, strong as an olive tree; Euryale, with a mind as wide as the sea; and Medusa, a mortal, the most beautiful of them all, whose name meant "rulerless."

They were known as the Gorgons, and they lived on an island far beyond the vast waters of Okeanos, in the direction of Nix, Mother Night. They were said to have golden wings and hands made of gleaming bronze—untamed, wild women not at all human, and older than the shining gods atop Olympus.

Some say that in the dawn days of the earth, Medusa challenged Athena in a contest of beauty. Outraged, Athena cursed her to become hideous, forever ending Medusa's arrogant dispute.

Yet others tell a different tale. One day, the dark-haired god Poseidon frothed up on the golden shores of the still-young land. There he found Medusa, who was indeed beautiful without compare. In the words of Hesiod, Poseidon "lay with her in a soft meadow among spring flowers." Shouldn't we all be so lucky. But you and I both know these are soft words, bedtime stories shaped by an old man's honeyed tongue.

Ovid tells a far more disturbing tale. Of all Medusa's beautiful qualities, her hair was her most prized. One evening young Medusa was lingering in Athena's temple, and as the golden sun dipped beneath the oceanic horizon, Poseidon found her there. Upon the marble altar, the god of dark seas ravaged her against her will. Athena turned away, hiding her "virgin eyes" behind her gleaming shield. Not even the goddess of war could witness such violence.

Poseidon took what he wanted and left as swiftly as he came. As he was an Olympian and technically Athena's uncle, she had no power over him. So Athena cursed Medusa instead. Her beloved hair became a writhing nest of serpents, tusks emerged from her mouth, and her milky skin became scaled and snakelike. Any creature that looked upon Medusa turned to stone. From then on, Medusa lived among the rocky cliffs on the island of Kisthene, high up in a cave with her sisters, where no one could hurt her again.

Until a hero came to call.

Ten thousand tides washed upon the island's shores, and ten thousand moons swelled to bright fullness. Centuries passed, and new men began to pour down from the mountains, finding their way into the olive groves and myrtle forests of Attica, drums and hoofbeats announcing their approach. And with them came new gods: sky gods, thunder gods, war gods. Their kingdoms sprouted from the earth like stalks of wheat. They flourished and became the people we now call the Greeks.

Among these people there was a king who had only one daughter to succeed him. Danae was her name, and tales of her beauty grew faster than her flowing hair. Yet King Acrisius grew anxious for a male heir, so he sent messengers to Apollo's oracle at Delphi—the serpent priestess known as the Pythia—to ask her whether he would have an heir. Acrisius found the Pythia's answer deeply disturbing: "A grandson you will have, though his fate is to kill you."

Frantic with fear, the king built a pit beneath the palace and sent his daughter to live within its depths, ensuring that she would never marry and never bear children. No children, no prophecy. In one final gesture of kingly reason, Acrisius lined the pit with bronze so that his daughter's internment might somehow be more respectable. She was a princess, after all.

But Zeus, far above, had his eye on beautiful Danae. Zeus knew that his preferred method of seducing mortals—transforming into a hot-blooded bull or stag and finding them alone in some quiet grove—wouldn't do here. So instead, Zeus channeled all of his potency into a rain of gold, and he fell upon young Danae through slats of her chamber, open to the sky.

Nine months later, Perseus was born in his mother's cell. Soon his cries were heard in the palace above. King Acrisius feared his fate was coming ever closer. The child must not live. So the king decided to build for his daughter and grandson a watertight wooden chest. He nailed it shut like a coffin, put them in, and threw it into the sea.

"What a curse would befall me," the old king mumbled, "if I were to murder my own flesh and blood. No, I am merely giving them to the sea. The gods will decide their fate. My hands are clean."

The churning Aegean tides carried Danae and her baby until finally they washed up on the shores of the island of Seriphos, where a lone fisherman dragged them to shore. For seventeen years the fisherman looked after the boy. But the fisherman's brother, King Polydictys, took Danae as a slave, seeking to bed and marry her.

The king was awed by Danae's beauty, and he waited for an open angle to seduce her. However, according to custom, as an unmarried youth Perseus was still living by his mother's side, which prevented the King from taking what he wanted.

The boy had to go, thought the king, and so he hatched a plan. One evening, he invited all the young men of the kingdom to the palace for a feast. Each of the youths of Seriphos gifted the king with a fine horse or some other token of their gratitude. But Perseus was poor, with not a lyra to his name, and when his turn came he was empty-handed and ashamed.

Polydictys expected this, and he sought to embarrass the boy even further by luring him into an impossible plot. With wine-stained lips and boastful tongue, young Perseus approached the king:

"I pledge to you, oh king, that I will give you anything in the land should you ask it of me."

"Well, there is one thing you could do," sneered Polydictys. "Bring me the head of the Gorgon, Medusa. Then honor shall be yours, and you can take your rightful place among the heirs of Seriphos. Show me you're a real man, and you'll gain my respect."

The young men in the hall laughed and pounded the tables with their fists, taunting Perseus for his fool's errand and his empty hands. Perseus stumbled home and determined to finally get himself and his mother out from under the king's yoke.

The next day he set out, traveling far to the north to the land of the Hyperboreans, seeking oracles and nymphs who might point his way to the fearsome Gorgons. He encountered oracles and nymphs, and their directions only pointed him farther into the wilds. While resting beneath the shade of an oak tree, two strangers approached him: a woman with piercing gray eyes, and a thin man with a cat-like smile.

The woman said, "Be not afraid, Perseus. We know of your quest and will help you complete it." Perseus realized at once that these weren't mere mortals, but gods—Athena and Hermes.

"I will aid you, and you will have my protection," Athena said. "Long ago did this vile creature compare herself to me in beauty. And long ago did she defile my temple. Cut off her head and be done with it."

Hermes gave to Perseus his winged sandals, a leather sack, and the Hood of Hades, a cap of invisibility. Lastly, Athena gave Perseus a gleaming sickle of adamantine said to have been used by Chronos himself to castrate his father, Uranos, at the beginning of time.

Athena then gave Perseus her bronze shield. "Do not look Medusa in the eye, or you will turn to stone like everyone else," Athena said. "Only gaze upon her through the shield's reflection."

Flying through the air with the aid of the winged sandals, Perseus sped across the ocean until he finally arrived on a remote island far to the west. The wind rasped upon its bleak shores, where twisted stone spires adorned barren hills. The stars moved backward in the sky, and the tides seemed to lap in reverse.

The next day he set out to find his prey. Up in the island's punishing hills, Perseus came upon a brackish lake. There he spied three old women dwelling in a cave near the murky lakeshore. They were not the Gorgons, but the Gray Sisters, immortal beings born old, their swanlike faces shriveled and pruned, sharing only one eye and one tooth between them. To find Medusa, Perseus would have to get past them.

Quietly, Perseus snuck up behind them. While one of the sisters was passing her eye to the other, Perseus snatched it from between their pale hands.

"Tell me where to find the Gorgons, Old Ones, and I will give you back your eye."

"Follow the path," croaked the Gray Sisters, their voices sounding in unison like the winter winds. Pemphedro, the oldest and smallest of the sisters, pointed her bony finger in the direction of the path.

"I thank you," said Perseus, and chucked their eye into the lake.

Soon, Perseus began to notice that the stones around him began to take on stranger shapes, animal-like, twisted, frozen in flight. A wolf, a lion, a rabbit, a fox, petrified in their tracks. Then he began to see stones in human form, their faces cemented in moments of unspeakable terror. Up the narrow path he walked until he came to another cave high up in a cliff overlooking the sea.

Within the cave he found the Gorgons—Stheno, Euryale, and Medusa— their bodies entangled in peaceful sleep. Perseus placed the Hood of Hades upon his brow, and with the winged sandals, he silently flitted into the cave. And there he beheld Medusa, sleeping peacefully before him. Perseus felt a twinge deep within his gut. He felt compelled to come closer to the beautiful, terrifying woman.

Perseus gazed at Medusa's face, horrified, enamored, enthralled. A lock of snake hair stirred in his direction, sensing his presence, and at the last moment Perseus remembered the words of Athena: only look upon her through the shield.

Close enough to hear her soft breathing, Perseus raised the shield, and as he gazed into the bronze reflection, Medusa's eyes slowly opened. As her eyes widened, Perseus took the adamantine sickle from its sheath, and with one movement, he cut off her head.

At once, Medusa's sisters awoke, shrieking. They stirred into a taloned frenzy, clawing at Perseus, bulging eyes aflame with rage. With one hand he grabbed the head of writhing snakes and stuffed it into the leather sack. Perseus ran from the screeching cries and gnashing teeth behind him and jumped out of the cave into the clear blue sky. The winged sandals whisked him away from the rocky sea below.

The cries of the Gorgon sisters roared across the oceans, haunting Perseus as he flew over distant lands. It is said that the sound of the sisters' wailing was so full of grief that it inspired Athena to invent the flute, which to this day beckons their ghoulish screams. After that day Athena would forever wear the face of Medusa on her breastplate as a warning to all who would confront her. For his part, Perseus became one of Greece's great heroes, using Medusa's head to turn his adversaries, including King Polydictys and the entire population of Seriphos, into stone. Violent delights with violent ends.

And here Medusa's story ends. But something happened when she died.

Out of her headless body emerged two beings: a giant named Chrysaor, bearing a golden sword, and a white winged horse, known as Pegasus.

It is said that Athena collected two drops of blood from Medusa's head and gave them to Asclepius, the god of healing. One drop would cause sickness and death, the other healing and new life.

Out of the monster called Medusa, all medicine was born.

Turning to Stone

Perhaps more than any other figure from Greek mythology, the image of Medusa is indelibly burned into the human psyche. Like shadows etched onto Hiroshima sidewalks, such a lasting imprint can only result from something like an atomic bomb erupting deep within our collective past. Medusa's alluring, monstrous image speaks to us from this place.

Medusa's story begins with violation. Of her challenge to Athena's beauty, not much is known. Hesiod, one of the main fonts of Greek myth, paints a picture of a carefree tryst between Medusa and Poseidon in a pastoral meadow. Yet the poet Ovid presents a much more compelling version of the tale: Poseidon rapes Medusa in Athena's temple, and instead of the powerful male god being punished for his deed, Athena punishes Medusa. A devastatingly familiar tale.

The Medusa myth speaks to trauma on every level, from the individual violations perpetrated on women every day to the collective trauma inherent in living in a patriarchal or "dominator culture," as writer Riane Eisler puts it.

I see three ways in which Medusa's monstrous condition and the lived experience of trauma survivors are intertwined. First, Medusa is robbed of agency. She certainly has no choice in her violation, nor does she choose whom she turns to stone. Medusa does not aggressively use her power to petrify, as Perseus would later do. Instead, one must look at her. Trauma robs us of agency by fracturing our ability to relate to the world in a coherent and consistent way. Instead, our choices become colored by what happened in the past, our actions guided in ways that often continue this cycle of harm.

Second, Medusa's gaze of petrification is also a gaze of isolation. She dwells with her sisters in a cave on a remote island, removed from the world. Perhaps she retreated there to keep herself safe or to protect the world from her gaze. Perhaps she found herself too hideous for polite society, the world of Athena and her "just" city, and hid herself away. Trauma isolates us within its calcified walls, which also serve to keep us safe. But there's a cost.

Trauma's petrifying gaze creates the antithesis of the very thing that might bring it healing. Instead of strengthening trust, trauma questions it. Instead of fostering safety, trauma disrupts it. Instead of building intimacy, trauma distances us from it. When looked at this way, trauma can indeed seem like a powerful curse.

Finally, Athena's curse makes Medusa invisible. One cannot look at her without turning to stone. Abuse can dwell unseen beneath the surface of an individual psyche, a family system, or a culture, sometimes for years or generations. Freud's discovery that most of his young female clients in high-class Viennese society had experienced horrific sexual abuse ignited his work on dismantling what he called their "hysteria," but it also disturbed him. Eventually, the pervasiveness of the abuse Freud uncovered became too overwhelming to rationalize, so he changed his theories to avoid addressing the realities being shared with him. Instead, he focused on sexual fixations in childhood and "wish fulfillment," incapable of embracing the horror he found his gaze fixed upon. Trauma, as we now understand it, would continue to go underground through the majority of the twentieth century, remaining mostly invisible until 1980, when the diagnosis of PTSD was formally added to the *DSM-III* for returning Vietnam War veterans.

On a psychological level, we could see Medusa's invisibility as a form of repression. She is exiled to a remote island, a distant region of the psyche, where the ego can comfortably deal with her confronting presence. Trauma is insidious because we hide it within the caverns of our subconscious where it might dwell for decades, slowly unraveling our lives and influencing our choices and perceptions. Only through the reflective process of deep inner work—psychotherapy, self-examination, and psychedelic healing, to name just a few methods—can the complex of trauma resolve. We'll explore that in more detail later.

It is interesting to note here that Athena is the one who curses Medusa. Poseidon is a powerful male Olympian and therefore not subject to Athena's retribution. So the punishment falls on Medusa, a beautiful young woman. Yet even Athena herself cannot bear to look at Medusa's rape, averting her gaze and preserving her "virgin eyes." Psychoanalysts might say that Medusa embodies the animalistic, sexual, and instinctive parts of ourselves, Freud's id, while Athena, goddess of wisdom, war, and the city, is connected to the superego world of popular opinion, protocols, and prestige. The public, civilized parts of ourselves cannot bear to witness these instinctive aspects of the psyche, the wet, snakelike impulses we all have. Medusa embodies something ancient and wild that the gods of civilization abhor.

Interestingly, Athena's sacred breastplate, the Aegis, also bears the face of Medusa, serving to ward off evil and perhaps any licentious gods who might seek to violate her. Medusa's face contains a key as to how we might face certain experiences of evil that have transpired in our own lives. When trauma is healed or integrated into the psyche, that means we consciously bear its mark upon our chest, an acknowledgment of the terror we have gone through and emerged from. Athena's Aegis is a symbol of strong boundaries and the parts of us that say with fierce conviction, "Never again."

Yet Medusa is not the only traumatized character in the story. Let's not forget the utterly appalling circumstances of Perseus's birth. His mother is imprisoned in a pit, where he is born, and then they are both promptly nailed into a box and set adrift on the sea by the very person who should protect them. Perseus grows up poor, with no father, and has to protect his mother from becoming the king's sex slave. Hardly a perfect childhood.

Yet Perseus deals with his pain in a decidedly masculine, extroverted fashion, through striving, success, recognition, and respect. Put him in a suit and tie, and you have a picture of the quintessential modern man, a Don Draper of ancient myth. He is also a symbol of the dissociating effects of trauma—a psychic defense by which trauma disconnects us from ourselves, our emotions, and our actions. His feet are not even connected to the ground. With the help of the winged sandals, he hovers above the earth, flying away on his quest, too fast for his past to catch up to him, what Robert Bly would call a "flying boy."

It is no mystery that Perseus, of all heroes, sought out Medusa, as people with deep trauma are often magnetized to one another. The connection forged through this strange attraction is today commonly called a trauma bond.

Throughout the myth, Perseus is directed by forces larger than himself. This can be a blessing when those forces are divine or transcendent. But in this case, Perseus—with his dissociated, almost trancelike psyche—is being guided by the will of the culture rather than the will of the soul. We can see the king, Athena, and even Hermes as symbols of external cultural powers that all want to have their way with us. When we are dissociated from our soul, we may find ourselves climbing ladders with nothing at the top, pursuing gold that turns out to be worthless, or wanting to behead anyone who cuts us off on the freeway.

Medusa and Perseus represent two ways that trauma disconnects us from our soul—one introverted, one extroverted. Jungian analyst Donald Kalsched, whose work in trauma spans nearly four decades, says the traumatized, dissociated psyche is open to the archetypal under-world, which the Italian poet Dante called the realm of *Dis*.

According to Kalsched, in the world of mental health "we are very familiar with 'Dis' as dissociation, dissociative identity disorder (DID), disavowal, disconnection, disease, even disaster, which means to become separated from your stars. Trauma is just such a disaster and the loss of one's guiding star is equivalent to the loss of one's soul or God-given spirit—one's true, spontaneous self" (2013, p. 87).

Kalsched's work explored an inner pattern he saw within his patients, which he called the "psyche's self-care system" (1996, p. 17). In essence, trauma causes us to hide and protect our core essence, "one's true, spon-taneous self," in order to prevent future harm (Kalsched, 1996, p. 17). When this core self is threatened, the psychic self-care system, much like the body's immune system, activates, defending us against real or imag-ined threats. In the case of a traumatized self-care system, the psyche overcompensates, essentially terrifying us into a state of risk avoidance, freezing us in place. We are turned into stone. These psychic forces can manifest in nightmares, intrusive thoughts, terrifying dream figures, and in the case of children, often as monsters.

On another symbolic level, we might also see the myth of Medusa as a metaphor for moving from the "reptilian brain" and its instinctual responses to the mammalian brain, which is responsible for our warm-blooded modes of social bonding, restraint, and emotionality.

Medusa's snake hair is perhaps her most memorable feature. It tells us that she is connected to something reptilian and primordial. A scientific examination of the reptilian brain would suggest that a snake's sole concerns are food and threat. They might be your pet, but they are not your friend. The reptilian brain is where the fight, flight, and freeze responses evolved from. It is the place in our neurology where we shudder and flinch when confronted with the unspeakable. When our reptilian brain is triggered, such as in a trauma response, the autonomic nervous system kicks into gear as well. Our heart and respiratory rates increase, along with other imperceptible changes in our bodies, emanating from some ancient cave deep within our skull.

The mammalian brain, however, contains the hippocampus—named after the Pegasus-like sea horse of Greek myth—which is largely responsible for memory and learning. The hippocampus is also connected to our limbic system, which allows us to feel complex emotions, bond socially, and regulate our instinctive reactions. Just as Medusa's headless body gives birth to Pegasus, so too does the human brain's development move from reptilian to mammalian, from instinct to emotion.

As trauma heals, the psyche gradually moves from the extremes of the reptilian brain's fight-or-flight responses into the limbic, mammalian brain, where relationship and emotional breadth are possible. We move from the impulse and hypervigilance of the snake coiled in its nocturnal cave to the sensate embodiment of the winged horse, morning light warming its skin, breathing in peace.

What Makes a Monster?

Monsters serve a powerful function in both culture and psyche. They are mythic expressions of our collective shadow, revealing to us that which abhors and violates the established order of things. Monstrous beings embody an instinctual, existential darkness that society can push against without reservation, thereby establishing itself as the light.

But who decides what is monstrous? And what is actually being killed when a monster is slain? To answer these questions, we must reach far back into the ancient recesses of history, to the foundations of Western civilization itself.

Nigerian writer Bayo Akomolafe speaks of monstrosity as a "cultural technology" that humanity needs in order "to define ourselves, to teach our children what not to do, to sound warnings about the future, to define the territorial boundaries of our habitats, and therefore carve out the wilderness, and to dream about the impossible" (2018). He goes on to describe the function of these impossible beings as "transversal disruptions of order," meaning that their very forms are meant to shock and upset society's neatly set table (2018). "[Monsters] have always been in dynamic interaction with the city that exiles them to the wilderness," he says (2018). In other words, monsters play essential roles for culture. They do not exist by accident.

As with many stories of monstrous beings, if we hold our lanterns a little closer to the tale we might see another layer of meaning encoded into the Medusa myth. Indeed, the slaying of Medusa speaks of a tectonic shift in the development of Greek—and therefore Western—culture, which emerges through the symbolic language of the story. The myth of Medusa gestures toward a cultural moment when the Great Goddess was decidedly suppressed in ancient Greece. The result of this conquest is a collective trauma from which the Western world is still reeling.

The first key is in the name of the hero, Perseus, which translates to "the destroyer" or "sacker of cities" (Graves, 1960, p. 17). I was surprised when I discovered that the bearded, curly-haired champions depicted on the terracotta amphoras of antiquity were actually descendants of invading tribes who flowed into the Grecian mainland from the northern mountains around 2000 BCE (Graves, 1960). These invading tribes, known as the Hellenes, were composed of four different groups that would come to populate the majority of Greece. By the time of Hesiod and Homer—the two most ancient sources of Greek myth—these tribes were already deeply embedded in the culture and landscape, establishing classical Greek civilization as we know it.

It's unclear who the Indigenous inhabitants of Greece actually were. Various sources name them as the Pelasgians or the Aeolians, likely seafaring peoples who came from the Levant and north Africa, along with an influx of Minoans from neighboring Crete. What we do know is that successive waves of invaders did indeed flow down from the north. And with them they carried new gods who lived atop mountains, inhabited thunderstorms, and animated the vast horizons of Asia Minor, which they swiftly conquered through an ingenious and deadly invention called the chariot.

Athena was the protector of cities and heroes. Born from Zeus's forehead, Athena is alive and well in our world: she wears a pantsuit, drives a Tesla, and is a cutthroat corporate executive. Athena's been with us the whole time, an appendage of the patriarchal sky gods and their systems of laws, ethics, and ways of thinking.

Medusa, on the other hand, embodies the instinctual, wild feminine that, according to many academic sources, thrived in the ancient world. Through that world's gradual adoption of patriarchal kingship and its associated gods, that wild feminine power became feared and suppressed. Riane Eisler chronicles these cultural shifts in her enduring book *The Chalice and the Blade*, describing the systematic upheaval of goddess-worshipping "partnership culture" in favor of sky god–worshipping "dominator culture" (1988). These cultural changes are also the main point of inquiry in Terence McKenna's book *Food of the Gods* (1993).

Ovid describes Perseus as *aurigenae*, or "born from gold." Gold is usually connected to the sun and to the masculine sky gods we associate with it. Perseus is directly linked, both genealogically and symbolically, with Zeus, patriarch of the sun and sky.

The moon, whose metal is silver, is profoundly woven with the archetypal feminine because of its twenty-eight-day cycle of waxing and waning. Ancient cultures predating the Greeks saw the archetypal maiden, mother, and crone in the moon's changing fullness. The moon embodies and symbolizes the Great Goddess of the ancient world, known by many names. The disciples of Orpheus even used the word *gorgoneion* to describe the moon's haunting visage (Kerenyi, 1980, p. 50). We can see in this being called Medusa an embodiment of this older feminine power that these proto-Greek cultures revered.

Medusa, it seems, is a far more ancient goddess than the myth fully reveals.

Three is the number of the Goddess. They say there are three Greek seasons. In the myth of Perseus, Medusa is one of three Gorgon sisters, and is guarded by the three Gray Sisters. Not even the gods can escape the will of the three fates—Clotho, the spinner, Lachesis, the measurer, and Atropos, the inevitable. In later times, Greeks worshiped the three goddesses Aphrodite, Demeter, and Hera—all faces of the one. Hecate was an ancient, three-faced goddess whom Zeus was said to revere above all others. Suppliants would find her on moonlit nights at the crossroads in the form of three wooden masks upon a pole, or as a goddess with three faces (Kerenyi, 1980, p. 36). Of her many names is "she-wolf," linking her to the wild feminine, and to powers far greater than the plough or hearth.

Medusa is connected to these ancient goddesses that the Greeks knew by many names and found ways to welcome into the Olympian pantheon. But Medusa herself was unwelcome there. Perhaps it was her innate sexuality, a reminder of women's freedom and power in a mythic world dominated by philandering males. Or perhaps Medusa symbolized an ancient priestesshood that flourished in Greece long before the invasions of the northern Hellenic tribes. What is clear is that certain aspects of the archetypal feminine continued to be revered, while others were cast out of the light.

Mythologist Jane Harrison illustrates that Medusa was once the triple goddess herself, whose priestesses hid behind a fearsome Gorgon mask to frighten away any profane trespassers against her mysteries (Graves, 1960). As in many ceremonies of the ancient world, blood was the most valued currency of the gods.

These priestesses embodied and were woven with what Clarissa Pinkola Estes calls "the dark feminine," an unflinching power to devour and descend into holy, blood-soaked rage. Kali energy, dancing on Shiva's lifeless body. When the *maenads*, the female followers of Dionysus, fell into their (likely psychedelic-induced) frenzies, they were said to rip apart bulls and men with their bare hands, overcome with the power of their wild god.

Perhaps that is what we see in the Gorgon's face: unbridled feminine power, confrontational sexuality, an earthly pulse that terrified her would-be conquerors.

British mythologist and poet Robert Graves distills Medusa's little-known legacy into one powerful sentence: "Perseus beheads Medusa: that is, the Hellenes overran the goddess' chief shrines, stripped her priestesses of their Gorgon masks, and took possession of their sacred horses" (1960, p. 17). We are all now living in the consequence of this mythic event.

To this day, monsters are still worshiped across Mediterranean Europe and many other parts of the world. Their horned, shaggy forms descend from the mountains at almost the same time each year across the northern hemisphere, often marking the winter solstice or New Year.

The bestial forms of the Bulgarian *Kukeri* are striking examples of this ancient custom still alive today on the Balkan peninsula, which includes mainland Greece. Farther west in Spain, the *Harramachos* de Navalacruz, the *Vaquillones, diablos*, and feminine *mascaritas* descend from the highlands with the frigid February winds, just in time for the Catholic festival of Carnival. The townspeople ask for protection and fertility from these old mountain gods, long eclipsed by the crucifix. The demonic *Krampus* of Germanic tradition threatens to steal and devour children in the midst of an otherwise joyful Christmas time. And the *Mari Lwyd,* a Welsh tradition, features a yuletide phantom in the form of a talking horse skull (more horses!) that demands food, ale, and song. Even in Japan, the New Year brings with it the monstrous *Namahage* spirits, beings that come to frighten children into behaving, and to bring blessings and protection to each home they assail.

Monsters pervade our collective psyche. Although the shape and texture of these frightening beings reflects the unique cultural landscapes of a people, the customs remain shockingly similar. Monsters are chthonic earth gods who demand to be known and fed, their fearsome appearances a reminder of nature's power and of humanity's need to pay it respect. A lesson that many of us in the modern West are slowly waking up to.

Perhaps a god becomes a monster when it has been left out in the cold for so long, so starved of praise and reverence, that it is reduced to a haunting shadow, terrifying us with the reminder of what we forgot. Pastoral spirits that we once nourished in exchange for strengthening every wheat stalk are now chemically poisoned ghosts who stalk our monoculture plantations, creating sickness as they are processed into packaged food. The primordial spirits of the old forests, rightfully feared and fed through ritual, now surge in seasonal flames that demand respect as they march toward the ever-encroaching grasp of the city. The Great River, which once fed thousands of villages along its rippling shores, is now siphoned into dams and polluted by factories. In the winter she floods her banks, consuming our houses and highways instead. Perhaps only when a culture has strayed so far from relating to these powers does it make sense to slay the very beings that used to keep us safe.

The Shield: Trauma-Informed Psychedelic Care, Part I

In my work as a psychedelic retreat leader, experience has unfortunately shown me that when working with a group of ten people, on average about 25 percent of them either revisit a past trauma or uncover one they didn't know they had. The amount of sexual abuse perpetrated upon people, especially but not exclusively women, is hard to comprehend.

That said, I've seen people make incredible progress and exhibit an awe-inspiring level of courage and tenacity when they begin to use psychedelic medicine to help them resolve and understand their trauma. While this might be the most terrifying thing one could do, the results are often astounding.

This is delicate work. Simply consuming a large amount of psychedelics, jumping into the deep end, and hoping that the experience will be healing is a brave yet risky move. I've known people for whom this extreme approach has worked, but I wouldn't recommend it. There is even a chance that psychedelic experiences can be retraumatizing, either due to lack of support, too high a dose, or lack of skillfulness or support on the part of facilitators.

The story of Medusa gives us several symbols that show what a trauma-informed approach to psychedelic healing might look like. The first is the shield. A powerful symbol of both protection and reflection, the shield is an archetypal image that we can integrate into our understanding of trauma-informed psychedelic healing.

Let's begin with protection.

In the mythos surrounding Medusa, there are many instances of the *apotropaic*—a ritual or object used to ward off evil. The crucifix, the Middle Eastern *hamza*, the Greek "evil eye," and the Egyptian eye of Horus are all apotropaic images. As discussed above, in the goddess's shrines of prehistoric Greece, Gorgon masks were worn to ward off anything that would profane the rituals taking place therein, her fearsome visage a sign to all those who would defile her power. Medusa's monstrous face served the purpose of apotropaic protection.

The shield is also a symbol of reflection—the inner work that trauma requires if it is to be healed, psychedelics or no.

Athena's shield protects Perseus from Medusa's petrifying gaze. The myth tells us clearly: one cannot stare the monster in the face and emerge fully alive. Reflection allows us to see trauma clearly without being overwhelmed or crushed by it.

Greek mythologist Karl Kerenyi described certain Greek initiation rites that involved this practice, requiring the young initiate to look at a mask mirrored in a silver vessel, an echo of the Medusa myth (1980). Each time we take psychedelic medicines, we gaze into that silver vessel. Reflected back to us is an image of our personal Gorgon: the unique elements of our lives that carry shame, darkness, and pain. The aim of psychedelic healing in the context of trauma is to provide both the reflection and the protection of the shield. The medicine itself becomes the reflector through which we gaze, allowing us to meet the piercing eyes of the Gorgon without turning to stone.

There is a certain paradox here. One cannot look upon the face of the monster and live to tell the tale. Yet only in clearly seeing what haunts us can we begin to reclaim our power from it and eventually heal. Somewhere between these two directives lives the courage required of us every time we take psychedelic medicines, especially if we are survivors of trauma.

This paradox is fitting because Medusa is born of paradox. She is both beautiful and monstrous, powerful and powerless, isolated yet entwined, mother and destroyer, giving birth through her death. The ability to embrace paradox speaks to an adaptable psyche that can stretch itself to encompass multiple truths, embrace new experiences, and experience new ways of being in the world without shutting down. Trauma might be considered healed when the psyche is capable of such flexibility and dynamism, embracing the complexity of truth and the undulating tides of the human experience—the exact opposite of turning to stone.

The Three Sisters: Trauma-Informed Psychedelic Care, Part II

Throughout this exploration of the Medusa myth, I have danced around a topic many have referred to as "the feminine mysteries." Far be it from me to say what these actually were and still are.

What I will say is this: sometimes women need to heal with women, men need to heal with men, and trans or genderfluid people need to heal with trans or genderfluid people. Whatever your identity, finding affinity groups where you feel safe is an essential element of deep healing.

When I spent a summer living in an Aboriginal Australian community as a young anthropology student, I often heard people refer to things as either "men's business" or "women's business." In their culture it was understood that there were certain ceremonies, especially around rites of initiation, puberty, and birth, that excluded people who were not of a certain gender. There were even certain places that men or women were not allowed to go or even look at because it was not for them to see. "Women's business," one of the older men would say, and that's all there was to it.

In Aboriginal culture it seemed to me that there existed a sense of awe-filled mystery for the other, a healthy reverence for the fact that not everything is shared because it's not meant to be.

Medusa lives in the refuge of her cave with her immortal sisters. The Gray Sisters watch over them from afar with what I can only imagine is a grandmotherly gaze, albeit with just one eye. In this story, as in many myths, we see women gathered together in ways that are both timeless and necessary.

While I have personally held space for women processing sexual trauma during many psychedelic sessions, as a male-bodied practitioner I would never assume this was a good idea unless my presence was requested, or unless we had a significant level of trust established beforehand. I've heard some women share that a grounding and protective male energy was exactly what they needed to feel supported during their journey. I've also had women ask me to leave. Both are valid. The delicacy of these situations cannot be overstated.

Medusa's Children

At the end of the story, Medusa's body gives birth to two radiant beings: Pegasus and the sword-wielding giant Chrysaor. To me this image of rebirth in the face of severe harm is the most miraculous and redeeming part of the entire story.

Jung might see Pegasus symbolizing what he called the "transcendent function"—a mystical force that generates healing between two people (usually a client and a therapist) like a chemical reaction. Is is also known as the "sacred third." In psychedelic healing, this sacred third can be the healing that emerges between the medicine itself and the person taking it, as well as between the journeyer and the guide. The transcendent function is a space where dualities fall away, creating a transpersonal container where boundaries may dissolve on levels we cannot yet comprehend.

Pegasus is the spirit of healing, forgiveness, and that mystical third thing that emerges when the rigid boundaries of the ego's defenses begin to soften. Those boundaries aren't inherently a bad thing. They may have once been extremely necessary—lifesaving, in fact—but they may not be necessary any longer.

Of Chrysaor, the giant with the golden sword, not much is known. But the image of the sword is often a symbol of decisive action, clear boundaries, and protection. Manjushri, the young bodhisatva of Mahayana and Tibetan Buddhism, is always depicted with a flaming sword above his head, meant to skillfully cut away illusion. Perhaps the golden sword of Chrysaor is the clarity that comes with self-acceptance, which also allows us to cut through the trappings of trauma. We might see Chrysaor as a masculine guardian living within us all, fiercely protecting our soul.

Pegasus also has his own compelling myth, with many echoes back to his mother's story. Pegasus once wandered and flew across the world, free of care. One day when he was grazing in the town of Corinth, a strapping young lad named Bellerophon sought to claim him for his own. A son of Poseidon (no surprises there), Bellerophon was a wayward youth, and much like Perseus was living far from home. But Bellerophon was no ordinary youth—he was on the run, fleeing home because he had murdered two men, including his brother. For the Greeks, these were unthinkable offenses to commit before the gods.

One day, a king asked Bellerophon to travel into the wilds and slay the monster, Chimera. Of course, he asked this to get him away from the queen, who had taken a liking to the boy. So Bellerophon wrangled Pegasus with a golden bridle that some say was given to him by Athena herself (again, no surprise).

I won't elaborate on Bellerophon's deeds; suffice it to say that he slayed the Chimera and continued his "heroic" work, making a name for himself across the known world. In fact, Bellerophon became so enamored with his own glory that "at the height of his fortune, [he] presumptuously undertook a flight to Olympus, as though he were an immortal; but Zeus sent a gadfly, which bit Pegasus under the tail, making him rear and fling Bellerophon ingloriously to earth. Pegasus completed the flight to Olympus, where Zeus now uses him as a pack-beast for thunderbolts;

and Bellerophon, who had fallen into a thorn-bush, wandered about the earth, lame, blind, lonely, and accursed, always avoiding the paths of men, until death overtook him" (Graves, 1960, p. 254).

Pegasus flings the conquering hero off his back. This is a powerful image, full of free will, empowerment, and the decision to no longer collude with powers or people that do not serve our highest good. Although Bellerophon is a hero of Greek antiquity, he is clearly not a good guy. Yet Pegasus falls under his sway. Haven't all of us at one point fallen under the spell of some powerful lover or boss, only to wake up months or years later realizing the toxicity of the situation? Abusive relationships, romantic or otherwise, are traumatic, and an example of falling under the golden bridle of Bellerophon.

Setting ourselves free of abusive people or dynamics can be extremely empowering. When we do this, we become like Pegasus, galloping into the blue sky. No looking back.

Skills

Wielding the Shield

What does it mean to face the monstrous in psychedelic healing? In my time as a psychedelic therapist, learning how to protect myself has been a vital growth edge. This essential yet seldom-discussed topic could be another book entirely. But I can summarize it like this: do not take on the monstrous elements of another person's experience.

This may be a bit of a far-out topic for some, but ask any seasoned facilitator and they'll tell you that a major risk of facilitating psychedelic work is "picking up stuff."

Sometimes this "stuff" is extremely subtle. You might feel exhausted and dazed after the session, or irritable or depressed. These might be signs that you've absorbed someone else's energy during a session. Sometimes this is quite overt. I can recall many sessions where I left feeling shaken, disturbed, or simply crushed by the weight of the trauma reliving itself before me. In psychotherapy, we call this *vicarious trauma,* which affects those who work with clients dealing with serious trauma. The results are fatigue, burnout, and depletion.

I cannot stress this enough: after every session or ceremony, especially the difficult ones, I always find a way to cleanse and reset my energy. In Indigenous healing traditions, there are specific tools for this, such as feathers, fans, perfumed Agua de Florida, aromatic smoke, fire, even certain songs and prayers. In the Shipibo ayahuasca tradition they use mapacho tobacco. In the Native American Church they often use cedar, among other tools. If you have European ancestry and feel connected to those blood ancestors, you may feel drawn to burn herbs they might have used, like rosemary or mugwort. The point is to find a practice that works for you.

When I worked in Jamaica I would swim in the Caribbean sea after each dosing session, letting the salt water and waves wash away whatever had just unfolded. I know, I know: not everyone is going to have a tropical ocean to jump into at the end of the day. But even getting into a hot shower or bath, perhaps with some epsom salts, can do wonders as you imagine all of the "stuff" from the session flowing down the drain.

Lastly, self-care is an ongoing and profound need for anyone involved in healing work of any sort. Wielding the shield means knowing when to say no, when to take a break, when to step back, and when you yourself might be needing help. The energy required to facilitate psychedelic healing is immense, and it requires deep recovery on multiple levels. Knowing when to raise your shield and how to take care of yourself will either make or break you.

Healer vs. Hero

You cannot heal someone's trauma for them. Not in life, not in therapy, and not in a psychedelic session.

When I work with clients, the person before me temporarily becomes my responsibility until the medicine's effects wear off. Even then, I hold a certain level of responsibility for my clients after the journey ends, all the way through the integration process, until our work together is done.

However, I don't take on the responsibility of healing their trauma for them. To do so would not only rob that person of their own healing but place me on a false pedestal, casting me as the one doing the healing, not them. Such a road leads toward the kind of overly heroic ego trips that are all too common in this work.

Believing that another person's trauma needs to be swiftly decapitated is not a good move either. Working with trauma requires a level of gentleness, patience, and care that moves at its own pace, which many have called *the pace of trust*. I've worked with people who, even after three large doses of psilocybin, were still not ready to face things from their past that they had alluded to in our intake or preparation sessions. It will take the time that it takes.

Pegasus Medicine

If you've ever spent time around horses, you'll know that they are extremely sensitive creatures who perceive even the slightest changes in breathing, body posture, and facial expression. They can often feel us much better than we can feel ourselves. Horses demand our full presence, and they immediately show us when we are off center.

Psychedelics do the same thing. People on psychedelics are in a heightened state of awareness. They can tell when I'm not present, or when I'm anxious or uncomfortable. Knowing this, I take into consideration even the most minute aspects of my presence, including my facial expression, body language, breathing patterns, and eye contact. In a strange way, being around people on psychedelics is very similar to being around horses.

And just like with horses, this is a delicate dance of direction and listening. We must learn to let the medicine do its work, not impose our own agenda, but keep track of where we are going. Make too many wrong moves and things can get out of hand real quick. This is all extremely subtle, and with it comes learning to feel the energy of the person before you and the energy of the space itself.

When Pegasus comes into a session, you can feel it. Something in the air shifts, and a person who moments before was wailing in abject terror finally exhales, their body releases, and some new tide washes over them. Things get very quiet. Like a healing presence, Pegasus is the spirit of deep relief, forgiveness, and transcendence. In moments like this, I pay close attention and do as little as possible.

The medicine of Pegasus is also about empowerment. I've seen countless people emerge from psychedelic sessions with some new clarity about a particular facet of their life—usually a relationship—that needs to end. Sometimes this takes the shape of admitting the toxicity of their situation or the ways in which they feel unmet or hurt. Anger and rage are fitting emotions here. Often, integration for trauma survivors involves taking decisive, even ruthless action in the name of their healing.

Risk Delight

The poet Jack Gilbert said, "We must risk delight.... To make injustice the only measure of our attention is to praise the devil" (2013).

How do we hold on to beauty in the face of the monstrous? This inquiry speaks directly to our philosophical understandings and spiritual beliefs as facilitators. Whatever your framework, whether atheistic and clinical or animist and shamanic, the task of the psychedelic guide, like any genuine healer, is to fiercely hold on to beauty and goodness, even when all hope seems lost.

"It has been said that there are no atheists in foxholes," wrote Donald Kalsched. "There are also few, if any, atheists among trauma survivors" (2013, p. 5).

There is, and will always be, a spiritual dimension to psychedelic work, despite how sterilized certain areas of this field may become. If the word *spiritual* ruffles your feathers, as it often does mine, you can think of this instead as a form of faith or trust in something far greater than oneself. Only by maintaining this connection to something can we continue to trust that healing is still possible, even in the darkest of places.

When I facilitate, I ground myself in a soil that I consider sacred. That's a complicated word, but it works for articulating how I approach this work. As facilitators, we need roots that go deep into our inner groundwater, so that we become oriented toward the soul, rather than merely toward the flowers of our ego. Flowers blow away in the wind. Roots can survive entire winters.

❉ ❉ ❉

One of the most profound healing traditions I've been fortunate enough to encounter is that of the Diné, or Navajo people. To the Diné, beauty is the source from which all healing flows. This understanding is reflected in their word *hózhó*, meaning beauty, harmony, and rightness. *Hózhó* can also be a prayer that is woven into a poetic tapestry used to heal the heart and ensure that every action henceforth is done in the way of beauty. This is what's known as the Diné "Blessing Way Prayer."

When all hope seems lost, when the immensity of suffering threatens to pull you into the maw of despair, don't lose sight of beauty. When you finally glimpse the dawn pouring through the cracks in the sky, when you, like Pegasus, at last emerge from the thunderstorm of your heart into the clear light of the sun, remember the words of the Blessing Way:

> *Hózhó nahasdlii.*
> *Hózhó nahasdlii.*
> *Hózhó nahasdlii.*
> *In beauty it is done.*
> *In beauty it is done.*
> *In beauty it is done.*

VI

The Trickster

Marginality, the Crossroads, and the Liminal Road

Treat everyone you meet like God in drag.

—RAM DASS

The Birth of Hermes

*L*ong ago in golden Arcadia, when trees and beasts and humans all spoke the same language, when the gods still roamed the earth, there was a nymph named Maia who lived in a cave. Like all nymphs, she was young and beautiful, though some say that she was, at the same time, a very old woman. One day Zeus spotted her from his throne atop Mount Olympus. Insatiable as ever, Zeus had to have her. As with so many of his conquests, we'll never know if he even asked, or if she answered. So at night, Zeus began to sneak away from the hearth-warm arms of Hera, his wife. Wasn't the first time. Wouldn't be the last.

From the beginning, it was a coupling born of mystery and darkness, scattered upon the rosemary breeze in the warm Grecian night. Yet Maia, who dwelt on earth in her humble cave, was left alone to bear the thunder god's secret child. After nine moons shone their fullness on her belly, Maia gave birth to a boy. But the moment Hermes was born, he slipped out of the cave into the brightness of the new day, where he happened to cross paths with a turtle. "Well now," Hermes said with a grin, "what a lovely creature you are. Better take you home with me and keep you safe. Trust me," he said with a wink.

But Hermes, tricky from the jump, killed the poor creature, scraped out its shell, found some cow hide, and voilà—he crafted the instrument called the lyre, born out of the first lie ever told. As he plucked the strings of his new toy, Hermes's mind quickly flew to his empty stomach. Only meat would do. He walked up the mountain to survey the surroundings. Helios' chariot had just begun to dip beneath the pellucid ocean, and Nix, the goddess of night, was wrapping her starry cloak over the land.

Hermes got wind that a precious herd of cattle grazed in the nearby hills, and in a blink he flitted there. But these weren't any cattle. These were the golden cattle of Apollo, his half-brother. Spotting the glorious heifers in the corral, he set them loose. As they mooed and snuffled their way out of the corral, Hermes maneuvered them in a zig-zag while he walked backward. A little ways down the road, Hermes fashioned himself a pair of light-footed sandals made of myrtle wood and tamarisk to hide his tracks.

As he led the cattle over the countryside, Hermes passed an old man working in his vineyard. "Well hello there!" Hermes shouted. "I reckon you'll have more wine than you know what to do with once those lovely vines bear fruit. That is, as long as we both agree that you didn't see what you saw today. Let's keep this secret between us." The old man wasn't sure what to make of a talking baby herding cows. In fact, he wasn't sure what he'd seen at all.

But soon Hermes led the cattle into a columned stable, nestled in the pastoral countryside. He rapidly made a fire from sticks—a technique he would later give to humans—and killed two of the golden cows, quick and painless. In the manner of a formal sacrifice he divided the meat into twelve equal portions, one for each of the Olympian gods—himself included, of course.

The sizzling meat had Hermes salivating. But in accordance with some ancient art lost to the ages, Hermes didn't taste a morsel. Instead, he set the most delicious portions of fat and flesh into an offering tray and placed it high on the mantel. The bones, hooves, and head he gave to the fire to consume instead of him.

Hidden once again by the cloak of night, Hermes returned to his mother's home, slipping in like mist through the keyhole of the simple door. Silently he crept back to his cradle and swaddled himself back up like the innocent baby he seemed to be.

But mothers always have a way of knowing when their sons are up to something, don't they? Maia said, "Where were you all night, sneaky boy? I see you are wrapped in your cloak of deception, lying through your teeth. I know whose cattle you stole. Do you want to bring Apollo's wrath upon us?"

Hermes, of course, denied everything. "You'll see, mother. Everything will be fine. Besides, do you really want to live like this in a cave? I've got bigger plans for us."

The light of dawn was cresting over the eastern ocean, shining the new day's glow upon the earth as Helios mounted his solar chariot. Radiant Apollo, immaculately dressed for the day, hair and skin freshly oiled, went to his sacred pasture to admire his prized herd. Immediately he noticed something was terribly wrong. Annoyed, he set out to find his stolen herd. Being the god of prophecy, he had a pretty good idea of where to look.

He soon passed the old man working in his vineyard and asked him what he'd seen. The fellow's reply was as confusing as the zig-zagged tracks of cattle Apollo was following.

The god sighed in bitter frustration. He had things to do, meetings to attend, and deals to close, and chasing cows was not on his agenda.

He followed the tracks and soon saw footprints made by no being he had knowledge of—neither man nor beast. At that moment, Apollo glanced up into the bright blue sky and beheld an eagle soaring directly above him. As the god of prophecy, he knew exactly what that meant: he was dealing with another son of Zeus.

The Far-Sighted Archer followed the confusing tracks, tracing them through gorges and canyons, all the way back to Maia's cave.

Ignoring the nymph, Apollo went straight to the cradle. "You there, child. I don't know who you are, but I know what you did. I can see farther than a hawk, soaring on the highest gust of wind. My bow can shoot straighter than the edge of a spear forged by Hephaestus himself. Don't lie to me, baby."

Of course, Hermes denied everything yet again, wriggling down into his swaddling blankets even further. "Look at me! I'm just a baby. I don't know what a cow even is, so how could I steal one? I swear by the shining brow of my father, I never touched your precious cattle. After all, I was literally born yesterday."

As Apollo watched Hermes lie to his face, a cold rage began to swell in up the usually aloof Olympian. "Well then, you little thief, let's test your mettle in the halls of Olympus."

With that Apollo scooped up the swaddled Hermes from his cradle and set out for the mountain of the gods. But Hermes had another trick up his sleeve— or rather, someplace else. Suddenly, he let loose in Apollo's hand an "ill omen, a ripe messenger" from the darkest depths, oozing down the golden god's pristine hand. Then Hermes sneezed an eruption of snot.

Shocked, aghast, offended, Apollo dropped the baby Hermes in disgust and sat down on the ground beside him. Immaculate Apollo was laid low, brought down to earth. Not knowing what else to do in a moment as outrageous as this, he laughed. Apollo looked into the young Hermes's eyes and suddenly saw between them the complex, beautiful, fraught, intimate bond we call brotherhood.

Afterward, Apollo brought Hermes to the hall of the gods. Zeus asked Hermes one final time about his theft of the sacred cattle, and for the third time, Hermes lied, and lied gloriously. Apollo and Zeus looked at each other and burst out laughing, delighted by the audacity and cunning of this irreverent little god. So entertained was Zeus that he welcomed Hermes into the ranks of the Olympians, excused his theft, and sent Apollo and Hermes on their way to collect the rest of the golden cattle.

Somewhere far out in the rolling pastures of Parnassus, Apollo and Hermes strolled down the dusty road at high noon. Taking a seat at a crossroads for a swig of ambrosia, Hermes took out his faithful lyre and sang an invocation to the muses and of the creation of the gods, including himself. Apollo was deeply moved and asked Hermes if he too might learn to play such an instrument. Thinking for a moment, Hermes placed one more card on the table. "Of course you can, brother! You can learn it in a day! Take it as a token of my love."

Apollo was so pleased with the gift that he gave Hermes his caduceus—the famous staff wound about with double serpents—and his whip, and he christened Hermes as the sacred messenger of the gods and the guide of souls. They shook hands, and with that, the deal was done.

It is said that Hermes still waits at that crossroads, and at every crossroads, where travelers still build small piles of stone in his honor. And there he waits, drinking with blues musicians and Coyote and whatever traveler might cross his path, still hungry for a deal.

Turtles All the Way Down

Moments after his birth, Hermes leaves the cave of his mother and stumbles upon an unsuspecting tortoise. Turtles and tortoises are animals with mythic connotations the world over, symbols of the world itself and of a cosmic order that the early Taoists saw encoded into their shells (which, according to some, formed the basis of the *I Ching*). In Hindu mythology there is a belief that the world is supported by four elephants standing on the great turtle Kurma. And of course, Native peoples across North America, specifically the Lenape, Anishnabe, and Haudenosanee, have long referred to their continent as Turtle Island.

Yet Hermes, in his infinite crassness and wisdom, tricks the turtle and turns its shell into the lyre. The fact that one who tricks and deceives is called a "liar" may be linguistically unrelated, yet the coincidence has Hermes's tracks all over it. Eventually, Hermes gives his instrument to Apollo in exchange for his own divine vestments of caduceus and winged sandals, cementing his role among the Olympians. Yet none of this would have happened without two beings bumping into each other at precisely the right moment.

Was it luck? Destiny? Divine providence? These unpredictable moments often speak to our own circumstances in ways that seem too strange to be merely accidental. Jung called these moments *synchronicities*: inexplicable coincidences that contain a meaning too uncanny and improbable to ignore. And to be sure, at the juncture of every synchronicity, whether it's luck or lovers or something entirely different, Hermes is in the air.

There's a strange thing that happens when you start spending time around psychedelics and people who ingest them. I know, I know, but hear me out. When psychedelic medicines are close at hand, synchronicities often begin to occur at a rate that is frankly impossible to ignore. Don't ask me how. It's just been my experience.

For instance, once I was about to sit for a man who was processing an immense amount of childhood trauma and abuse. After ingesting his first dose of psilocybin, he made his way to his journey spot: a chair perched on an isolated rock several feet above the calm Caribbean sea. Just as he was sitting down to begin his trip, he stood up with a start, feeling his phone ringing in his back pocket. As he looked at the phone, his face went white, his eyes widening in shock. Staring at the phone in disbelief, he turned to me, exasperated, and said, "My mother just called me. I haven't had a relationship with her in fifteen years. Why is she calling me now?"

This is only one of a countless array of synchronistic encounters and inexplicable connections that I've witnessed around these medicines. Perhaps you've encountered a few yourself. Synchronicities are inexplicably woven around psychedelic experiences; not always, but often enough to name here. A material-reductionist explanation might assert that synchronicity is a result of a more agile mind's ability to see loose connections and associations because the brain's "default mode network" has been reset. A purely psychological lens would say that perhaps it is the contents of the unconscious bubbling up to the surface. A mythopoetic lens would say that it is the archetypal Trickster, who invites us to dwell in the space of "both/and," of paradox and mystery. Perhaps synchronicity is all of these things, and none, and more.

Neurology and New Worlds

Neuroscientist and psychedelic researcher Robin Carhart-Harris' land-mark 2014 paper "The Entropic Brain" highlighted the ways in which psilocybin decreases blood flow to an area of the brain called the default mode network, enabling novel connections between neural pathways normally routed through this cognitive superhighway.

Psychedelics upset the apple cart of our normal cognitive function-ing, and by introducing a bit of pharmacologically mediated chaos, they make room for new and different neural connections to take shape. Of additional interest here is Carhart-Harris' discussion of psychedelic states being "poised at a 'critical' point in a transition zone between order and disorder" in terms of consciousness (2014, p. 1). This "transition zone" is the domain of all trickster gods. We can find them anywhere that roads, worlds, and even neural networks collide.

We can even see the many studies showing the promise of psyche-delics (e.g., de L. Osório et al., 2015; Hamill et al., 2019) for treating addictions in the light of trickster myths. Whatever epiphany arises during the psychedelic experience that might finally help someone kick a long-held habit marks a shift from one way of thinking to another, one neural network to another, and, mythopoetically speaking, one arche-typal way of being to another. True recovery marks both an end and a beginning—and Trickster dances at the crossroads between.

Two-Faced Gods

Trickster is responsible for helping us see a third way out of our predic-ament. In myths from all over the world, Trickster wisdom teaches the folly of binary thinking. In one story of Eshu, the trickster god from Nigeria's Yoruba people, the god painted his hat white on one side and black on the other, as if wearing two faces at once. Riding down a narrow lane between two fields one day on a fine horse, the villagers saw him and began to quarrel about what color his hat was. Some were certain they saw a white hat, while others were confident it was black. Fighting ensued, and the previously peaceful village erupted into bitter conflict.

Soon, Eshu returned to scold the villagers for their literal "black and white" thinking. Amid their self-righteousness and conviction, they forgot to honor Eshu, which, for the Yoruba, was required before starting anything new, or even claiming something to be "true" at all. Because in the eyes of Eshu, what is true from one side may appear completely opposite from another.

For Eshu, two things can be simultaneously true and false at the same time. But humans have a way of complicating things when they forget this fundamental, quantum-level fact.

Eshu's lesson is social as well as psychological. When we can stretch our perception to embrace truths outside of rigid ideologies, when we can allow our mind to bend itself around some unknown barrier of belief or threshold of imagination, Eshu is dancing with us.

When we are depressed, anxious, or enraged, what is the likelihood that we have fallen into the binary trap of rigid perception? How often do our minds fixate on the way we think life should be—or worse, the way it should have been?

Every time the words *should, can't, always,* or *never* are involved, we can be sure that some part of the psyche is stuck in a binary that makes no place for Trickster's revitalizing flow. It is no small wonder that there is so much division in our culture today. There is no room for these ancient gods of the in between. Every time we cling to self-righteousness, Trickster shakes his/her/their head and tsks their tongue. We can witness their displeasure in the breakdown of community that seems to also be a regrettable outcome of the internet age.

Psychedelics are frequently referred to as "nonspecific amplifiers." Like Grof's notion of psychedelics as *abreactives,* the term *nonspecific amplifier* refers to the idea that psychedelics do not create *specific* effects within the psyche, but rather amplify what is already dwelling within. While there are of course some predictable effects, a familiar arc, and an expected duration with a given substance and dosage, it is almost impossible to foresee the content of this experience. At their core, psychedelics are always unpredictable. They are, in this sense, archetypal tricksters, who both create and destroy the world through their deeds and mistakes, and both help and hinder the efforts of humans. Tricksters are two-faced gods of chance who live between worlds, helping us see all sides of a situation, embracing multiple realities at once.

That fact alone should give anyone pause before approaching these powerful plants and compounds. And despite the recent uptick in clinical research activity, we are nowhere closer to understanding the subjective or phenomenological effects of psychedelics than we were a century ago. The way psychedelics function in the deep psyche (not the brain) still remains a mystery.

Many times I have been with clients who seemed to be in a state of bliss for hours, then suddenly cracked open with grief or pain. Other times, people who expressed complete trust and confidence at the start of a journey might suddenly spiral into a nearly psychotic paranoia, or emerge from their inner world with some emotive eruption completely opposite from the state of inner peace they were saturated in moments before. The psychedelic psyche can reveal many personas or parts hidden within an otherwise collected exterior.

This unpredictability is possible with every psychedelic encounter, but especially at higher doses. Facilitating psychedelic journeys can often have a tenuous, slippery feel. Say the wrong thing, use the wrong tone, even make the wrong facial expression, no matter how subtle, and you may run the risk of sending someone down a road of confusion and doubt, profoundly altering their experience. In these moments, Trickster is dancing in the spaces between, watching and waiting.

The Liminal Road

In ancient metallurgy, mercury—the metal of Hermes—was combined with base metals to help release the gold that might be trapped within. After this alchemical process was complete, the mercury would emerge, unchanged. Like young Hermes walking backward with his stolen cattle or on his many journeys down to Hades and back, the planet Mercury appears to traverse backward several times a year the dreaded Mercury retrograde. Perhaps these parallels drew early Hellenic mystics and their cultural descendants, the medieval alchemists, to link the elemental mercury—quicksilver—to that wandering planet and the only Olympian able to traverse all three worlds at once. The medieval European alchemists distilled this Hermetic quality in the enigmatic phrase *eadem mutata resurgo*: "though changed, I arise the same."

This image of mercury's ability to enter into the heavy, dark *prima materia* of base metals and emerge once again unscathed is also a powerful metaphor for the role of the psychedelic guide. The *psychopomp*, the guide of souls, is one of Hermes's many roles. As patron god of guides and travelers, Hermes and all trickster gods could also be seen as patrons of anyone who ventures into the psychedelic realm.

Karl Kerenyi wrote, "The journeyer is at home while underway, at home on the road itself, the road being understood not as a connection between two definite points on the earth's surface, but as a particular world. . . . He who moves about familiarly in this world-of-the-road has Hermes for his god" (2020, pp. 32–33). The liminal road is a world unto itself, a distinct space that is neither here nor there; and in almost every myth and psychedelic journey, it is the place where transformation most readily occurs.

Across world mythologies, the Trickster is most commonly depicted as being "on the road," traveling between villages on some misadventure, encountering and engaging with the messy unpredictability of life's crossroads. Coyote's travels across North America often begin with him traversing some desert road amid the sagebrush. Loki regularly travels to the mead halls of Jötunheim, the realm of the giants. Eshu trots through village pastures to teach those who forget his power. Raven flies up to the house of the sun and throws down light to the dark world below. In all of these stories, we find Trickster moving from one realm to the next and back again.

Anthropologist Victor Turner studied rituals of initiation across the world, fixing his gaze primarily on the middle phase of these rites of passage, which he called the *liminal*. The word stems from the Latin *limen*, or "threshold"; accordingly, Turner linked liminality to "death, to being in the womb, to invisibility, to darkness, to bisexuality, to the wilderness, and to an eclipse of the sun or moon" (1995, p. 95). Citing culturally marginal figures like the court jester, the traveler, the wandering Jew, and the lone stranger from films about the old American West, Turner claimed that liminal figures play roles in human culture that, although essential, are often maligned and misunderstood. Trouble seems to follow them around. Or vice versa.

Up until quite recently, psychedelics and the people drawn to them have always been liminal outsiders or literal outlaws. They likely didn't know it at the time, but their magic bus trips and fugitive escapades helped birth what we now understand as "psychedelic counterculture," the movement that is perhaps most responsible for bringing psychedelics out of the locked box of government research into the hands of the people. And just like Hermes, it all began with theft.

Sacred Theft and the Birth of Psychedelic Counterculture

The birth of Hermes is a mythic invocation of a sacred theft that changed the entire Greek pantheon and cosmos. The American psychedelic counterculture was also born of theft and sacred transgression. And if we look closely at this history, we will find Hermes's winged signature at every turn.

The discovery of LSD-25 by the Swiss chemist Albert Hofmann is a moment in history that echoes Trickster's cunning laughter and earth-shattering repercussions. Hofmann, who first synthesized LSD-25 in November 1938—less than a year before the outbreak of World War II— would shelve his discovery for four and a half years, until he felt some inexplicable intuition to revisit the molecule. Hofmann undertook the first intentional LSD trip on April 19, 1943. Recalling the incident,

Hofmann said, "I did not choose LSD; LSD found and called me." That call, we could say, was a call from Trickster, entreating him to reach for that fateful molecule he had given birth to—which in turn gave birth to one of the greatest cultural shifts the world had seen in centuries.

Ken Kesey, famed author and the beloved captain of the Merry Pranksters and their acid-fueled 1964 bus journey across the United States, first encountered LSD through another bizarre series of events. Kesey volunteered to take part in a series of LSD experiments at the Menlo Park Veterans Affairs hospital in 1959—one of many covert projects connected with the notorious government mind-control research program known as MK-ULTRA—which means Kesey's first encounter with LSD was actually facilitated by the CIA. He enjoyed the experience so much that he volunteered for the night shift at the hospital for the explicit purpose of being able to ingest and eventually steal more LSD.

Just imagine: wandering around dark hospital corridors, high on acid, listening to the echoing cries of disturbed patients at a time when psychiatrists prescribed lobotomies just as easily as they now prescribe pills. This experience eventually inspired Kesey to write his 1962 novel *One Flew over the Cuckoo's Nest*, establishing him as a literary celebrity and inevitable psychedelic provocateur. Despite the CIA's best efforts to contain LSD and bend it to their will, their research backfired, eventually fueling a tectonic shift in American culture. Yet in true Trickster fashion, some say that was their plan all along, though I don't agree.

Kesey began to share his stolen fire with close friends and other early psychedelic luminaries. From 1965 to 1966, Kesey's literary notoriety and psychedelic evangelism coalesced into a series of live music events up and down the West Coast known as "Acid Tests," where often-unwitting participants would take doses of LSD averaging around 300–500 micrograms: three to five hits of the cleanest acid imaginable, concocted by the famous acid chemist Owsley "Bear" Stanley. The house band for these parties was a little-known group of San Francisco ragtags who eventually called themselves the Grateful Dead.

Back on the East Coast, Harvard psychologists Timothy Leary and Richard Alpert began researching psychedelics in 1960. Often sharing psilocybin and LSD at intimate gatherings with their students under the guise of "research," Leary and Alpert were inspired to critique and eventually dismantle the psychological establishment and its emphasis on pathology, illness, and reinforcement of questionable societal norms. They would eventually both be fired from Harvard for giving psychedelics to undergraduates, violating one of the only boundaries of their research. Build a wall, and Trickster will find his way around it, sometimes through ethically questionable or downright dangerous methods.

Eventually, Leary and Alpert (who later became Ram Dass) moved to the Millbrook Estate, a mansion in upstate New York owned by several young oil heirs to the ultrawealthy Mellon family. These unlikely benefactors bankrolled Leary and Alpert and allowed them to continue their "research." Millbrook became a nexus for psychedelic culture on the East Coast, hosting the acid chemists Nick Sand and Tim Scully, along with their partners Jill Henry and Alice Einhorn, as well as a rotating cast of legendary countercultural intelligentsia including Allen Ginsberg, Jack Kerouac, Alan Watts, Ralph Metzner, Charles Mingus, and even an ill-fated visit from Kesey and the Pranksters on their bus journey.

This bizarre redistribution of wealth from a high-class oil dynasty to a marginal assemblage of obscure intellectuals, renegade psychologists, and straight-up outlaws has the covered tracks of Hermes all over it. Cattle have always been a symbol of wealth, from the Maasai in east Africa to the ancient Norse. We can also see Hermes's theft of Apollo's golden cattle as a redistribution of wealth, channeling Apollo's lofty and far-seeing abundance to Hermes's pedestrian, and far more human, realm.

Kesey's theft of LSD from a secret CIA-funded experiment, Leary and Alpert's ethically ambiguous transgression of Harvard's research boundaries, and the unexpected flow of American dynastic oil wealth into the hands of the radical vanguard of the psychedelic revolution marked a radical shift in our own cultural cosmos that we are still coming down from, more than half a century later.

Leary's public notoriety and psychedelic proselytizing would continue to grow as he sounded the clarion call to "turn on, tune in, and drop out"—the unofficial mantra of the psychedelic '60s. Richard Nixon would eventually label Leary "the most dangerous man in America" precisely for his advocacy of psychedelic consciousness, which in every regard represented transgressing and dismantling the power structures and social norms that conservative white men like Nixon embodied and fiercely protected, even when faced with their own hypocrisy.

Kesey and Leary ultimately ended up paying a price for their sacred theft and transgressions. Both of them landed in jail multiple times, with Leary eventually becoming a fugitive after breaking out with the help of the Weather Underground, another radical movement composed of college students seeking to change the foundations of American society. Their lives were not all peace and love; in fact, one could say that Trickster chose them for the task, that they were fated for this archetypal position and fully lived it, come what may. Perhaps that's why we still know their names today.

Hermes is never punished for stealing his brother's cattle. He's way too sly for that. But Prometheus, a Titan from an earlier generation of gods, paid dearly. Like Raven from many Native mythologies in the Pacific Northwest, Prometheus stole fire from the gods and gave it to the humans, whom he pitied. For his betrayal, Zeus chained him atop a mountain and sent an eagle to peck out his liver every day for eternity. Prometheus's fate, along with the fate of early luminaries like Kesey, Leary, and countless others who dedicated their lives to psychedelics, could be seen as a warning to us all: if you want to steal fire, and if you want to give light, prepare to get burned.

Today, as the "psychedelic renaissance" continues to unfold, we would be wise to remember these moments in psychedelic history where Trickster thoroughly had his way, for better or worse. Coyote visits the land of the dead and comes back, datura flowers behind his ears, dancing in the purple sunset. Raven laughs atop a cedar tree, stealing fire from its locked box in heaven and throwing it down to earth. Hermes walks backward in the dust, leading Apollo's golden cattle toward some roadside attraction, changing the world forever.

If the CIA couldn't contain this stuff, what makes us think we can?

Secrets

The realm of Trickster also encompasses night, and all of the mysterious, mischievous, and sometimes malevolent things that occur under its blanket of quiet darkness.

My personal history of consciousness alteration began as a young adolescent discovering cannabis in the forested hills of Portland, Oregon. After procuring a glass pipe I heard was stashed in some lavender bushes near my home, I began sneaking out at night. Cracking open the antique door at the end of my mother's basement art studio and breathing in the cool, moist night air, I would smoke cannabis far too powerful for my nascent brain, relishing in the secretive ritual of intoxication that I conducted for myself. Not quite sneaking out like mist through a keyhole, but a hidden psychotropic ritual nonetheless.

The outlaw history of psychedelics and plant medicine—from their federally illegal status in the United States to the persecution and murder of midwives, folk healers, and Indigenous people going back centuries—meant that for a very long time these medicines had to be shrouded in secrecy. Any culture of secrecy is a culture of survival, usually in the face of oppression and violence. The cunning and creativity required to keep these traditions alive for so long amid such oppression is, in part, a blessing of Trickster.

I once heard a story about how the water drum and gourd rattle became the two primary instruments in Native American Church ceremonies. In the late 1800s, when the United States still considered Oklahoma to be "Indian country," the Native American Church was formed by the famous Comanche war chief Quanah Parker. During this time, federal officers and soldiers would "patrol" Indian country, making sure that the natives weren't practicing their traditional religion or outlawed ceremonies like the sweat lodge or the Ghost Dance.

As the peyote ceremony grew in popularity, the people knew that they needed to practice their rituals in secret. In the event that a reservation officer came around, they could quickly take the skin off the metal water drum, put it above the fire, and say they were simply making soup. The rattle, which some say was originally made out of a metal tin, appeared as a simple salt-and-pepper shaker. Nothing to see here, officer. *Heyoka* blessings once again.

Secrets play an immense role in the process of psychedelic healing. Very often we might know something unconsciously but require the aid of a psychedelic medicine to bring it into awareness. Whatever was previously unknown, dwelling in the unconscious, emerges into the upper world of our conscious awareness. This previously unconscious material crosses a threshold within the psyche, doing something that only Hermes, Raven, Eshu, and other trickster gods can do.

As a psychedelic therapist, I've seen people struggle and fight for hours on end only to reveal some deeply held secret they could no longer hold. Extramarital affairs, incidents of abuse, silent betrayals—when bottled up, these experiences slowly ferment into the sicknesses that can lead people to seek psychedelics in the first place. When this is the case, the medicines seem to bring people right to the last place they want to go. And often, relief from the ordeal only comes when the secret is finally expressed and brought into the light of consciousness.

Medicine from the Margins

Marginality has always been a core value of depth psychology and Trickster mythologies. Dreams exist at the margins of our consciousness and direct our attention to marginal areas of the psyche that we would rather not see. Tricksters are gods of the road, travelers, edge walkers and eccentric vagabonds who don't quite fit in at the banquets atop Mount Olympus; nor do they find themselves at home around the village hearth (though they'll happily help themselves to morsels from either table). We can always find Trickster at the borderlands of the village, of the cosmos, of the psyche itself. Or rather, that's where Trickster finds us.

Trickster mythologies are often teachings that speak to the necessity for human culture to embrace and maintain a relationship with the marginal wilds of the natural world and the soul itself. In countless fairy tales, an ailing kingdom is revivified by the heroine or hero taking a journey beyond its boundaries, like the girl in the Lindworm story. The medicine needed most is almost always found in the dark forest, not in the comforting lights of home.

The Jungian concept of the *anima/animus,* which implies that different genders psychologically contain one another, subverts modern culture's basic understanding of gender. Queer, trans, and nonbinary people may find a mythopoetic patron in Trickster, for across world mythologies Trickster embodies the in-between spaces of gender and sexuality. While most often showing up in cultural narratives as male, Trickster frequently shifts into other bodies, sexualities, and genders. Loki transforms into a female horse, mates with a giant, and gives birth to Odin's eight-legged steed, Sleipnir. Eshu often appears as both male and female, with multiple forms of genitalia. In stories from the Winnebago tribe, Coyote transforms into a woman at will. In alchemical and Greek traditions, the union of Hermes and Aphrodite sublimates into a nonbinary being known in the classical texts as the Hermaphrodite. While this is now seen as a stigmatizing term, its origins might speak to a mythic root of queer and trans identities.

Trickster embodies and lives multiple identities at once. Changing and eschewing gender is an essential function of trickster gods, who do so through a mythic drive to create something new and unexpected. Queerness, of course, isn't something new, but old as the myths themselves.

Neurodivergence and conditions like autism spectrum disorder (ASD) and attention-deficit/hyperactivity disorder (ADHD) are also marginal (and marginalized) states of functioning experienced by an increasing number of people. Many people, especially those with autism, receive messages all the way from childhood telling them that they are different, deficient, or somehow don't fit in with the standards of neurotypical culture.

As they sit in the back of the classroom or in a quiet corner of a bar, neurodiverse people are also prone to novel ways of thinking and experiencing the world that do not conform with mainstream, neurotypical avenues of perception and cognition. Alan Turing, widely regarded as the progenitor of computer science, was both gay and likely autistic, and he suffered immensely in his life because neither identity was welcome in the world around him. Many other geniuses, like Leonardo Da Vinci, Albert Einstein, Emily Dickinson, and Carl Jung, have all been characterized as either eccentric, hyperfocused, antisocial, reclusive, or simply bizarre, and may have actually been autistic.

The gifts we've received from these groundbreaking thinkers is beyond measure. The role of neurodivergent people in culture at large is one of profound creativity and visionary ingenuity—precisely the role that Trickster figures play in myth. And, like their mythical counterparts, they don't always "fit in" because their unique medicine derives precisely from their experience at the margins of the psyche and brain. One could even make the case that neurodivergent people's ability to think in novel and nonconforming ways puts them at the cutting edge of human evolution.

The margins of culture are almost always responsible for the greatest breakthroughs in art, philosophy, and spirituality. Black culture, marginalized and oppressed in American and European society for centuries, has birthed some of the most enduring art and music of the modern era.

On every level, medicine comes from the margins. From an ecological perspective, the borderlands between different climates and ecosystems harbor the greatest levels of biodiversity, and therefore the greatest potential for fascinating adaptations. The practice of permaculture values the margins as one of its central principles, understanding this archetypal principle that is echoed throughout ecologies.

Human culture gets into trouble when things gravitate too heavily toward anything *mono*, anything decidedly one-sided. *Mono*cultural fields of wheat need to be doused in pesticides simply to survive. *Mono*theistic religions have clashed with each other for centuries over who knows what anymore. *Mono*tonous politicians drone on as they defend *mono*polistic corporations hoarding increasingly obscene amounts of wealth. Meanwhile, Trickster waits in the margins, flipping a coin, biding their time.

Psychedelic Capitalism and Other Bad Jokes

There are psychedelic substances, experiences, music, art, and literature. There are psychedelic philosophies, ethics, worldviews, and subcultures. And there are traditional and modern practices of psychedelic healing and exploration. Psychedelics dissolve boundaries and reveal the soul. And then there is capitalism: an economic system dominated by private corporations entranced with the ideals of infinite growth, resource extraction, consumption, and the bottom line of profit. Capitalism engulfs, confines, and extracts the soul from whatever it consumes.

Like "military intelligence" or the "music business," the convergence of the words *psychedelic* and *capitalism* creates a philosophical paradox. We are currently witnessing how this conundrum will commingle in an age defined by increasing wealth disparity and unchecked extraction. The balance will undoubtedly be precarious.

In the heart-wrenching internet graphic art piece *We Will Call It Pala*, artist Dave McGaughey tells how one woman's vision to start a psychedelic clinic collides with the profit-driven ethos of Silicon Valley and the cold-blooded demands of venture capital investors. As the story progresses along its all-too-likely trajectory, she faces the monstrosity she unwittingly created. Grieving for her seemingly naive vision, the heroine laments, "There is no medicine strong enough to blow a corporation's mind." This is because, despite their legal standing in our society as persons, corporations are not conscious beings. A corporation can never have a mind-altering or heart-opening experience; and although the etymological roots of the word boil down to "body," a corporation will never feel a thing.

Art may be one of the best arenas where we might be able to predict how the alchemical vinegar of psychedelics will merge into the oil-laden waters of capitalism. It is said that art can serve either as a hammer or a mirror for society. Even once a great work has been absorbed by capitalism— a Banksy or a John Cage or a van Gogh—the impact of that work can still resonate within the psyche and catalyze an inner shift, no matter how many coffee mugs it's been plastered onto.

Art is able to at least partially escape the trap of capitalism because it exists between two realms. Art takes form in our physical reality, but it also lives within the imagination and is formless. Art can transmit ideas, imparting messages that transcend the tangible and time-bound. Art changes culture and evokes emotion even if we've seen the same image a thousand times. Art is dangerous.

Lewis Hyde, in his book *Trickster Makes This World*, argues that artists have evolved to become the trickster figures in our modern era (2010). Charting the work of figures as diverse as Marcel Duchamp, Bob Dylan, and Frederick Douglass, Hyde explores the very nature of the words "art" and "artist," tracing their etymological origins back to the Latin *artus*, which means "joint" or "juncture"—Trickster's domain. Hyde says the "artus-workers" of our modern era now play the role that Hermes, Raven, and Coyote played in their own cultural mythologies as gods of the threshold, the trick, becoming the oft-misunderstood hammer or mirror of the culture.

Art stops being art when it emerges from a commodified, controlled, and overly conformist environment. The spirit of art is to buck these conventions and shatter the gallery glass that contains it. Psychedelics are no different. As more corporations and financial interests attempt to stake their claim on psychedelics, whether by the creation of "novel" compounds or by attempting to patent the most basic elements of psychedelic therapy, as chronicled in various reports in *Vice*, they too will be confronted with Trickster's archetypal urge to break convention (Love, 2021). As we have seen, psychedelic substances seem to have an agenda all their own, escaping labyrinthine hospitals and laboratory shelves, and are guaranteed to escape the rigid boundaries and outdated structures imposed upon them, despite our best efforts. Like great artists and their mythological forebears, they cannot be controlled.

Skills

The Guide Is Not the Hero

Hermes might visit Olympus, but he doesn't live there. Kerenyi says, "Hermes is deliberately kept at a distance from every heroic happening. . . .

Fame has no part in his world. Hermes's skill in the *Iliad* is strictly that of the most unheroic evasion" (2020, pp. 26–27).

The role of the psychedelic guide is not heroic or exalted. Chances are, if we're getting off on finding ourselves surrounded by notoriety or receiving some lofty status from the work, we may have taken a wrong turn. Yet we live in an ego-driven culture. Heroics form the basis of Western cultural mythologies and therefore permeate our psyche as a desirable archetype to embody.

The Trickster is like a balm for a culture inflamed by the heroic ego. The guide is not the conquering warrior, the exalted healer, or the star of the show—they don't do something to those they guide. Rather, they are along for the journey, entering into a highly relational space that is the antithesis of heroic exploits and represents a desperately needed counterpoint.

Expect the Unexpected

Trickster loves to remind us of their power the moment we forget it. Put another way, the more we think we *know* something—the way a certain psychedelic experience is going to go, for instance, or how someone will respond to a particular medicine dose—the more we invite Trickster to remind us of his presence. As nonspecific amplifiers, psychedelic medicines work in ways that are nonlinear, often irrational, and rarely conforming to a materialist, biomedical framework. There must be room for the unexpected, the messy, and the unknown on your altar; otherwise Trickster may come through and kick the whole thing over.

Embrace Synchronicity

Healing is nonlinear, defies logic, and can break all conventions of rationality. Synchronicity plays a fascinating role in psychedelic work that I hope will always remain a mystery. I always try to keep a space open for the uncanny or miraculous. Often, synchronicities occur when the natural world has something to say during a psychedelic experience. A fated hailstorm mirrors someone's inner turbulence. The hoot of a hidden owl draws our attention beyond ourselves and out into the liminal darkness of the forest. An iridescent butterfly lands on your arm at the perfect moment, or a humble caterpillar crawls across your hand and becomes a symbol of the journey to become the very butterfly glimpsed before. All of these things, in the right frame of mind, can become unique, synchronistic events of immeasurable consequence.

Don't Get Too Holy

Thou shalt not take thyself too seriously. I once heard of a Lakota medicine man who would play weird tricks on people during his ceremonies. Some people loved it. Some people never came back. His advice? "Don't get too holy."

Hermes shits on Apollo's hand. Loki cross-dresses as other creatures. Eshu wiggles his way through a multiplicity of genders and appearances. Sheela na Gig, whose wide grin graces old Irish churches, flashes her genitalia at the world. Coyote is sent running a thousand times with his tail between his legs. There is a vital and refreshing link between Trickster, humiliation, humor, and humility. We have a lot to learn here, especially in the healing professions, where we all probably take ourselves way too seriously.

Stay Human

Above all, keep to your ethics. Remember, archetypes are amoral, their actions not grounded in the social norms of humanity. We mortals, on the other hand, are strictly bound to a set of rules and boundaries that must be adhered to for the sake of everyone involved. Even as Trickster energy flows in and around psychedelic medicines and experiences, do not lose sight of what is ethical, what is safe, what is kind, and what is human. Trickster is unpredictable and will happily have their way with you, as they have done with so many wayward journeyers who paid dearly for their crossroads bargain. Too many have invoked Coyote or the *Heyoka* as a way to excuse their shape-shifting moods and questionable behaviors. Staying human means we must never lose sight of the things that make us so, especially when playing with Trickster's stolen fire.

✳ ✳ ✳

It was said that one could petition Hermes for aid by leaving an offering at one of his roadside shrines, covering one's ears, and walking away. When you finally opened your ears, the first thing you heard was Hermes speaking back to you. The fine print is that one had to be firmly outside the bounds of the village and marketplace before listening for the messenger's reply. I believe the modern term for uncovering one's ears too soon is an "echo chamber," and we all know how helpful those can be. Especially in the age of social media and increasing polarization, Trickster delights when we can lean into the paradox of "both-and." When Eshu's hat can be both black and white.

As I write this, I am traveling in Mexico. Having traveled all over the world for a large part of my adult life, I can say this: traveling is a dance between protection and vulnerability. While on the road, we are constantly subject to the whims of Trickster, and like the Fool card of the tarot, are perpetually opened to the unknown. The liminal road makes fools of us all.

Vulnerable uncertainty is a notion that I try, and often fail, to integrate into my daily life. Trying to make space for the hat (or cloak) of many colors continually brings me to the edge of my comfort zone. Things might get a bit messy. And I have to trust that Trickster is teaching me through the mess. Vulnerable uncertainty is a cornerstone of my work as a therapist and psychedelic guide, and perhaps the most rewarding element of my intimate relationships. Every time I sit with a client about to undertake a psychedelic voyage, I feel myself returning to this vulnerable precipice of the known.

So now I wonder: what might it look like to bring this principle of vulnerable uncertainty and Eshuic ambivalence into our broader relationships and communities? How might Trickster dance with us if we allow them more space in our daily lives, especially when we are rubbed the wrong way by someone's viewpoint or opinion?

Somehow, I don't think Trickster would approve of the vitriol and righteousness that is now the standard communication style in our internet age. I don't claim any truth here, but let's call it a hunch: we disrespect the gods when we dismiss each other. Instead, there's a floral whisper in my ear pleading that we sit down at the table together under the bougainvillea blossoms, pour some mezcal, and talk long into the night.

We can pray to other gods for help in the morning.

VII

The Guide

Power, Authenticity, and Inner Authority

Heavy is the head that wears the crown.

—SHAKESPEARE

The Sorcerer's Apprentice

*O*nce upon a time there lived a powerful sorcerer. Everyone in the village knew not to trouble the white-haired conjurer. A hush fell upon the villagers whenever he walked down the muddy lanes, where hearth smoke and alehouse banter parted around his shape like a ship through fog. He didn't need to say much.

This sorcerer had an apprentice, a young boy who labored in his workshop. Every day, the apprentice mopped the floors, scrubbed the kitchen, fed the fire, and swept up piles of luminescent dust. Chop wood, carry water. We all know this kind of work. With nothing to show for his efforts, the apprentice began to feel—like many of us begin to feel when we're immersed in such tasks—bored.

One day, the old man left his workshop, leaving the apprentice to safeguard his elixirs and feed the cauldron fire. After a long morning of cleaning ashes from the hearth, with more work still before him, the apprentice had an idea.

He crept through the workshop, shifting around glass alembics and rare animal skulls, and found his way to the magician's private chamber. There, on the cluttered table, the apprentice spied the object of his desire: the sorcerer's wand.

Without a second thought, he grabbed it. When he came back to his old broom, he knew exactly what he was going to do. Glancing down at the wand in his hand, he felt some newfound power surging up his arm.

He raised his arm, and with a flick of his wrist, he beckoned the broom to life. The apprentice was shocked as the broom shot up and proceeded to whirl with a life all its own. The young apprentice guided the broom to fetch a bucket and follow him down the stone stairs to the well in the cavernous basement. Somehow, the broom managed to fill the bucket on its own and went back up the stairs, pouring the water into the cistern that the apprentice had begrudgingly filled so many times before. Dunk, Splash. Dunk, Magic!

A smile crept across the apprentice's face as he contemplated the power he now possessed. Impressed by his newfound abilities and pleased with the spell he seemed to have so easily conjured, the apprentice decided to take a well-earned nap.

But suddenly the apprentice woke from his sleep to find water gathering around his feet. As he looked, he saw the broom pour yet another bucket of water into the already overflowing cistern.

Jumping to his feet, the apprentice rolled up his sleeves, raised the wand and, just as before, flicked his wrist in the broom's direction. Yet this time, nothing happened. The broom continued its manic dance, and the water continued to pool upon the floor. Dunk, Splash. Dunk,

Perhaps I was holding it incorrectly, the apprentice thought. He focused his mind and once more flicked the wand. Nothing.

Third try. The apprentice adjusted his stance, took a deep breath, and tried with all his might to will the broom back into its previously inanimate state. Again, nothing.

The apprentice realized he needed to do something drastic. He frantically scoured the workshop for something that might work. Perhaps a cursed Egyptian talisman? Or maybe a Tibetan dagger carved from a rinpoche's femur? He rummaged through the sorcerer's study, looking for instructions that he knew he wouldn't find, realizing that he had put into motion something he did not have the power to stop.

Running back into the workshop, he grabbed his axe. The broom was simply a piece of wood, was it not? The apprentice ran to the broom, and with one clean blow, cleaved it in two.

Breathing a sigh of relief, the apprentice collapsed back into his chair, grateful that he had solved the problem. He settled in and drifted back to sleep.

As the apprentice dreamed of wealth, success, and even more power, something was stirring in the workshop. Pieces of the broom, still enchanted by the apprentice's spell, were shaking themselves back to life and growing in size. Where there was one broom, now there were many. Without stopping, the brooms continued their task of fetching buckets of water and pouring them into the overflowing cistern.

Abruptly awakened by the rush of cold water, the apprentice found himself immersed in the flooded workshop. The apprentice looked around desperately for a solution, found himself utterly alone, and realized that he was literally in over his head.

At that moment the workshop doors flew open, and the old sorcerer beheld the disaster that had unfolded during his absence. Without hesitation, he commanded the brooms to stop. In response to nothing more than a muttered word, the brooms became lifeless sticks once more. The water retreated back down the well like the tide, books stacked themselves back together, and the workshop magically returned to its old, familiar arrangement. He didn't even need the wand.

With one glance at the young apprentice, the wizard knew all he needed to know.

The Sibling Society

This simple folktale, which traces to medieval Europe and the Middle East, is said to have roots that reach all the way back to ancient Egypt. It has much to teach us about power.

From the beginning of the story, the old sorcerer, who may have been preparing the young apprentice for deeper knowledge, leaves. Once again, myths often reveal the value of elders, who can help to temper the overly ambitious, ego-driven flush of youth. As with fire, if you're playing with psychedelics, or anything filled with a power beyond your control, it's best to learn from those who've been around a while—those whose hands maybe have a few scars from their own experiments gone awry.

True elders are hard to come by. In the world of psychedelic healing, many of our elders are slowly fading into the twilight of their years or already waiting gleefully for us on the other side. We may find them living a humble life of ceremony near Mesa Verde or the Rio Ucayali, far from the glow of city lights. Perhaps this drought of eldership accounts for why so many modern psychedelic explorers find themselves in remote Indigenous communities in search of a teacher. This was certainly the case for me.

Wherever the elders are, this story tells us what can happen in their absence. The young apprentice looks around, sees the elder's vacant seat, and believes themselves ready to claim it as their own. Because of this void of genuine leadership, the apprentice is drawn to claim power they have not rightfully earned. They claim authority without the authenticity to back it up. A person who lives in such a way is like a tree with no roots: sooner or later, it's going to come crashing down.

Robert Bly referred to this pervasive trend as the *sibling society*: a contemporary cultural condition whereby people who are young in body or spirit look to each other for guidance because the elders are nowhere to be found. It's not just the blind leading the blind; it's the uninitiated initiating the uninitiated.

In Indigenous cultures, becoming the village shaman or healer was usually not a job people wanted. This immensely difficult position might have entailed a childhood illness or spiritual burden that left them isolated or painfully misunderstood. Ancestral spirits might harass or demand things of this person, which could lead to a life on the margins of society, away from the troubling eyes of the village. (A certain snake-haired goddess comes to mind.) One's community could just as easily celebrate you for healing their sick child, or blame you for that very sickness, whispering behind your back a word met universally with fear: *witch*. There is a reason that the shaman lives in a hut at the edge of the village. It wasn't a glamorous gig and was understood to be just as much of a burden as it was a blessing. One did not eagerly claim the title of shaman or healer. It claimed you.

In the Shipibo tradition, a qualified *onanya*, or ayahuasca healer, spends years in isolation in the jungle, sacrificing what little material pleasures they might otherwise enjoy in order to complete many painstaking plant *dieta*s. The *onanya*-to-be forgoes sex, salt, sugar, alcohol, spices, oils, and most human contact—all of which bring us comfort—in order to learn from the plants themselves, making a pact with these powerful spirits. Fasting, cleansing, and ceremonial work are all elements of the Shipibo *dieta*, which is aimed at stripping down one's mind, body, and spirit enough to establish relationship with the ethereal energies of certain *plantas maestras*, or teacher plants. This cannot happen without a severe tempering of the ego and its pride—energies that the Shipibo would identify as *cruzado*, or crossed against the energies of the plants. To *cross* a plant during a *dieta* is a serious misstep that can result in sickness, madness, and even death. Immense sacrifice was, and still is, a foundational aspect of this tradition.

The Shipibos, not immune to pride themselves, understand the multilayered function of the *dieta*. They often refer to the "cleaning" that occurs during ceremony and the *dieta*. While there is certainly a level of physiological and somatic cleaning that occurs through drinking ayahuasca, there is an equal if not greater depth of psychospiritual purification that the *dieta* facilitates. The ideal end result is that the person undergoing this experience is prepared to relate to their newfound power in a balanced, tempered way. Having engaged in just a few months of this practice myself, I can personally attest to the grit, difficulty, and immense sacrifice required to undergo it. Nothing about the *dieta* is easy or glamorous.

In the Native American Church, there is no training program to become a road man and lead an all-night peyote ceremony. While I can only speak from what my own teachers have said and from what I've observed around this tradition, here's what I understand: one puts their time in, slowly learning through proximity to elders and other relationships within the tradition, until one is asked to lead a *meeting*. Putting on just one peyote meeting requires countless tasks that are often imbued with many layers of ancestral and spiritual teachings. There are often stories attached to why things are the way they are, which is also the responsibility of the road person to know and transmit as they see fit. Becoming a road man or woman takes years of sacrifice that are difficult for most people to even comprehend.

My understanding of these roles is superficial at best. But from what I've learned and observed, the responsibilities of a road person are immense. They must learn how to prepare the firewood, how to build and manage the fire, how to move the coals into their proper shape, and how to put up the tipi in its correct form down to the most minute detail. They must learn how to prepare the medicine, how to sing the songs for different parts of the ceremony, how to work with both positive and challenging energies and spirits, and how to see what is occurring in the fire and the ceremonial space itself. They must master each ritualistic step of the all-night ceremony until finally they receive their "altar" or "fireplace" from an initiated road person and elder. These are only a fraction of the outer responsibilities required of this role.

The Native American Church is as much a way of life as it is a spiritual community, as well as a symbol of the perseverance and strength of Native peoples. It is also a living example of the time it takes for someone to authentically step into a ceremonial leadership role in an authentic way. In the "psychedelic renaissance," where anyone with a handful of mushrooms and an Instagram profile can fashion themselves as an elite shaman, the traditions of the *red road* have much to say about what true leadership requires.

Being "told by the plants" that one should serve psychedelic medicine is not a legitimate path to leadership in any Indigenous medicine tradition I have ever encountered. Claiming the title of shaman, guide, or healer without any contact with elders or mentors is a symptom of the sibling society. We all must proceed with caution.

Potions of Power

The second thing that happens in the story is that the apprentice sees an opportunity to claim power. He picks up the wand, but he hasn't earned the right. The results are catastrophic. Such is the situation with so many people in positions of power across the globe. Perhaps the most dangerous situations arise when people claim authority without having done the inner work that can ground and balance it. This is only amplified in the modern psychedelic world, where anyone can suddenly claim the role of "leader" and go about their business unchecked. But how does one earn this power in a good way, and what does being grounded in one's own inner authenticity actually mean?

Victor Turner examined the role of power in the processes of initiation, paying specific attention to how experiences of liminality reorganize and reshape power within both individuals and cultures. Initiation, wrote Turner, "tempers the pride of the incumbent of a higher position or office. . . . Liminality implies that the high could not be high unless the low existed, and he who is high must experience what it is like to be low" (1995, p. 97).

Initiation prepares people for any actual power that may await them upon their return to their community. Our culture is not big on "tempering pride." Yet the study of myth, Indigenous cultures, and psychedelic healing traditions shows us how such tempering is profoundly necessary when it comes to our relationship with power.

This has nothing to do with how many cups of ayahuasca you've drunk. It has everything to do with the condition of your heart, the amount of grief you've metabolized, and whether you've actually taken the time to learn from teachers, elders, and the psyche itself. This isn't a trophy that you get just for showing up. You have to earn it.

In the West, we are obsessed with claiming power. The United States was founded on a conflicted mythos of empowerment, liberation, and rugged individualism. Yet anyone who has remotely paid attention to history will quickly point to the many flaws in this narrative and how this power was only won through the genocide and suppression of Indigenous people and those sold into bondage. Like it or not, this is the story of power most Americans are living by.

But it wasn't always this way. Power in an integrated, initiatory context is achieved through authentically earning it, a task that is recognized, facilitated, and therefore trusted by the community. Let's not forget: for power to be real, it has to be agreed upon by a community of others. A lone individual conflating their delusions of grandeur with power isn't strength, it's psychosis.

Authentic power is inherently relational, and therefore must be in service to the very relationships that support it. Along with this comes responsibility to a real community of people that can remove this power if it is abused. *Accountability* is another word for this reciprocal aspect of power.

By "accountability," I'm not talking about the fallout from scandal or being "canceled." I'm talking about how authentic power operates within a functioning community. Collectively, our culture might be so far removed from such an understanding of power that it seems alien to imagine a world where the community actually determines who and what receives power. But once upon a time, this radical notion was called a *democracy*.

Without real ties to a community, people in positions of power are far less likely to be held accountable. Engaging in psychedelic work without real ties to a community and avenues of accountability is dangerous. This is why cult leaders and other abusers isolate themselves and the people under their sway. An abusive practitioner can simply pull up stakes and head off to the next hippie town where nobody knows their name or history—a far-too-frequent occurrence in the psychedelic world and beyond.

Leadership Archetypes and the Psychedelic Guide

What happens next in the story is that the apprentice falls asleep after claiming his newfound power, becoming literally unconscious. Unconsciousness is where abuse of power begins. The result in the story, and in real life, quickly spirals out of control.

Psychedelics, and all drugs for that matter, are saturated with power. A single drop of LSD can send you on a twelve-hour voyage, a dusting of MDMA crystals can heal trauma, and trace amounts of fentanyl can kill. Because of this, being in close proximity to this power also contains certain archetypal qualities. Archetypes, as Jung noted, are also crystallizations of power, which, like all drugs, can just as easily expand and enliven the psyche as they can overtake and consume it. In depth psychology, this phenomenon is known as archetypal possession.

According to Jung, this occurs when the archetype unconsciously "seizes hold of the psyche with a kind of primeval force and compels it to transgress the bounds of humanity. The consequence is a puffed-up attitude (inflation), loss of free will, delusion and enthusiasm for good and evil alike. This is the reason why men have always needed demons and cannot live without gods" (1972, pp. 70–71). We all have seen instances of archetypal possession, knowingly or not. Celebrities going off the rails, high on their own self-importance and fame. Tyrannical leaders becoming even more unhinged as the walls close in. Religious fundamentalists on fire with manic zeal. We can also see archetypal possession orbit close to our own lives: a relationship dynamic that oscillates between fiery passion and toxic disdain, an inexplicable phobia or obsession, or anything that causes us to act beyond our control. All are signs that some archetypal force is inhabiting the psyche.

Within the field of psychology, watching one's own ego inflation is ideally a constant practice. Being able to laugh at oneself, see parts of oneself as ridiculous, and maintain a sense of humor about one's own life and work can be a powerful practice to counter self-inflation. For many therapists and psychedelic practitioners, myself included, this often looks like a refreshingly dark sense of humor in a world that has the potential to drown you in heartbreak.

As more people begin flocking to the field of psychedelics, the risk of inflation is even greater, for psychedelics put one in exceedingly close proximity with power.

Below are three archetypes that I have observed in various "psychedelic personas" over the years. Many of these archetypes I have seen embodied in real people working in the psychedelic world, while others are more amorphous energies I've felt with certain "healers." Just like the illuminated face and perpetually dark side of the moon, each archetype has two sides: a mature or integrated form, and an unintegrated or shadow form, resulting in a total of six archetypal forms. You may find these archetypes resonating in yourself, or you may see them in others. We are not defined by them; we simply need to be aware of them.

The Guru and the Sovereign

Terence McKenna famously said, "Avoid gurus. Follow plants" (2015).

Although figures like Leary and Alpert certainly flirted with guru energy, the "guru" archetype has certainly been around since well before the wild days of the 1960s. Yet unlike the early pioneers of psychedelic counterculture, who put their lives and careers on the line, the current field of psychedelics has the potential to become awash with people drunk on their own power (and possibly still high from the night before).

I once saw a friend who owns a psychedelic retreat center post an ad looking for facilitators. After listing the job qualifications, the ad said, "No guru complexes!" I couldn't help but laugh. This is a known phenomenon in the psychedelic world, and it is deeply problematic.

The Guru is the shadow of the archetype of the Sovereign.

In its integrated form, the Sovereign—the Emperor and Empress cards in the tarot—is an archetype of abundance, fertility, wealth, care, support, family, safety, celebration, and blessing. The Sovereign arche-type flows from our inner authority, located at the very center of the psyche, what Jung called the Self. The Sovereign is the embodiment of right relationship to power.

Like a loving parent or attentive mentor, the Sovereign watches over their realm with love and care. The Guru, on the other hand, forces the world to conform to their will—a vision to which they are committed despite whatever harm may come in its wake. In the context of psyche-delic healing, this can play out directly with clients or collaborators. This archetype can also manifest through the space where the actual work occurs. Is there a special lofty seat that the leader always needs to be in? Is there a lack of flexibility in terms of who can speak or contribute to a space? Are there certain unspoken rules, codes, or dogmas that permeate the environment? Are people vying for attention from the leader? These are all signs that the Guru archetype may be present.

The Guru strongly believes that they know what is best for someone else. The Sovereign knows that within each person exists an inner healer, an emergent knowing that is directed toward wholeness, even if we don't understand it. This is called the "inner healing intelligence," a notion developed by Stanislav Grof and elaborated on by Michael Mithoefer in what is now the MAPS MDMA therapy training protocol, which is used across the world (Mithoefer, 2015). The Guru mistakenly believes that they are the ones doing the healing. The Sovereign knows that given a safe, loving, and well-held container, they can empower people to heal themselves.

The embodied authority of the Sovereign recognizes that within each person lives another Sovereign—an inner authority that must be met in collaboration, not domination. The Sovereign archetype is about power *with*, not power *over*. In its integrated form, the archetype of the Sovereign, the King and the Queen, is highly relational. The Guru, the shadow King/Queen, or the Tyrant is antirational and ultimately oppressive.

Jewish mystic and philosopher Martin Buber wrote about what he called the "I-Thou" relationship: a cornerstone of humanistic psychotherapy that sees the therapeutic relationship itself as an inherently loving, and therefore healing, force. Between two beings, wrote Buber, lives the divine. "Love is between I and Thou. . . . Love is the responsibility of an I for a Thou," he said (1958, pp. 14–15).

I always strive to approach my work with this "I-Thou" relationship in mind. For me, it means respecting the fact that there is something much larger at play between me and my client. At the most foundational level, the client is already whole. It is the job of the medicine, and at times the facilitator, to help people realize this fact.

The Dark Sorcerer and the Wounded Healer

In the Amazon, I heard it said that every shaman who has the power to heal also has the power to kill. There is a fine line between the two. Just as the dose is the difference between a medicine and a poison, somewhere on that same spectrum dances the archetype of the Dark Sorcerer and the Wounded Healer.

The Dark Sorcerer is an archetype that occupies and perpetuates disconnection. The Dark Sorcerer represents the lofty intellect disconnected from the embodied heart, raw power disconnected from relational responsibility, and alluring appearances disconnected from the unpolished truth.

No one sets out to become a sorcerer. It's not an archetype we consciously walk into. People find themselves unconsciously consumed by this destructive energy because bad things happened to them: abuse, betrayals, loss, grief—in a word, trauma. The Dark Sorcerer is a healer whose wounds have been ignored for so long that they begin to fester, and the only thing they can do is wound others, reproducing their trauma. When this archetype finds power, gasoline pours onto an already uncontrollable fire.

The Dark Sorcerer archetype is what enables someone to rationalize abuse in ceremonial or therapeutic spaces. Especially in instances of sexual abuse, the Dark Sorcerer is so possessed by their power that they rationalize the abuse itself by believing it will bring healing, that it was somehow what the client was needing or asking for all along. The Dark Sorcerer cannot take accountability because the power they possess is bolstered by the hierarchical disconnection they create within their community. Taking real accountability would render the Dark Sorcerer powerless; therefore, they avoid it at all costs.

In many Indigenous cultures, a person deemed a sorcerer by the community would often be subject to exile or even death. During my time with the Shipibo and other Indigenous cultures, the topic of sorcery was always right around the corner. My teachers would speak of "attacks" coming from other shamans, often hundreds of miles away. Sickness and bad luck was usually chalked up to *brujeria*, which a bitter rival might send their way. While black magic and sorcery seems to be a ubiquitous part of the Indigenous shamanic world (at least in every tradition I've encountered), the *brujeria* situation in Peru was clearly exacerbated by the exploding market of ayahuasca tourism.

We could easily decry this apparent despoilment of what we might otherwise see as a "pure" Indigenous cultural sphere, but this is a colonial lens. Without asking the Shipibo, this perspective insists that they, and indeed all Indigenous peoples, should exist in some kind of suspended animation that conforms to a European notion of who Indigenous people should be: poor, living in a hut, and disconnected from the "outside" world. This lens also robs the Shipibo and other Indigenous people of their right to profit from a tradition and medicine that are rightfully theirs.

It should also be mentioned that many of these traditions can weaponize the label of sorcerer as a way to explain the unexplainable, placing blame on a human being for what those in the Western world might see as simply a matter of health or bad luck. It has happened that successful people have been labeled sorcerers out of jealousy or personal rivalry. The consequences can be immense. In the context of this book, I am speaking from an archetypal and metaphorical perspective, not a literal one.

The Dark Sorcerer archetype heals by being brought back into community. In a famous story from the Haudenosaunee peoples of what is now upstate New York, an evil sorcerer named Tadodaho was finally healed when the clan mothers brought him into their village and combed out the snakes from his hair. The community, especially the feminine, was the medicine this sorcerer needed in order to finally make peace. Only when surrounded by loving people can our minds—our mental serpents that only care about themselves—be massaged into something more relational, more empathetic, and more dedicated to healing. This story eventually ends with the people forging what came to be known as the Great Law of Peace, which was the precursor to American democracy and the powerful Iroquois Confederacy.

The Wounded Healer archetype is painfully aware of their own wounds and the wounds of the world around them. Where the Dark Sorcerer seeks to smooth over these wounds with illusion and manipulation, the Wounded Healer understands that their soul's vulnerability is what often facilitates the healing itself. Where there is no wound, there can be no healing. As Rumi said, "The cure to the pain is in the pain" (1995, p. 205).

The Wounded Healer is no stranger to suffering. In fact, you could say that it is their very relationship to suffering that creates this capacity to heal *through* the wound itself. This is a primary reason why suffering is such a ubiquitous element of initiation rites across the world. Sometimes this process can take years. But in time, the wound becomes a channel for whatever precise medicine is required by the circumstances of their client or community. The Wounded Healer dutifully tends to the depths of their own wound, their own sadness, their own grief, and the space it occupies. All of this directs us toward the soul.

This is not to say that the Wounded Healer lopes around bleeding all over the place. They don't parade their wounds for people to gawk at, nor do they need someone to rescue them from their pain. But they don't hide it either. The most powerful healers I've met walk with a limp, literally or metaphorically, and often refuse to be called healers in the first place. They are honest about their incompleteness. They can laugh at themselves, and weep just as easily. The Wounded Healer works to heal themselves first, even if they must learn to live with a wound that will never completely mend.

The Eternal Youth and the Wise Elder

Peter Pan—flying ever higher, continually seeking the next quest, refusing to grow up, and instead choosing to live in the dramatic dreamworld of Neverland—is the quintessential image of the Eternal Youth. In depth psychology, this archetype is known as the *puer* (or *puella*) *aeternus*, the eternal boy or girl. In the psychedelic community, one does not have to look far to see this archetype dancing with people. Self-described "biohackers," usually white dudes obsessed with extending their youth, are magnetized to psychedelics for productivity purposes and the "hacks" they perceive these medicines might offer them in their perpetual quest for optimization and perfection. The entire biohacking phenomenon could be seen as a *puer* fantasy, obsessed with the pursuit of youth, seeking the Holy Grail as quickly as possible while bypassing the quest. But there are no shortcuts in this work.

Programs in which people believe they can get a rapid online certification to become an "expert" or "shaman" are entranced by the archetype of the Eternal Youth, which always seeks the quick and easy path. While this sort of behavior has today become commonplace, there used to be a word for people who peddled this kind of unearned authority: *charlatan*.

The Eternal Youth is the archetypal foundation of the sibling society. Bly often referred to "flying boys"—youthful archetypes of escapism and aloofness—appearing throughout myth and fairy tales. Being "high" and constantly needing to alter one's consciousness is another method of flight that many people use to escape the heavier realities here on earth. Symbolically, we could even see a superficial relationship to feathers in various New Age ceremonial circles as an indication that the Eternal Youth archetype is present. When sincere Indigenous cultural practices become a fashion statement, you know that the energy of Eternal Youth is in the room.

While the Eternal Youth is mostly concerned with themselves, the Wise Elder is concerned with their community. By way of initiation, the Wise Elder becomes less and less self-focused and more oriented toward service of others. The Wise Elder teaches and shares what they've learned for those who seek it out. It is natural that an initiated psyche seeks to help support the initiation of others.

Yet another reason why elders are so necessary in cultivating psychedelic leadership is that they can serve as examples for what a right relationship with power might look like. Many (but not all) of the medicine elders I've known carry a lightness and humor with them and seem to hold their power lightly, or not at all. They have nothing to prove and are not seeking to meet their own emotional needs through those they serve. Power naturally gathers within them the way water settles into a still pond—impersonal, gentle, and brimming with vitality. It becomes a source of abundance for all who drink from it, a Well of lifegiving waters.

The Wise Elder also knows grief. They can relate equally to the depths of the Underworld as they can to the summit of the Sacred Mountain. Part of their role is simply to support and bless others as they navigate the many twists of life's labyrinth because they've been there before. Yet despite this, the Wise Elder still preserves some of the sweetness, playfulness, and hope of the Eternal Youth. Otherwise, life will leave us bitter and cynical. The name of the ancient Chinese sage Lao Tzu, it is said, translates both to something like "old master" and "ancient child." It is in this paradox, on the precipice of age and youth, joy and suffering, and hope and despair, that the Wise Elder makes their home.

Skills

Examining Our Relationship to Power

Psychedelics are crystallizations of power. Stay in proximity to this power long enough, and it will magnify your relationship to it, pointing directly to the parts of this relationship that need attention. No one is immune to, above, or past this process. Power is an archetypal energy that affects everyone in strange ways.

Ecofeminist author Starhawk talks about three types of power: *power-over*, *power-from-within*, and *power-with*. "Power-over is linked to domination and control; power-from-within is linked to the mysteries that awaken our deepest abilities and potential. Power-with is social power, the influence we wield among equals" (1987, p. 9). Symbiotic patterns in nature exemplify power-with relationships, which embrace collaboration, transparency, and participation. The "three sisters" method of Indigenous agriculture, where corn, beans, and squash all grow together in a supportive dance, depicts a power-with dynamic in a beautiful way. The corn provides a stable stalk for the bean vines to climb upon, while the wide leaves of the squash cover the soil, keeping it moist. The dynamic relationality of ecosystems shows us what true power-with relationships might look like.

Some questions to ask yourself when examining your relationship to power:

▼ How does having power make you feel? What thoughts or emotions arise?

▼ Can you recall a moment in your life when you felt completely powerless?

▼ Can you think of examples of power-with relationships or systems that inspire you?

▼ Who or what embodies healthy leadership archetypes to you? This can be a real or fictional person, an animal, or an aspect of nature.

▼ What would tempt you to abuse your power?

▼ What community structures can you surround yourself with that can offer you reliable reflection?

▼ Whom do you trust to offer you clear and honest feedback?

Doing Your Own Work

Examining your relationship to power is also an introspective act. Therefore, doing your own work, especially with psychedelic medicines, becomes an ethical requirement of any psychedelic facilitator or healer. I'm not saying you need to be tripping all the time. Rather, it is an ethical imperative to maintain an ongoing relationship with the medicines you are serving others or claiming to "carry."

Would you trust a pilot who is scared of flying? Would you take a prescription from a doctor who doesn't believe in pharmaceuticals? There is a question that occasionally arises in certain corners of the psychedelic world: does a psychedelic therapist need to have personal psychedelic experience in order to be a worthy guide? I would emphatically say yes.

While working as a psilocybin retreat leader in Jamaica, it was an unspoken agreement among the team that periodically taking mushrooms was simply part of the job. Not only did we need to test each new batch of mushrooms we were offering clients, but the nature of the work also requires a relationship and familiarity with the medicine that can only be built by taking it. Imagine the countless hours spent in psychedelic space by the many Indigenous practitioners mentioned at the start of this chapter. All of that time is an investment in this relationship between human and something decidedly more than human.

Doing your own work does not exclusively refer to psychedelic work, either. Having practices for looking inward, receiving honest reflection, and returning to one's center are what's important. This could be therapy, meditation, men's or women's circles, or other forms of council circles, for instance. Doing this work in community is a vital aspect of this spiral road.

Community

The more community you can surround yourself with, the more people whom you trust enough to offer clear and sometimes harsh feedback, the less likely you are to unconsciously act out your shadow material when it comes to power.

As a psychotherapist, I meet with a mentor at least once a month in order to process my experiences and share what is alive for me personally. We do dream analysis, discuss my personal life, and explore the endless pathways of depth psychology. I also do this in a group, which has the added bonus of reflection from diverse perspectives. In therapy-speak this is called "supervision" because a professional therapist subjects themselves to the watchful eyes of trusted peers and elders in the field. It is an extremely valuable process that I believe should be a requirement of any psychedelic guide and facilitator, especially in our new era of legal, regulated use.

As legal prohibitions continue to loosen around psychedelics in many places, the risks of building community around psychedelic healing are hopefully becoming much less of a concern.

Here are a few ways you can build community around psychedelic work:

- ▼ Start a professional consultation group for other facilitators or guides in your area.
- ▼ Start a peer-led journey and/or integration group.
- ▼ Create opportunities to gather and share skills, perspectives, and reflections with each other.
- ▼ Get creative. Make art together. Throw a potluck. Create opportunities to engage in genuine community building that go beyond the field of psychedelics. Be human.

Projection

Power magnetizes both conscious and unconscious psychic material. When doing deep work with people, some of this material will inevitably take the form of a projection: a feeling or story someone has about you that is not entirely based in reality, but emerges mostly out of their own unconscious psyche.

CASE STUDY: *Sarah*

Sarah had spent years of her life in Saudi Arabia. Her partner at the time came from a wealthy Saudi family, and as a white American woman she found herself immersed in a culture vastly different from her own. Over the course of the retreat, Sarah became more and more withdrawn and eventually couldn't even look me in the eye. During a group integration circle, she shared that I reminded her of her brother-in-law, a powerful, vicious man who she felt "wanted to destroy her." Something about my mannerisms, posture, or tone reminded her of this terrifying figure from her past. Especially the way I was sitting, she said, with one leg crossed, my sandal pointing vaguely in her direction, caused her to think I was deliberately showing her the bottom of my foot—an egregious sign of disrespect in Arab culture.

This felt equally awful and awkward. I thanked her for telling me, apologized that she was feeling uncomfortable around me, and asked if I had done anything to make her feel unsafe. While I didn't actually *do* anything, Sarah said, my mere presence was enough to make her feel unsafe. Of course, I was saddened and disturbed hearing this; the fact that someone felt unsafe with me, regardless of their reasoning, felt terrible. In turn, I felt my own need to feel safe, as a part of me felt somewhat attacked, causing my own protective parts to click into gear. Another part of me wanted her to feel differently, to realize that she was projecting, and to no longer look at me as a frightening oppressor. This was a difficult moment for us both.

Over the next few days, I gave her plenty of space and made sure she was surrounded by female facilitators she felt safe with. By the end of the retreat, she apologized, naming that she had indeed been projecting. While her projection was nothing to apologize for, I'll admit how relieved I felt hearing that. For the rest of our time together, I felt her energy shift into a much more grounded, relaxed place. Finally, she was able to look me in the eye with a soft, gentle smile.

I share this story to illustrate how strong and also how impersonal projections can be. Sure, something in my innate mannerisms may have triggered Sarah. Equating me with an imposing Saudi billionaire was a bizarre comparison I've never received before, or since. It shows how unrelated projections can be to reality, as well as the depth of the emotional material they are connected to.

Projections can be positive, too. I've had clients say incredibly flattering things to me that my ego loved hearing. Yet overwhelming praise can veer toward idealization that is just as subjective or unreal as its negative counterpart. Charismatic leaders thrive on these idealized projections, as do the shadow archetypes of the Guru, Dark Sorcerer, and Eternal Youth. Often, their empire comes crashing down when their followers come to the shocking realization that the idealized figure is yet another flawed, ordinary human being.

I'll admit, it feels damn good to be showered in praise. It balances out all the difficult and emotionally taxing aspects of this work. But to take this praise with anything less than a grain of salt runs the risk of ego inflation and grandiosity. (We'll talk about that more in chapter 8.)

Lastly, we need community to help us discern if something is just a projection or actually an unconscious part of ourselves that we are unable to see. Simply writing off challenging reflections as projections is a tricky road that can enable all sorts of manipulative behavior. Before labeling something as a projection, it is your responsibility to ask those around you for feedback. But if you are grounded in yourself, ethical in your behavior, surrounded by a trusted community of peers, doing your own work, and willing to receive hard feedback, then you're doing good work.

Self-Care for Guides

I'm still figuring this one out myself. For therapists and psychedelic facilitators, self-care is the foundation upon which everything else stands. But for those of us with a penchant for giving, the last person we usually give to is ourselves. I'm not going to pretend I have this one figured out or drum up tired clichés like telling you to do more yoga or take a bath.

What I can personally speak to, however, is experiencing a level of burnout I never knew was possible, and what I learned from it. These simple mantras speak to some hard lessons I've learned. You can revisit them when the going gets rough or when you've found yourself frustrated, struggling, or exhausted (as you inevitably will). I hope they serve you well:

Recovery is real. One day of psychedelic facilitation may not equate with the same amount of time required to recover. Don't underestimate how much recovery time you need. Which leads to my next point:

Remember the frog in the pot. Burnout creeps into your life slowly. Sometimes we don't realize we're getting cooked until we suddenly discover we have no energy left for our closest relationships and find little joy in our work. Our coping mechanisms and self-soothing strategies might slowly become more toxic. The things we know are good for us start to fall by the wayside. We become emotionally reactive, raw, or flat. These are all signs that we are burned out. Recognize them and take a break before you get cooked.

Mistakes are human. What matters is how you show up for the repair.

Be gentle on yourself. Self-compassion is vital. Perfection is not required.

You can lead a horse to water—but not beyond. Everyone is on their own journey, and their choices often have very little to do with you. There is a limit to what we can do for another person. We must do our best to serve others without an attachment to the outcome.

❋ ❋ ❋

To quote the Irish poet John O'Donohue:

May you have a mind that loves frontiers
So that you can evoke the bright fields
That lie beyond the view of the regular eye.

May you have good friends
To mirror your blind spots.
May leadership be for you
A true adventure of growth
    (2008, p. 151).

VIII

The Sacred Mountain

Vision, Ecstasy, and Becoming Nobody

The smaller we come to feel ourselves compared to the mountain, the nearer we come to participation in its greatness.

—ARNE NÆSS

Eagle's Gift

*O*utside, *it is bitter cold. Inside, a small fire wraps you in warmth. Outside, arctic winds howl. Inside, seal skins and caribou hides hang from whalebone rafters in the cramped shelter, blubber crackling on the flame. Outside, blue aurora lights haunt the boreal night as glacial stars flicker their transmissions from the ancestors' hearth. Inside, an old man stirs in the corner, clears his throat, and begins to speak,*

Let me tell you a story . . .

Long ago, there was a hunter. Skilled in the ways of the bow, he knew a thing or two about the wild. One day, he spotted an eagle, high up in the sky. He nocked his arrow, drew his bow, and shot it down.

Walking up to his prey, it dawned on him that this was no ordinary creature, but a great eagle, huge, the likes of which he had never seen. He took it back to his village and divided it up for everyone to share. The whole village was delighted to share in such a feast.

But something in the hunter knew that this creature required a special sort of honor because it was no ordinary eagle. So he spent days working to preserve its body, delicately drying its skin, making sure to treat its feathers gently so it retained its lifelike presence. From then on, any time the hunter ate, he put some meat into the eagle's claws. After every kill he made, he offered a small piece to the eagle too. As time went on, he became an even greater hunter.

One day, out on the tundra, the hunter saw two men on the distant plain. Strangers. As they came closer, he noticed something odd about them: on their thick hoods, they had carefully sewed the snouts of foxes, one of them red, the other white. He could hardly see their faces.

"Come with us," the strangers said. "We've been sent for you. Don't ask questions."

Realizing he didn't have much choice in the matter, the hunter agreed. They walked on in silence. Across the crunching snow they went. Up the river gorge they went. Into the quiet forest they went. Suddenly one of the men turned his fox snout to the hunter and asked, "Tell me, friend, what is it you desire in this life? What do you really want? Because soon you will meet someone who will give you everything you could dream of, but they will require something in return."

"All I want is to get home safe," said the hunter nervously, realizing how far he was from anything he recognized.

On they went, deeper into the wilderness, until the Red Fox turned and growled, "We'll never get on at this pace. Close your eyes."

They grabbed the hunter by the hands and began to run. Faster and faster they went, so fast that the hunter's face felt like it was being blasted by a storm from the northern sea. So fast they went, it felt as if they left the ground entirely.

When they slowed, the hunter felt the earth beneath him again. He opened his eyes and realized that they were now high up in the mountains, far from even the most remote hunting grounds of the caribou people. They were far away from everything he knew.

"Come, we are not far now," White Fox barked. And further up the mountain they went.

As they neared the summit, the hunter began to hear a strange sound. Thump thump. Thump thump. As they climbed, it grew louder and closer.

Thump thump. Thump thump. It was as if the ground itself was pulsating.

"What is that sound?" asked the hunter.

"That is the beating of a mother's heart," the White Fox said.

The hunter was confused but kept silent.

After some time, the Red Fox turned to the hunter, "Do you remember when you shot that eagle out of the sky? That big one? Well, that is the sound of its mother's heartbeat. We are getting close now. Soon you will meet her. She will want to give you gifts, but remember, she will want something in return."

The hunter was terrified. What was going to happen to him? What if she wanted to punish him? Had he made a grave mistake? He should have never gone with these strange fox-men. He should have never shot that eagle. All he wanted was to go home.

Finally, high up on the mountain, they reached a small settlement, hardly a village at all, just a humble cluster of dwellings. To his amazement, the hunter was treated to a sumptuous feast of the finest caribou meat, along with delicious whale fat. The wind was calm, the sky was clear, and they sat outside on the snow—not the custom of his people, but a beautiful sight this high up the mountain.

Then he heard the sound again: Thump thump. Thump thump.

Suddenly before him stood Mother Eagle. The hunter realized that his heart, too, was beating. But to his great relief, Mother Eagle received him with such warmth, such noble graciousness, that his fears began to melt away.

She spoke:

"Hunter. I honor you for the way in which you treated my son. It is no crime to kill an animal, as long as its soul is honored, which you have done. And for this, I offer you a gift. Tell me, hunter, what is it you desire?"

He fumbled for his words.

"All I can ask for is a safe journey home. Please, that is all I wish for."

"That is well and good," said Mother Eagle. "I desire some plaited sinew string. Surely a hunter such as yourself would have that gift for me?"

The hunter was at a loss. Where was he going to find sinew string so far from his home? Surely he couldn't find anything like that here. He looked at the ground, embarrassed. But suddenly he thought of his arrows, which were all lashed together with sinew. He took out his arrows and began unwinding the sinew string from them, removing the sharp tips, dismantling them one by one, until finally he presented Mother Eagle with the string.

"Thank you, hunter," said Mother Eagle. "These two men are my sacred messengers, whom I sent to find you." As the hunter looked at them, he realized that they weren't normal men at all, but fox-spirits, whom the people say still play tricks on unsuspecting hunters to this day.

More food was shared, and soon the hunter began to prepare for his long journey home. Before departing, Mother Eagle spoke to him a final time.

"There's one last thing, hunter. When you return home, I ask that you gather your people to honor the life of my son, the eagle you killed. Hold a dance in his honor. Hold a festival in his honor. Gather the seal people, the caribou people, the salmon people, the whale people. Gather them all together, so that they may trade and smile and exchange gifts with each other, as we have done here today. This is all I ask of you."

The hunter promised Mother Eagle that he would. Eager to get home, he hoisted his pack onto his shoulder and prepared to begin his long journey home.

"Hunter," said Mother Eagle, "take with you these gifts. They contain immense value, the likes of which you have never seen. Just make sure that you do not place them on the ground until you reach your home."

The hunter thanked Mother Eagle, agreed to her strange request, and accepted the gifts: two simple bags made out of the thin skin surrounding a caribou's heart. One pouch was filled with caribou ears, the other with the ears of wolves and wolverines. The hunter, skilled in crafting, knew these animal parts were worthless, but he said nothing. He tucked them into his pack, thanked Mother Eagle, and left with the fox-men.

They took him back the same way they had come, as if flying through the air. When he landed again and opened his eyes, the hunter looked around and realized they had returned to the very place where he first met them. When he turned to bid the strange messengers farewell, he saw only the white, drifting snow.

As he made his way back to his village, the hunter found himself needing to rest after what he had just experienced. As he sat down near the banks of a river, he saw a flock of swallows flitting around the water who had made their nests in the clay wall above the riverbank. They flew with such gracious beauty, such delicate precision, which somehow he had never observed before. They danced and twirled over the river, gliding in the crisp air. The hunter felt an inexplicable joy kindle somewhere within him, under his caribou skins.

And then, he saw something very strange. Suddenly, all the swallows soared into their nests. A moment later, wolf heads emerged from the holes, staring down at him, into him, through him. The hunter was stunned. And then, as if by magic, the vision vanished. The hunter found himself looking at an ordinary riverbank, water flowing calmly below. Blinking, the hunter wondered if he had truly lost his mind. Perhaps he had imagined all of it: the swallows, the wolf heads, the fox-men, the mountain, and Mother Eagle. In his confusion, he dropped the two caribou-heart bags onto the snow.

Suddenly, the seemingly worthless gifts transformed into massive sacks stuffed full of the finest caribou hides, pounds and pounds of delicious meat, and valuable pelts of wolves and wolverines. They were so heavy and plentiful that he could not possibly carry them back home. Mother Eagle's gift, which seemed worthless, had turned into the greatest wealth imaginable.

When he finally returned home, the hunter sent out all the young men from the village to collect the sacks of skins and meat. And ever since then, the people of that land would gather together to exchange gifts and trade, to dance and sing, and to share food and stories—all under the watchful eyes of the eagle, who gave the people the gift of joy.

The Price of Vision

Step by step, we climb the steep ascent. Through the twisting pathways of the labyrinth, we at last find stillness at the center. After the harrowing journey into unknown darkness, the golden light of sunrise warms our weary face. When the dust clears and tears flow, when we throw down our burden by our blistered feet, we may finally glimpse the shimmering vastness that unfurls in all directions, singing back to us in a thousand secret voices:

Welcome to the Sacred Mountain.

In this visionary tale from the Iñupiat or Inuit people of the Alaskan Arctic, we follow a hunter into the upper world, fox spirits accompanying his flight to a mountain peak, where he encounters a numinous being, Mother Eagle, who gifts him with a ceremonial vision and many other forms of wealth. This story is saturated in mythopoetic meaning that teaches us something about the nature of vision, ecstasy, and mystical experiences.

Today, amid the continual hunt for the next spiritual download or ego-obliterating "hero's dose," we would do well to hear a subtle lesson contained within this myth: there is no getting something for nothing.

It's an easy message to forget, especially in the age of Amazon Prime delivered to your doorstep. But the myths, and the Indigenous traditions, remember: everything given must be paid for. Every animal killed, every ear of corn harvested, every tree cut down. There is also a cost for every vision we might be lucky enough to receive during our lifetime. Vision requires us to be in reciprocity with the powers of the Otherworld if we want the blessings of these experiences to actually stay with us.

At the story's beginning, the hunter shoots a massive eagle out of the sky. Instead of catching some big fish or creature from the Great Below, this story instead orients us upward, in the direction of the spirit. The hunter immediately recognizes the gift from spirit contained within his prey, and he acts accordingly, offering the fallen eagle morsels of food each time he eats, a small portion of every animal he kills.

This simple act of animistic reciprocity speaks to this lesson of exchange. Knud Rasmussen, an explorer from Greenland, collected this story, along with some of the most detailed accounts of traditional Inuit life. His work also included interviews with a famous Inuit shaman named Aua, who said: "The greatest peril in life lies in the fact that human food consists entirely of souls. All the creatures that we have to kill to eat, all those that we have to strike down and destroy to make clothes for ourselves, have souls, like we have, souls that do not perish with the body and which must therefore be propitiated lest they should avenge themselves on us for taking away their bodies" (Rasmussen, 1932, pp. 55–56).

The spirits of animals, and all things human beings depend on, must also be fed. For the Inuit and many other earth-honoring cultures, this was quite literal. The modern world is a universe away from such a life-style. But the animistic principle remains the same: there is no getting something for nothing. To forget this spells disaster, for after going hungry for so long, these other-than-human beings will seek to "avenge themselves," perhaps by burning down a town in wildfire, or maybe swallowing it in a torrential flood.

For Indigenous societies, this exchange was not merely a psychological or spiritual reality, but something woven into their everyday lives. Disrespect the spirits, disrespect the sacred, and you might just find yourself without food during a harsh winter.

One could call this the necessary "chop wood, carry water" that must occur after a visionary experience. We build a certain rapport with what we are shown, cultivating a chain that links our normative consciousness back to the transpersonal perspective we've been lucky enough to glimpse. This process between hunter and eagle is ongoing. The hunter demonstrates the devotion required to ground and integrate the gift he received from higher realms. There isn't much glamor here, but there is discipline.

Discipline: to be a disciple of something greater than oneself. Being a disciple locates one in a place of listening and being willing to receive instruction. Putting in the road miles, the ten thousand hours, submitting to the full initiatory ordeal, completing the long training—it's all discipleship. For me, this has looked like graduate school, unpaid internships, costly training programs, student loans, and years spent learning from and investing in teachers from all walks of life. For others, the discipleship process will look different. The point is that for the teachings to stick, you must have some skin in the game.

Flying to the Upper World: Mythopoetics and the Mystical

The archetypal Sacred Mountain is deeply embedded in the collective unconscious as a place of revelation and ecstatic vision. The mythical mountains of Meru and Kailash in Hindu and Buddhist traditions are said to be the template for every temple across Asia. In the Judeo-Christian religions, Mount Sinai and the Temple Mount represent pinnacle moments where God spoke to prophets. In Navajo cosmology, their vast homeland is hemmed in by four sacred mountains, one in each direction. Black Elk, the Lakota visionary and medicine man, received the guiding vision of his life on what is now called Black Elk Peak in South Dakota's Black Hills. The list goes on.

Every steeple-crowned church, every temple across the world, every pyramid, however great or small, is a symbolic manifestation of the Sacred Mountain. Marie Louise von Franz writes, "A widespread symbol of the land of soul is the mountain, which understandably came to stand for the unconscious since one imagines that their tops are often covered in mist, and reach—like a transition—into heaven. The gods manifest or reveal themselves on mountain peaks" (2020, p. 65).

And we can be sure that it's in no ordinary state of consciousness that the gods reveal themselves to us. Ecstasy is a precondition for revelation. No, not the drug. The word *ecstasy* comes from the Latin *ecstasis*, meaning "to stand outside one's self." In true ecstatic states, *we* leave. There is not much of *us* left, as our entire perception becomes filled with the immense, all-encompassing pulse of creation. Or *ecstasis* might take the form of deep presence, a moment so singular and profound that the mind is perfectly stilled while some vast primordial truth whispers into our ears from the Great Beyond.

"Flying" to the upper world is a classic motif in myths across many cultures, especially those versed in trance states. In the upper world, spirits or gods can be contacted and sometimes consulted. Gifts might be given, or stolen. The Tsimshian people of the Pacific Northwest have a creation story in which Raven brings light to the world by flying through a hole in the sky and into the house of the Sky Chief. Turning himself into a cedar leaf, Raven is drunk by the Sky Chief's daughter, who becomes pregnant, eventually giving birth to a child. As baby Raven grows, he wails and wails, gesturing toward the box on the wall where he knows the Sky Chief keeps the light. Thinking him only a harmless baby, the Sky Chief's wife gives baby Raven the box of light to play with, after which he quickly transforms back into his feathered form, flies back down to earth, smashes the box, and releases daylight for the people.

While Raven is inherently a trickster and Promethean thief, the point is that there is power contained *up there*. In our story of the hunter, there is also immeasurable value in the upper world. The people down below need whatever is *up there* (*out there, down there, over there*), and the myths give a clue about what this could be: spiritual light and illumination, instructional revelation, material abundance, cultural vitality.

Taking psychedelics is not a requirement or recipe for experiencing *ecstasis*; far from it. You could fast on a mesa for four days, burrow into darkness for a week, or listen to the howl of wolves under the full moon and enter *ecstasis*. Yet psychedelics are ancient and reliable tools for apprehending these mystical states. Even still, there is no guarantee, nor should a "mystical experience" be seen as some benchmark of value when taking psychedelics. The medicines themselves don't make ecstatic states occur. They simply offer the psyche the opportunity to become less encumbered and to enter them on its own. It's a difficult pill for Western culture to swallow, but it's worth repeating: there is no getting something for nothing. We are not entitled to anything.

Psychedelic medicines are long overdue to be respected as valid methods of accessing ecstatic and mystical states. The notion that a "drug-induced" mystical experience is somehow less valid or less real is rapidly deteriorating in the face of emerging research.

One woman I worked with was a participant in Roland Griffiths's 2017 study in which he gave psilocybin to long-term meditators. Seeking to explore psychedelics in a less sterile and clinical context, she decided to go on an extended psilocybin retreat, which is how we met. Midway through the week, she shared that she had finally experienced what she'd been seeking all these years: a truly cosmic experience of complete oneness, far surpassing anything she had touched in decades of meditation. "This was just, beyond," she told me. "And it couldn't have happened without the meditation. It prepared me for it. But this was something else."

Research into mystical experiences and psychedelics frames these myths in an even more intriguing light. The Mystical Experience Questionnaire (MEQ-30) is a research tool that psychedelic studies frequently use to measure the levels at which a person's experience could be considered phenomenologically "mystical." Developed by Walter Pahnke and Bill Richards and utilized by the late Roland Griffiths in his Johns Hopkins studies on this subject, the MEQ-30 measures factors that comprise these expansive states of consciousness. Those factors include a sense of "internal unity, external unity, noetic quality, sacredness, positive mood, transcendence of time and space, and ineffability" (Garcia-Romeu et al., 2015, p. 5). While much of this research simply confirms what Indigenous cultures and mystical traditions have known for generations, it's a necessary validation of these "archaic techniques of ecstasy," as Mircea Eliade called them. Of particular interest is Griffiths's research revealing the necessity of mystical experiences in effecting lasting improvements in both mental health and addiction outcomes, referenced above. These ineffable moments can permanently change our lives and ripple outward to affect everyone we know, not just ourselves.

And still, the gifts we receive atop the mountain will always ask something of us in return.

Mother's Heartbeat

As the hunter approaches Mother Eagle's luminous domain, he begins to hear a heartbeat, as if emanating from the earth itself. Some say that the heartbeat is the original drumbeat and that all drumming is an approximation of this carnal rhythm surging through blood and bone. The Iñupiat people are no strangers to drums, which they still use in their ceremonies.

Interestingly, Inuit peoples are one of the few cultures on earth who have no documented history of working with psychoactive plants, due to the harsh growing conditions of the Arctic. Yet the extreme landscape may have been consciousness-altering enough. Months of impenetrable darkness and ice, followed by months of sunlight and sprawling vistas, would have likely required their imaginal perceptions to expand and contract depending on the intense pulse of the seasons. What could be more psychedelic than spending half the year under the haunting lights of the aurora borealis, followed by months of nearly constant sunlight? Their spiritual cosmologies and imaginal world may have mirrored these extreme shifts, resulting in one of the most profoundly shamanic cultures on earth.

Like many peoples of the far north, the drum was the vehicle their shamans used to traverse the higher, lower, or outer realms, contact spiritual beings and guides, and receive instruction that would ensure their community's survival. Indeed, people across the world use drums to induce altered states of consciousness. Our story offers a clue as to how one might access the upper world of Mother Eagle.

Another reading of the thumping directs our attention to our own hearts and the fact that the hunter soon began to feel his heart beating in time with Mother Eagle's. On a symbolic level, the message is simple: the heart is the gateway to the mystical. On a more literal level, we can understand this phenomenon as *entrainment*, when two rhythms begin to naturally synchronize by mere proximity to the other, like two off-kilter metronomes slowly finding the same beat.

When the soul opens to the mystical, something happens to the heart. In the myth, the hunter's heart becomes entrained to a force much larger than himself. The "beating of a mother's heart" could speak to many things. It could be a symbol of a return to childlike innocence or helplessness that can occur when we step into the mystical, or the overwhelming love a child feels for their parent, and vice versa. The hunter could also be attuning to the archetypal heartbeat of Mother Earth, the pulse of all life, upon which we utterly depend.

Though she wears many masks, Mother Eagle is a powerful being known throughout the world. Gaia, she has been called, or Shakti, or Shekhinah. Demeter, Coatlicue, Spider Woman, Hathor, Parvati, Brigid, Yemaja, and Mary. She is the Great Mother goddess whom all mothers embody, the source of all life. Yet she gives as easily as she takes away, as von Franz reminds us: "The Great Mother can be frightful, dark, and destructive, as well as good, cherishing, supporting, giving, and warm; a wise woman—the guardian of all things past, and knowing about the future" (2020, p. 275).

Perhaps this is another lesson within the myth: without attuning to the heart, without listening to its subtle murmurings that pulse within our being, without remembering that everyone alive shares in this primordial rhythm, we will never be able to receive the gifts atop the mountain.

Becoming Nobody: The Arrows and the String

Something very significant happens when the hunter finally meets Mother Eagle. The fox-men have told him that she will want something in return for her gifts. He is speechless, wracking his brain for where he might find sinew string so far from home. And yet there it is, right under his nose.

This is a theme that repeats itself across mythology and folklore: the least likely thing, the humblest of creatures or people, something previously unwanted or discarded, becomes the essential key that unlocks everything. The unlikely hero or heroine speaks to the unseen value hidden in the mundane, and the fact that spirit might be dwelling in the last place we think to look.

By dismantling his arrows, the hunter deconstructs the very thing that makes him who he is. He sacrifices the most essential element of his identity in the face of the ineffable, surrendering the sharpest aspect of his ego, his source of power and prestige, abandoning a social role and persona that has served him up to this point but now needs to be released in the face of the numinous. As he unbinds his arrows one by one, we can imagine the hunter on his knees before the towering presence of Mother Eagle. One reading might lead us to see the unbound arrows as an image of emasculation or castration. Especially when instigated by the Great Mother, this Freudian interpretation makes a strong case. Yet I prefer to see this in a deeper mythopoetic light: the hunter must dismantle his sharp-pointed ego-edges, his destructive power, in the face of something far more powerful.

Psychedelics can often serve to "soften" people's edges, making them more psychologically flexible instead of rigid, introspective instead of relentlessly extroverted, and emotionally fluid instead of monochromatic. Yet these benefits only come after we give up these tired ways of being and dismantle some of our own "arrows" atop the mountain. The persona's sharp exterior must give way to the soft underbelly of the soul.

The arrows the hunter dismantles are the same arrows that shot Mother Eagle's son out of the sky. Is this a reckoning for his past deeds? Is this his karma? He's certainly worried that it might be. The hunter had no idea what it meant when he shot the eagle out of the sky. But he immediately recognized its importance and acted accordingly. If he had disrespected the eagle in the beginning, this would most likely end up being a cautionary tale. But Mother Eagle forgives him, thanking him for respecting the natural order of life. The hunter has a clean conscience. He's done good work.

I've found that mystical experiences are unlikely to occur if someone is completely out of alignment with their soul or is living in a way that is profoundly incongruent. Often, people will have to churn through various layers of psychospiritual concrete, trudge their way through the underworld, and face unmetabolized emotions like grief and sadness before any kind of experience atop the Sacred Mountain is possible. Even then, there is no guarantee. We are lucky if we have one or two of these experiences during our lifetimes.

This unforeseen circle with the young eagle, the arrows, and Mother Eagle also speaks to the unexpectedness of mystical encounters. They escape our misguided attempts at engineering or willing them into being. There is no dosage formula, no miraculous combination of molecules, no elaborate ritual that will guarantee a mystical experience. They operate in accordance with an unfathomable logic. But people who have these experiences often say afterward that it felt as if everything in their life had been leading them to this point. Because it had been.

Dismantling the arrows might also mean that we do not derive an egoic satisfaction from mystical encounters. Rather, it asks us to cease knowing, to no longer be experts or "authorities," and stop being capable masters of our own domain. When we find ourselves recalling the number of "countless ego-deaths" we've experienced, or regaling someone about how many cups of ayahuasca we've been able to stomach, we can be sure that some of our arrows still have yet to be dismantled.

Perhaps, as we stagger down the mountain from Mother Eagle's domain, we become less and less "ourselves" and more and more of the mystery. In my own life, some of the deepest people I've ever encountered—Aboriginal elders smiling in wheelchairs, Navajo road men with twinkling eyes, blind Zimbabwean musicians living atop mountains of stone—have said the least. If they did talk, it was almost always through jokes. "Talking backwards," as I've heard it called—a Native American saying describing how a *Heyoka* will talk around something in such a way as to never approach it directly, sometimes even saying the opposite of what they mean. But underneath the confusion lies a certain protection for the sacred, for to speak of something in a profane or casual way damages it. We cheapen something by speaking of it too freely. Some things are simply not meant to be shared. Don't talk away the magic.

Wolves' Ears and Caribou Hearts

The final gift Mother Eagle gives the hunter is two bags made from the sack surrounding a caribou's heart, filled with the ears of wolves, wolverines, and caribou. Thinking they are worthless, the hunter packs them away and forgets about them. Only when he places them on the ground, against her instructions, does he fully comprehend their true value.

We return to that mythic motif of something that seems worthless actually containing immeasurable value. Yet again, the hunter is in possession of something he does not fully understand. To claim that we "know" what a certain experience is ever truly about—especially one in which our usual ways of knowing are thrown to the wind—is to define and therefore limit its value. Some experiences may take years to bear fruit, slowly germinating in the fertile soil of our subconscious. Each of us is staggering back down the mountainside with secret bags of wolves' ears.

It is an interesting detail that Mother Eagle's gifts are contained in bags made from a caribou heart sack, or pericardium. Anatomically speaking, all mammals' hearts are contained within this fibrous double membrane. In Chinese medicine, there is an entire meridian devoted to the pericardium, seen as the "protector of the heart" and the bridge through which spiritual transformation occurs. In this tradition, an individual moves from being driven by ego and survival fears to being motivated by transpersonal perspectives through opening themselves to the natural flow of life and death, which occurs through the pericardium channel.

Can anything truly be considered mystical if it is disconnected from the heart? If compassion does not play a central role in mystical experiences, if the heart is not intimately involved, then it might not actually be "mystical." Just like Mother Eagle's gift, the heart is where we carry the blessings of such experiences.

This moment contains another lesson about mystical experiences: we will all inevitably forget what occurred atop the mountain. Whatever awe-inspiring vision was shown to us, whatever transpersonal revelation we glimpsed, will slowly fade into the background of our psyches and become no more than a distant memory. Life will resume its familiar pulse, and all the problems we left down in the valley will be waiting for us upon our return. The bills still need to be paid.

And yet, and yet, and yet . . .

Something of the eternal remains with us long after we leave its ineffable embrace. We are marked by such experiences, or at least we have the potential to be. The impact of just one of these encounters can shape our lives forever in its wake.

Original Instructions

Before the hunter leaves the mountain, Mother Eagle asks him to hold a festival in honor of her son. She offers a set of instructions and stipulates that the hunter must implement them once he is back among his people. Traditional festivals of trade and bartering held by the Iñupiat people, as well as one particular dance about swallows and wolves, are linked to this story. The mystical and the mythical are not abstractions. They are qualities that influence our daily lives, consciously or not. And both myths and mystical encounters contain instructions for what to do once we descend the mountain.

The late Oglala Lakota medicine man Leonard Crow Dog, and many other Native American spiritual leaders, have spoken about what they call the "original instructions." These ancestral teachings and traditional ceremonies were received by their ancestors in visions, considered sacred messages from the creator, and enacted through ceremonies and rituals that continue to this day. Ceremonies like the sun dance, sweat lodges, vision quests, pipe ceremonies, and many others are said to have been handed down directly from the creator into the hands of "holy people," who then shared these visions with the tribe. Along with these ceremonies came spiritual philosophies and ways of living that formed a complete spiritual vision of a people striving to live in reciprocity with the earth and the more-than-human forces that animate it.

It is important to name that traditional religious ceremonies practiced by Indigenous peoples are very different from personalized, mystical experiences that psychedelics evoke for modern, Western people like myself. Through the hyperindividualized, capitalist lens of modern culture, such "instructions" become complicated. Things can get weird. Just because someone "saw" something in a vision doesn't make it true or even a good idea. When left unchecked by community, accountability, and integration, many of the "visions" people might have through psychedelics can veer toward narcissistic inflation (which we will discuss shortly).

That said, in the proper context, psychedelic-inspired mystical experiences can indeed offer truly valuable guidance. Modern Western people might see these instructions as guidance for living in greater harmony with themselves, their close relations, their body, and their landscape. If these instructions or visions cannot be grounded in the tangible realities of everyday life, then we are missing the most important ingredient in psychedelic healing: integration. The messages received atop the mountain begin to take root by continually integrating them into the intimate tapestry of our lives.

CASE STUDY: *Ryan*

Ryan was a young financial professional from San Francisco who wanted to explore higher doses of psilocybin for personal growth. He shared that he didn't have much in the way of "deep issues" to work through, despite a fraught relationship with certain family members and difficulty maintaining intimate relationships. Ryan lived a fast-paced lifestyle and was, by some measurements, extremely successful.

Over the course of our work together, Ryan experienced higher and higher levels of expansive revelation. His psychedelic journeys were graceful and smooth, hardly requiring any assistance from myself or others. By the end of his first two journeys, he was experiencing a notable boost in self-confidence and enthusiasm. In fact, he even experienced a flood of new business ideas and practices he began implementing immediately, sending dictated voice notes to his assistant a thousand miles away.

Ryan was a genuinely kind and respectful person, yet over the course of our retreat many of the other participants began feeling uncomfortable around him. They began to chuckle to themselves as he became more grandiose. He began to speak frequently about his business success and life philosophies, and he was extremely excited about the role he saw psychedelics playing in the world. For the life of him, he could not figure out why certain people simply couldn't stand to be around him.

After his third dose, I approached him as he stared blissfully toward the sea. "How was it?" I asked.

"Beautiful," he said. "I know exactly what I need to do. I feel incredible, unstoppable. I own the world now."

Ryan left before our final integration session because he felt he "didn't need it." He never said goodbye to anyone.

Skills

Shadows of Ecstasy

Every light casts a shadow. Ecstatic and visionary experiences, as we have seen, can offer immensely valuable insights that can support us and our wider communities. Mystical experiences are part of our spiritual birthright and are important elements of living a complete human life. We all deserve such rapture at least once in our lives.

Yet there is an unforeseen dark side to ecstatic experiences that can become especially visible when magnified by psychedelics. These shadows of ecstasy are partly responsible for the many abuses of power that occur in psychedelic spaces, as discussed in chapter 7. While abuses of power are certainly morally concerning, the shadows discussed below, though problematic, can be seen as expressions of unintegrated or wounded parts of the psyche still seeking wholeness.

All of these "shadows of ecstasy" are the result of the hyperindividualized, disconnected state of modern Western culture. Mystical experiences undergone in isolation can just as easily drive one toward psychosis as toward healing. On a foundational level, the healing balm that these shadows require is community and belonging.

Inflation

At their root, these "shadows of ecstasy" are a result of what depth psychology calls "ego inflation." Confronted with our smallness, sometimes the ego needs to inflate or bolster itself in order to protect us from an experience that might be utterly overwhelming. A core function of visionary and ecstatic experiences is to actually regulate and temper the ego. We are put in our place, so to speak. Like an allergic reaction, inflation resists this tempering.

In the modern psychedelic world, I've heard people speak about "ego death" like it's a competitive sport. I'm sure the irony is not lost on you, either. This "psychedelic ego" is about deriving a sense of power from mystical experiences and using them to bolster one's already shaky sense of self. Eventually, one becomes like a tree with no roots. I've found that the more entitled someone feels to have a "mystical experience," viewing the sacred like some badge to pin onto their jacket lapel, the less likely it is to actually occur. The soul delights in humility. A wise dharma bum, friend to derelicts and outlaws, himself no stranger to the mystical, once said, "Blessed are the meek, for they shall inherit the earth."

Sometimes inflation is a necessary or natural phase to move through. Like a maturation process, inflation can serve to bolster confidence and firm up our conviction. I couldn't have even begun writing this book unless I was a little inflated. But if the energy of inflation cannot shift and evolve, cannot ripen and mature into a fruit that can nourish other people, eventually it will rot.

Blinded by the Light: Ontological Addiction and Spiritual Bypassing

If we climb the Sacred Mountain again and again, we get accustomed to the view. It only makes sense that we'd seek even higher peaks, always angling toward the spectacular. Called "ontological addiction" by psychologist Edo Sonin, this style of spiritual seeking becomes an addiction-like pattern wherein the insights and feelings of awe we encounter in peak states become something we crave; yet in the end they only serve to reinforce our identity and belief systems (Van Gordon et al., 2018). When we're in this state, it's not enough to meet Mother Eagle once. Instead, we need a daily ritual of returning to her domain through a variety of consciousness-altering substances or pursuits. Somehow I don't think she would be too pleased.

In New Age and neoshamanic circles, where people seem to live from one psychedelic ceremony to the next, perpetually oriented to the next "download" or "healing," it's not hard to see ontological addiction at work. As much as I am an advocate of psychedelic medicines, I am equally an advocate of stepping away from them. In my work with clients, after someone has undertaken several psychedelic sessions, I often suggest that they spend a long period of time not taking psychedelics, usually six months to a year. This allows the dust to settle in the psyche, so to speak, and gives time for one to actually start implementing whatever instructions they might have received atop the mountain.

Spiritual bypassing is another name for a similar phenomenon. A term coined by transpersonal psychologist John Welwood, *spiritual bypassing* can be defined as using one's spiritual practices or beliefs to avoid dealing with the more difficult, shameful, or painful aspects of their life. Taking psychedelics is easy. Facing our pain, resolving our relational patterns, changing daily habits, and finding meaning and beauty hiding within the mundane is hard. To continually orient to what is easy, exciting, or *feels good* might be a sign that we're using psychedelics as a way to bypass our shadow and suffering. Either that, or we've become addicted to the view from Mother Eagle's domain. It's only a matter of time before she kicks us out of the nest.

The Messiah Complex

"I've received a message and need to tell you about it."

"A higher dimensional truth has been revealed to me that is going to change the world."

"Everyone needs to hear this, experience this, and understand the message!"

"I've been chosen for a sacred mission that I must share with you."

Are these the sayings of a cult member, a religious fundamentalist, or someone freshly back from a psychedelic trip? When the messiah complex is at work, it's hard to tell. That alone should speak to the danger of this archetypal complex that lurks behind the bright lights of mystical experiences.

Some travelers who spend time in the lands of Israel/Palestine develop what is called Jerusalem Syndrome, a condition where they become convinced that they are the second coming of Christ, are receiving transmissions of the Torah 2.0, or have suddenly found the answer to the millenia-long conflict surrounding this region and other global issues. Psychedelics can trigger the same energy in the psyche.

The messiah complex, extremely prevalent in wide-eyed New Age circles, can express itself in subtle and overt ways. Overtly, we can all think of people overcome with an almost religious fervor after a particularly powerful psychedelic journey. Some say that Timothy Leary became hooked by this complex as he was christened as the "high priest" of the psychedelic '60s. On a more subtle level, this can look like someone convinced that they should become a shaman or psychedelic guide after only a handful of experiences. The messiah complex is dangerous because it can enlist other people in its radically inflated mission. These are the basic ingredients of a cult.

In many Indigenous traditions, people coming back from powerful ceremonies, be it a four-day vision quest or a year-long *dieta*, are often instructed not to talk about their experiences with anyone. There is deep wisdom here. This directive serves to stifle any urges to proclaim your specialness, and it redirects the mystical nature of the experience back into the individual's soul. By not sharing about a mystical experience, we protect its sacredness. By keeping its substance to ourselves, we might actually bring home its medicine, rather than forget it by the riverside.

Narcissism

Inflation, when left unchecked, becomes narcissism. The subject of narcissism and psychedelics could be an entire book by itself. As a psychedelic therapist, I have seen these medicines actually make narcissism worse, like in the case of Ryan mentioned above. As nonspecific amplifiers, psychedelics only serve to amplify what is already indwelling in someone's psyche. Therefore, someone with extremely narcissistic traits will likely find themselves even more convinced of whatever self-aggrandizing story they are already in. Every narcissist is a hero in their own mind.

While the term has gained immense popularity and become another pop-psychology buzzword, *narcissism* is actually a spectrum, an element of personality that we all have in varying degrees. In many cases, psychedelics can serve to reduce narcissism through ego dissolution and mystical experiences.

Yet true narcissism, or "narcissistic personality disorder," is a beast that even the most seasoned psychologists have difficulty treating.

Psychedelics only serve to inflame this already dangerous inferno. Many of the abuses that have come to light in psychedelic circles are linked to unchecked power stemming from narcissism.

※ ※ ※

Mystical experiences and ecstatic states are gifts bestowed on us from forces far greater than we can comprehend. To continually try to pillage this realm for our own ends disrespects the very forces we seek to be blessed by. Mother Eagle is kind to the hunter during his visit. She might not be so kind if he were to come back every week, expecting the same welcome and the same gifts.

Dwelling in the "spirit of the gift" can also bring us into an ecstatic state, according to author Lewis Hyde (2007). After all, what are visions if not gifts mercifully sent to us from the Otherworld? Hyde says, "When we are in the spirit of the gift we love to feel the body open outward. The ego's firmness has its virtues, but at some point we seek the slow dilation, to use another term of Whitman's, in which the ego enjoys a widening give-and-take with the world and is finally abandoned in ripeness" (2007, p. 21).

The forces that dwell atop the mountain require that we leave something of ourselves in their sky-filled realm so that we might open to that "slow dilation." Our notions of "self" must expand to encompass the wider pulse of "give-and-take with the world," which animates it and fills us with ecstatic participation in something far greater than ourselves.

Instead of elevating us toward ever more grandiose heights, the Sacred Mountain asks us to become nobody.

IX

The Tree of Life

Animism, Climate Change, and the Ensouled Earth

I praise what is truly alive,

what longs to be burned to death.

—GOETHE

Völuspá (the Prophecy of Ragnarok)

*L*isten. I will tell you now of the bright days of ages past. And I will tell you of the dark days yet to come. I will tell you of the great gods and how they will fall in flames and how the earth will come to an end. Does this trouble you, Odin? Yes, I know you, grim-face, hooded one, gray wanderer. I know you, old one-eye. And I know where you hid the other eye, deep beneath Mimir's well, in exchange for his wisdom. And yet now you seek my knowledge? What do you want of me, Allfather? I knew you before you were even born. Listen.

I will tell you of the great ash tree, Yggdrasil, speckled in white, the nine worlds living upon its branches: Asgard, of the Aesir gods; Vanaheim, home of the wise Vanir; Jötunheim, the realm of giants; Alfheim, the realm of elves; Midgard, the world of men; Svartalfheim, where dwarves dwell; Muspelheim, where there is only fire; Niflheim, where there is only mist; and Helheim, where the dead go who do not die in battle.

Dew falls from Yggdrasil's ever-green leaves, nourishing the valleys below. Atop the tree lives an eagle, gazing down upon creation, and at its base slithers Nidhogg, the serpent, who gnaws upon its roots. And down, down below the great tree bubbles the waters from the Well of Wyrd, where three old women— the Norns—spin the fates of all.

I was there at the very beginning of creation, before the earth, before the sea, when there was only Ginnungagap, the great void. I was there when the earth was created, made from Ymir's blood and bones. Those were the dawn days of creation—the moon soft as calf skin, newborn stars glimmering in the night. And then the gods came. They met in the green valley of Ithavoll, where they built their kingdom. And one day, they found two humble pieces of driftwood, Ash and Elm. You breathed life into them, Odin, and created humankind. The bright gods in those early days had no concerns.

And then everything changed.

One day, three knocks rapped on the hulking doors of Odin's hall. The golden doors groaned opened, and standing before them was a woman from another race of gods, the Vanir. They called her Gullveig, or "Gold Lust," for they did not know her true name or purpose in visiting. She stayed for a time, seeking secret counsel with Odin. But soon the Aesir began to whisper poison words about her in dark corners when the candles burned low.

The Aesir attacked Gullveig, piercing her with spears. Then they set her body aflame. Yet each time she was reborn from the ashes. Three times they burned her, and three times she would live again. Often-killed, yet ever-living, they said of her. She became the one known as Heith, Shining One—a powerful sorceress who foresaw good things. Skilled in magic and seidr— spellcraft—she was a wise woman of prophecy. Her power began to rival even that of Odin.

The Aesir gathered again in council, wondering what to do with this goddess and her Vanir kin who had begun gathering near Asgard. In the midst of their deliberations, Odin kicked open the doors of his hall, hoisted his spear, and threw it over the Vanir host below, initiating the first war. But the Vanir knew war-magic, and they surrounded the Aesir. Slowly, Asgard's walls, built through yet another act of trickery, began to crumble. Finally, Thor picked up Mjolnir, his war hammer, and put an end to the fighting. The Aesir and the Vanir declared a truce, but no one knows what became of Gullveig. Some say she fled east, into the ironwood forest of Jötunheim. Others say that she still lives among the Aesir and is the one they now call Freya.

I saw when bright Balder, Odin's son, most beloved of all the gods, was killed by that harmless tree, mistletoe, and his hapless brother Hoth. I saw how Loki spun this deceit, how Odin cast Loki out of Asgard and bound him beneath the earth for his treachery. And there Loki will remain until Ragnarok, when he will break free and ride the death-ship into harbor, leading an army of giants.

Then there will be no warmth, no summer. Only winter after winter, a black sun on a red horizon. Desperation and deceit will grow in the hearts of humankind. Many will feed their lives to the wolf. Men will become oathbreakers, murderers, and seducers. I foresee a dark time, a time of despair, a time of chaos, a time of confusion. Serpents will close in around once-joyful halls. Brother will fight brother, cousins will no longer be kin, and the world will become filled with ashes. An age of the axe, an age of the spear, an age of storms, an age of wolves. Shields will shatter. Betrayers will rule before the world sinks into the sea.

The wolf Fenrir, Loki's brood, will howl in fury. He will break free of his bonds and consume the sun. The giants will rise and beat the mountains as their war drums. The earth will quake with thunderous cries. Heimdall, the watchman, will raise the Gjallarhorn to his lips, and for the first and last time, sound its dreadful tone. The board is set. The game begins. And Odin seeks counsel from Mimir's head, down at the well where he gave his eye so long ago.

The world tree trembles. The giants shake its trunk. If you listen, you can hear it sigh.

From the east a frigid wind will blow as Hyrm, the frost giant, wields his glacial shield. Food will not grow in his wake. The Midgard serpent will churn the oceans before the tides rise. All of Jötunheim will roar. Elves and dwarves will cower beneath their doors of stone.

Surt, the unstoppable flame, will march with his burning sword from the south, scorching the land. Flames will devour the forests. The mountains will crumble beneath his feet. The skies will be torn asunder as Surt's flame turns the sun black and ashen snow covers the earth. Everything will flicker, and wither, and die.

Odin will fight Fenrir. Frey will battle Surt, the flaming one. Thor will wrestle the Midgard serpent, heaving it up from the sea. Thor will kill the serpent, yet will stagger nine steps before its venom stops his heart. And you, Odin, you too will die, finding your end in the mouth of the wolf you tricked into bondage. Humankind will fall with Thor and be wiped away from the dark earth.

Stars will fall out of the sky. The earth will sink into the sea. Flames will devour the leaves of Yggdrasil as a great bonfire reaches toward the sky. This is the fate of the gods.

Yet that is not the end . . . I see the world rise from the sea a second time, adorned in green. Lifegiving waters will flow down the mountainside, and eagles and fish and all the creatures of the earth will find life again. Two humans will live: Life, and Life's Yearning. They will take refuge in the hollow of Yggdrasil's scorched trunk, and there they will survive. Trembling in the great tree, they will endure the doom of the gods. And when the earth is new again, humankind will be reborn.

The new morning sun will crest over the horizon, warming the green valley of Ithavoll. Vidar and Vali, sons of Odin, and Magni and Modi, sons of Thor, will find their way to that grassy plain. Balder and Hoth will live again and join their kin in the morning light. And there they will find the towering bones of the Midgard serpent. There they will remember the deeds of Thor. There they will share stories of one-eyed Odin with his secret knowledge of the runes. And then, in the glistening grass, they will look down and find the golden game pieces they once played with so long ago. Strange, they will think, that the pieces look so much like themselves and the old gods.

Hoth and Balder will exchange a knowing smile, while Magni and Modi tap a cask of mead, somehow saved from the cataclysm. The board is reset with the golden pieces, and with a clack of their drinking horns, the old game begins again.

Climate Change and the New Gods

Several years ago on a late December night, a cold wind blew down from the north into the valley that holds my home in Portland. Our winters are known to be mild; a bit chilly and rainy, with maybe a few days of snow. But this was different. The howling air that surged down from the Canadian tundra that night carried with it a bitter cold that I had rarely experienced there. It was a vicious, arctic beast, instantly turning city streets into ice sheets, and brought with it the very real possibility of death for those left unprepared. Indeed, many did not make it through the night.

Looking at the weather radar on my phone, I zoomed out, trying to get a sense of the storm. I kept zooming out, and out, and out, until the screen before me filled with a deep purple hue, depicting a monster that had crept steadily southward, constricting the majority of North America in its icicled embrace. At that moment I realized that I was looking at a frost giant, a gargantuan being straight out of the sagas, whose freezing breath transformed the world overnight. When a giant rolls into town, everyone is keenly aware of its presence.

If you live in the north, you know this feeling. I call it the "snow day effect," when extreme weather seems to synchronize everyone's psyches, directing our awareness toward what feels like a heightened level of connectivity. People are suddenly tuned into their visceral needs for warmth, food, and shelter. The streets become anarchic pathways devoid of all lines, where yesterday's rules are disregarded as people walk and play freely. Your pipes might freeze, or your power can fail. And miraculously, neighbors actually begin to rely on each other.

The tropics have their own version of this when hurricanes threaten to make landfall, something I experienced while living on Jamaica's south coast. Extreme weather levels the playing field, for better or worse, by inhibiting our business-as-usual ways of functioning and bringing our attention to our immediate needs and closest relationships. Nothing clarifies your priorities like a force of nature rattling your walls.

For the world that birthed the *Völuspá*, extreme weather was a force worthy of immense respect. Today, as fatal frosts, rampaging wildfires, and catastrophic flooding begin to overwhelm much of our planet, the climate is again emerging as a god that demands respect. Ask anyone who has lived through a natural disaster, and they will tell you about the unstoppable power of these forces. These are giants of frost, flame, and water coming to call. They demand our attention, and they won't ask for it nicely anymore.

This is one of the many urgent messages I hear echoing out of the *Völuspá*. And as glaciers continue to melt and forests continue to burn, these beings that modernity exiled so long ago will only grow louder and more insistent until humankind can reweave our bonds of kinship with them and the untamed earth from which they emerge.

The Twilight of the Gods

The *Völuspá*, the ancient Norse prophecy of Ragnarok, comes from the *Poetic Edda*, a collection of ancient oral poetry that forms the foundation of Norse mythology, as well as from the *Prose Edda*, written down in Iceland sometime in the thirteenth century by Snorri Sturlson (Crawford, 2015). In the story, Odin awakens a *völva*—a Nordic seeress or shamaness—from beyond the grave to ask her to share her knowledge about the end of the world. Odin, always insatiable for knowledge, is told of his fate and the fate of the world as we know it.

The *Völuspá* is at once a creation myth, a chronicle of collapse, a battle saga, an apocalyptic prophecy, and a promise of rebirth. Through a series of betrayals, violence, and natural disasters, the world tree, Yggdrasil, is set aflame as the world is submerged beneath the churning sea. It is a frighteningly accurate myth for our times, which are fraught with greater polarization, public violence, and increasingly vivid encounters with ecological destruction.

A story that foretells the end of the world might seem like an odd choice to talk about the Tree of Life. Yet the *Völuspá* is perhaps the myth we most need to hear today. It is a deeply unsettling tale precisely because we are witnessing it play out before our eyes. And while our planet continues to unravel in ways that are shockingly similar to the imagery in the myth, psychedelic medicines have the potential to sow the seeds (or spores) of renewal and reconnection in the knowing soil of our psyche. Despite initial appearances, the myth of Ragnarok is a story about interconnection and what happens when the interwoven relationships between people and planet break down. Psychedelics are medicines of reconnection, and as we will see, they may be able to shepherd us back toward recognizing that all beings are indeed our kin.

Threads of Kinship

Like many ancient cultures, ancient Norse society was saturated with violence. War, blood feuds, and ritual sacrifice were everyday aspects of their world, and their mythology reflects this. Yet at the same time, pre-Christian Nordic culture was highly animistic, and perhaps like all Indigenous peoples, it saw the living world as full of sentient intelligence and worthy of respect. Their world was infused with an inextricable sense of entanglement, embodied through relationships with the ravens, wolves, mountains, and rivers that wove through their everyday lives.

Due in large part to portrayals in contemporary popular culture and the stories that have made their way down the centuries, it is easy to see Nordic culture as simply blood-crazed Vikings with cool hairstyles. Yet animistic kinship was the thread that bound their world together. Unravel this kinship, and you unravel the world.

The Desouled World

A defining condition of modernity is our unraveled kinship with the natural world. To understand how modern Western culture arrived at its radically disconnected state, we must go back to a period in European history ironically called the Age of Enlightenment.

Cultural ecologist and philosopher David Abram writes, "According to the central current of the Western philosophical tradition, from its source in ancient Athens up until the present moment, human beings alone are possessed of an incorporeal intellect, a 'rational soul' or mind which, by virtue of its affinity with an eternal or divine dimension outside the bodily world, sets us radically apart from, or above, all other forms of life" (1996, p. 47).

This thread would eventually be grasped by René Descartes, who, along with a cohort of even more zealous theologians, sought to expel any last vestige of an earth-based, animistic perception from Western consciousness. One of the many results of this shift was the separation of what he considered thinking—and therefore living—subjects (i.e., humans) from unthinking—and therefore dead—matter (i.e., nature). James Hillman referred to this period as the "desouling of the world," the fallout from the legacy of Descartes, which "required that subjectivities be purged from everywhere and everything except the authorized place of persons: the rational Christian adult. To experience otherwise was heresy and witchcraft" (1992, p. 5).

And "witchcraft" it certainly became. Across the world, countless people were executed for believing that a tree or stone might have something to say. The Spanish, in their bloody conquest of the New World, saw Indigenous peoples' animistic worldview as proof of their allegiance to the devil, deserving of wholesale slaughter or conversion at the tip of a spear—a colonization strategy sanctioned by Pope Alexander VI in 1493, just one year after Columbus sailed the ocean blue. This madness continued for centuries. It was not until 1978 that Native Americans were allowed to fully practice their religion, when the American Indian Religious Freedom Act was passed after nearly five hundred years of oppression. Yet ask many Native folks, and they'll likely tell you that the inquisition continues to this day.

The Witch's Pyre

Culturally speaking, the Western world is still wiping soot from the smoldering witches' pyre off its bloody boots. In the *Völuspá*, the story begins with a literal witch burning when the Aesir sought to murder Gullveig, whose true identity is shrouded in mystery. When I first dove into the source material for this myth, I didn't know what to make of Gullveig, and I felt disturbed by the way she was treated. Even in Neil Gaiman's beloved *Norse Mythology*, her name is never mentioned. It's unclear why Odin and his kin turned on Gullveig. What we know for certain is that it happened long ago, well before the events of Ragnarok, in the early days of the gods. It is also intriguing that the narrator of the story could be considered a witch herself, and that Odin needed her specifically to relay the tale. Three times they burned Gullveig, and three times she rose from the ashes. "Often-killed, yet ever-living," the texts say of her. Gullveig is indestructible, withstanding both spear and flame. Her power clearly extends far beyond these simple methods of destruction. What often dies yet is born anew, over and over? What is cut down every year with the scythe, only to sprout again? Look no further than the ground beneath your feet.

Gullveig's attempted murder is the first break in kinship bonds that the Aesir make, which eventually seals their fate. Their betrayal sparks the first war between them and the Vanir gods, which is a little-discussed yet pivotal moment in the Norse sagas. Just who are the Aesir and the Vanir? We won't ever be sure, but some scholars have speculated that the Aesir were that old familiar tribe of warlike sky gods, brought to Scandinavia by early waves of Germanic invaders (Branston, 1980). The Vanir were possibly a more localized, place-based clan of gods associated with the earth and its cycles of fertility—old magic. Frey and Freya, the two notable Vanir gods, are associated with these very things.

The reindeer-herding, culturally distinct Indigenous Sami people, who still populate Scandinavia's far north, were certainly living in those mountains long before the Germanic-speaking Norse arrived from the south. We can only guess how those initial meetings went. But odds are there was some bloodshed. It is even possible that Gullveig became the goddess Freya, patron deity of magic, love, sex, beauty, and yes, gold. Throughout Norse mythology, Loki often uses Freya's beauty and sexual vitality as a bargaining chip or object of scorn—a response still experienced by countless women who embrace their own sexuality and innate power. We can see both Freya and Gullveig as embodiments of feminine earthly power and as emanations of the earth. Clearly, the Aesir were terrified by this golden woman who contained a power far greater than the hammer or spear.

We can also see Gullveig's name, "Gold Lust" or "Gold Thirst," through a prism of meaning. To assume she is simply interested in material gold doesn't look nearly deep enough. As we've discussed before, gold is a solar metal. Illuminating, light-giving, and all-seeing, golden sunlight is literally the energy of life itself, a sacred commodity in a land that spends half the year in darkness. After she rises from the ashes a third time, she is crowned with a new title: Heith, "Shining One." We don't know why Gullveig arrived at Odin's hall, but she leaves as a transformed, brighter being. Her new "shining" form may suggest an element of spiritual illumination or inner radiance, a quality Odin sought for himself when he hung on Yggdrasil for nine days and nights, questing for the runes. Gullveig may also be the personification of two other alluring substances: gold itself, which needs to be refined through a process of repeatedly melting it down and reforming it; and mead, or fermented honey, which can "light a fire in the head," as the Irish say. Both of these substances were held sacred by the ancient Norse and across all of Europe. But we will never know for sure.

In the end, the Aesir betrayed Gullveig, committing the first murder, which sparked the first war the world had ever known. Odin, the "gallows god" who claimed all who died in battle, was likely pleased with the destruction, which secured his place as Allfather, the ruler of the gods.

But at what cost? Psychologically speaking, we are all still living with the consequence of Gullveig's murder and exile. We feel it as a great sadness that saturates anonymous city streets, a mournful longing whispering on full-moon nights, a grief too great for our wildly disconnected bodies to comprehend in isolation. This is the price of living in the "desouled world," a world that lost—or killed—its soul long ago.

Anima and Animism

Indigenous author and biologist Robin Wall Kimmerer writes, "It has been said that people of the modern world suffer a great sadness, a 'special loneliness'—estrangement from the rest of Creation. We have built this isolation with our fear, with our arrogance, and with our homes brightly lit against the night" (2015, p. 358). Kimmerer clearly links contemporary mental health issues with the West's long history of estrangement from the natural world. Yet the fallout of the desouled world extends far beyond our individual psyches, as Kimmerer demonstrates. It seeps into our rivers and groundwater, creeps into our food systems, and cracks apart swiftly melting ice sheets.

The climate crisis we currently face is a natural consequence of this desouling. If the world is indeed a living being, as it is for countless Indigenous cultures, then the atrocities and violence we inflict on her would be unthinkable. Theodore Roszak, who coined the term *ecopsychology* (along with *counterculture*, interestingly enough), wrote, "If we could assume the viewpoint of nonhuman nature, what passes for sane behavior in our social affairs might seem madness. But as the prevailing reality principle would have it, nothing could be greater madness than to believe that beast and plant, mountain and river have a 'point of view'" (1992, p. 13).

Embracing these diverse "point[s] of view" is the foundation of animistic thought. *Animism*, a word the academic establishment once used pejoratively to reduce complex systems of Indigenous knowledge, now seems to be the best term to describe a worldview that I believe holds the key for truly reversing the climate crisis and our incomprehensible treatment of the earth. Simply put, animists are people who recognize that the world is full of persons, "not all of whom are human but all of whom are worthy of respect" (Harvey, 2006, p. xvii). Recalling the legacy of Descartes, religion scholar Graham Harvey writes: "At the heart of the matter is the opposition between 'persons' and 'objects.' Persons are those with whom other persons interact with varying degrees of reciprocity. Persons may be spoken *with*. Objects, by contrast, are usually spoken *about*. Persons are volitional, relational, cultural, and social beings. . . . People become animists by learning how to recognize persons and, far more important, how to engage with them" (2006, p. xvii).

For even the most devout rational materialists among us, psychedelics seem to have an undeniably personlike quality to them. I've witnessed hardened investment bankers and CEOs grapple in wide-eyed wonder with the seemingly intelligent being they just encountered after ingesting a relatively small amount of unassuming *Psilocybe cubensis* mushrooms. I have personally heard the feathered language of ayahuasca whisper into my ears; felt the instructional, elderly energy of peyote directly point to areas of my life where I needed to get my shit together; had tricks of perception played on me by the cosmic prankster that lives inside every molecule of LSD. These are not poetic metaphors, but lived experiences.

Nature, Consciousness, and Psychedelics

At the 2023 MAPS Psychedelic Science conference, I heard Roland Griffiths, the distinguished psilocybin researcher, speak to a massive auditorium of eager listeners. Griffiths, a career scientist and devoted empiricist, deemed the psychedelic experience "essential to the survival of our species." As I listened to this frail, radiant man speak to an enraptured crowd of psychedelic investors, scientists, therapists, and media professionals, I felt as if this message was his last transmission to the world, an impassioned plea to broaden our understanding of the importance and scope of these substances and to begin to see them as necessary tools to help ensure our continued existence on this planet. My eyes welled as I witnessed the demure Griffiths, whittled down by cancer in his now-oversized blazer, absorb a standing ovation from a thousand hearts. He passed away just three months later.

Of all the momentous studies conducted by Griffiths, the one that he chose to highlight during his talk demonstrated something remarkable for the Western mind that animistic cultures have known all along. This 2022 study, poignantly titled "A Single Belief-Changing Psychedelic Experience Is Associated with Increased Attribution of Consciousness to Living and Non-living Entities," documented how for over 1,600 people, psychedelic experiences greatly increased their belief that nonhuman entities contain some element of consciousness (Nayak & Griffiths, 2022). The more "mystical" the experience ranked, the higher the likelihood that these attributions of consciousness would increase. Finally, the study showed that this belief did not wane for participants even years after the experience itself.

Another psychedelic study from 2019 conducted by psychedelic, ecological, and neuroscientific researchers Hannes Kettner, Sam Gandy, Eline Haijen, and Robin Carhart-Harris concluded that a sense of "nature relatedness was significantly increased 2 weeks, 4 weeks, and 2 years after a psychedelic experience" (p. 1), and that the frequency of lifetime psychedelic use was positively correlated to a baseline sense of nature relatedness in healthy participants. Summarizing their findings, the authors of the study explored how psychedelic experiences can do more than facilitate the fabled ego-dissolution experience; it also instilled something they called "self/nature continuity or overlap" (p. 13).

This is a wonderfully academic way of saying that people felt themselves intimately connected to nature, and nature intimately connected to them. Such findings should not be taken lightly. While the promise of psychedelics for treating issues of mental health is immense, I believe, along with Griffiths, that their potential to reconnect our psyches to the natural world and imbue it with a sense of animistic sentience is an even more vital role that these plants and compounds can play, both for the healing of individuals and for our collective survival.

I'm not naive enough to think that if more people simply ate psychedelics then the climate crisis would suddenly be solved. There are no answers, clear solutions, or action steps I can offer here. I'm afraid we're well beyond that. All I can do is pay close attention to what I feel the myths and medicines are saying and try to discern with my best guess where this subtle pathway might lead us. We're deep in the bush now, and your guess is as good as mine.

If generations of ceremonial plant medicine use by Indigenous people was not sufficient evidence, the research confirms that psychedelic medicines can help bring humans into a deeper relationship with the more-than-human world. But this is just a glimmer of hope, not a solution. Nothing will change with the advent of the "psychedelic renaissance" unless an animistic perspective is brought into the center of this work. Without creating meaningful doorways for Indigenous people and earth-honoring perspectives to inform the practice of psychedelic healing, it will remain squarely in the province of the desouled world, in the realm of anthropocentrism, medicalization, capitalistic extraction, and finding itself once again on this lonely island of disconnection known as modernity.

Returning to Harvey's definition of animism, I see three important shifts that this sort of perception might offer us in this era of climate collapse.

The first natural outcome of an animistic perspective is that it inherently requires one to offer respect to beings (or "persons") that dwell beyond the human sphere. This includes trees and rivers as much as it does psychic forms previously thought to be "imaginary," whether they're understood as inner "parts," ancestors, spirits, or certain places on the earth. Respect means that we stop trying to tell something what it is and that we listen intently to the stories and perspectives contained within the field of our attention. It also means that we give something back to the things (or persons) that give us so much.

Second, an animist perspective requires that we, especially Americans, begin to shed a layer of our pathological individuality, for animism implies being enmeshed in a web of interrelations with beings containing levels of consciousness equally valuable as our own. We can begin to locate our lives, experiences, and identities in this web of being, which extends far beyond the vicissitudes of the human mind. Surely we could learn a thing or two from a cedar tree or mountain.

Third, and most importantly, it means these beings support us, and we must support them as well. Because with relatedness comes responsibility.

Kimmerer writes, "Cultures of gratitude must also be cultures of reciprocity. Each person, human or no, is bound to every other in a reciprocal relationship. Just as all beings have a duty to me, I have a duty to them. . . . An integral part of a human's education is to know those duties and how to perform them" (2015, p. 115). Just what are these duties, and what needs to be performed? I haven't a clue. All I know is that there is something important that happens when we turn our attention back toward people, places, and cultures that have been around much longer than ourselves. Myths contain such wisdom, as do old-growth forests, as do ceremonies of healing.

CASE STUDY: *Maria*

I once had the privilege of working with a young woman named Maria who was born in Romania. She lived in an orphanage there for the first two years of her life until an American couple adopted her and brought her to the United States. Maria had no knowledge of her birth mother or family, other than that they were Romani (the people pejoratively referred to as Gypsies).

Maria had struggled with severe depression, anxiety, and PTSD, resulting in a cascade of symptoms and issues that severely limited her capacity to fully engage in life. When I met her she had recently undergone gastric surgery to help her manage her weight. Although she was in a loving relationship, Maria struggled with intimacy and would regularly find herself shutting down in trauma responses, falling into wells of despair, isolating herself from those around her, and coping in self-destructive ways.

On her second dose of psilocybin, Maria found herself experiencing something she was utterly unprepared for. Eyes closed, rocking back and forth, she suddenly found herself back in the Romanian orphanage of her early life. She described everything in vivid detail, from the feeling of her soiled diapers, to the details of the ceiling, to the dismal smell of the room. She was somewhere around two years of age, and she felt utterly alone. Somewhere, a distant voice called out her Romani name, "Maria Leonora . . . Maria Leonora . . ."

Tears flowed down her olive skin as she cradled herself, rocking back and forth while immense waves of grief and fear flowed through her.

After an hour or so, Maria imagined herself going into the orphanage, picking her two-year-old self out of the cradle, and comforting her, letting her know that she was going to be okay and that she was going to be given to a loving family that would care for her, support her, and keep her safe. In her vision, she carried her younger self out of the orphanage and back home to the United States.

On Maria's third and final journey, she went even deeper. She found herself immersed in total darkness, unable to see anything, but hearing strange, distant sounds echoing in her awareness. She heard shouting in a foreign language and breaking glass, and she felt a visceral twinge of fear. She realized she was in her mother's womb, experiencing the violence that permeated her mother's world. Then she saw her mother, whom she had never met—yet whom she also resented. Maria felt her mother's profound regret and sadness at having to give her up for adoption. She also felt for the first time her mother's love, flowing from her desire to give Maria a better chance at life. Maria understood that her mother didn't want to bring her into a life that would be saturated with abuse, which would surely have been her fate if her mother had kept her.

For the first time in her life, Maria was able to make peace with her mother's choice. She forgave her mother and found herself connected to her and her Romani roots in an entirely new way.

A year later, Maria is more physically and mentally healthy than ever, happily married to her long-term partner, and recently gave birth to her first child.

Skills: The Tree of our Life

Roots

As in Maria's story, psychedelic medicines can open profound pathways for ancestral healing and reconnection. Try as we might, none of us can escape the realities of our ancestry, birth family, and genetic heritage.

Our ancestry and family are the roots of the tree of our life. Connecting to these roots can provide us with emotional, psychological, and spiritual nourishment, just as a tree's roots draw upon groundwater and minerals buried beneath the earth. These roots are also a vital source of support, grounding our lives in a rich terrain that extends far beyond our individual psyches, connecting us to an ancient web of relatedness that extends backward in time, back to our earliest ancestors, to eons far beyond our comprehension.

For some, like Maria, ancestral roots may require immense healing on an individual level, where there are wounds and cycles of harm that need resolution. For others, their ancestral roots might require more creative forms of reconnection. My own ancestors experienced the traumas of the Holocaust and the Irish potato famine, which I have revisited and experienced through my own psychedelic journeys. Going back even further, many of these ancestors experienced centuries of marginalization and colonization, none of which is unique to my identity. In facing our own ancestral wounds, we can eventually find ourselves facing collective traumas that the vast majority of humanity has experienced at some point in time.

Trunk

As a tree grows, it slowly accumulates layers upon its trunk, visible in the rings that detail its journey through the seasons. We too add layers as we age, both physically and psychologically, forming patterns that constitute our lifestyles and personalities, for better or worse. These habits and ways of relating form the foundation of our lives and become inscribed into our bodies and psyches.

Tree trunks are primarily supportive and protective. The rough bark of a tree serves to insulate the precious sap that flows within, carrying vitality to its upper branches, which might be hundreds of feet above the ground.

Psychologically, we each have defenses and coping strategies to help us navigate everyday life. Many of these might have served us when our skin was thinner, or during a harsh winter or traumatic period; but they may have lost their usefulness as we've grown. All of our patterns and habits constitute the totality of who we are.

Psychedelics can help us reexamine all of the ways in which we support our lives, revealing the weak points where our trunk is not as strong as we thought, or reaffirming the goodness and support that we have worked so hard to create. Psychedelics can either serve to strengthen or compromise one's psyche, a quality that Jung and others referred to as *ego strength*.

The foundational trunk of one's life, encompassing supportive relationships, stable housing, consistent income, and a relatively healthy lifestyle, must be taken into account when determining if psychedelics are going to support—or compromise—someone's growth.

Branches

Tree branches radiate in all directions, like the neural pathways one can revitalize and expand with the aid of many psychedelics. When we are stuck in rigid thought patterns or immersed in anxiety and depression, we are like a tree with only a few branches. During and after a strong psychedelic experience, though, current research demonstrates that neural plasticity can greatly increase (Carhart-Harris et al., 2014).

The tree's branches support the nine worlds of Yggdrasil. The great world tree contains multiple realities and expressions of existence that are as different from each other as night is from day. It was said that the eagle perched on Yggdrasil's crown, and Nidhogg, the serpent wound around its roots, were mortal enemies—and that a playful squirrel named Ratatosk climbed the tree every day, exchanging their hate mail. They might not like each other, but they depend on the same organism for their existence—a simple teaching with profound implications.

One tree can contain an untold plethora of beings, from microscopic to mammalian, all finding a common home in the branches and trunk that link them together.

Tree branches demonstrate the complexity of interdependent relationships, which whole ecosystems depend upon. The giant sequoia tree, for instance, generates an entire ecosystem high above the earth, creating its own misty weather patterns in its canopy, which feeds a variety of lichens and mosses. It can even build its own soil in the deep crofts at its junctions, where new seedlings can germinate and grow in this unique world of branches and clouds.

How can we branch out to support those around us? As we wake up to the fullness of our interrelated lives, a question we can return to for guidance is this: who and what are we supporting, and who and what is supporting us?

Leaves and Flowers

Ralph Metzner likened the leaves and flowers of the Tree of Life to the thoughts and ideas that form in the minds of human beings. Metzner wrote, "As the health and beauty of the leaves and flowers are a function of the nourishing sap rising up from below under the influence of light and warmth, so, we may suggest, the health and vitality of our thoughts and images are a function of how unobstructed their connectedness is to the instinctual nature 'below,' and of the mental and emotional acceptance and support they receive from 'outside'" (1998, p. 204).

Leaves literally eat sunlight. They are powerful agents of transmutation. Chlorophyll converts the sun's rays into energy through photosynthesis, which has no direct parallel in humans, but we might see it as a metaphor for inspiration. We don't know where inspiration comes from, but many artists will likely tell you that it flows from somewhere entirely beyond them.

Creativity and inspiration are ways to celebrate and speak to the spirit and the soul. Ecstatic inspiration is one of the many gifts that psychedelics can offer, as we have seen. If we're lucky, the divine will speak back to us.

Finally, leaves are reminders of life's fleeting nature. Their cycles of blooming, fullness, and decay direct our attention to our own mortality, the preciousness of our time here, and the limited time of those we love the most. As the crisp winds of autumn touch our skin and the leaves begin their yearly dance downward to meet the newly moistened soil, we are surrounded by tiny teachings of red and gold, each a reminder of life's fleeting presence.

Fruit

Fruit has always been a symbol of abundance, fertility, and new life. Sweetness and sensual richness are inherent elements of all fruits, as their ripe flesh and sultry perfume bring our senses into intimate participation with life. Connecting to our senses brings us into the present moment.

When I mindfully offer a fruit to a client freshly emerging from an epic voyage into the beyond, I invite them to savor the miracle of a simple fruit. It might be the best thing they've ever tasted.

There is also an inherently sexual and creative element to fruits. The desire to create or offer something meaningful to the world can be seen as the fruit of a psychedelic experience. I've seen this crystallize in the literal desire to have children for people who had written off that path. Other times, creative fruits might take the form of a new artistic project or business idea.

Ultimately, the real fruit of a psychedelic experience is about serving others. Service is the apex of integration and can be seen as the gradual ripening of a process that begins as "self-growth" but ends up being much more about collective healing.

Fruits contain the seeds of new beginnings. The fruits of our actions ripple across time and space, affecting much more than our present-day reality. In many Native American cultures, there is a profound respect for the Law of Seven Generations, originally a principle of the Haudenosaunee or Iroquois peoples that required each decision of the tribe to be made in consideration of the seven generations that came before and the seven generations yet to come.

⁕ ⁕ ⁕

As glaciers continue to melt, forests continue to burn, and the sun continues to rise red on the horizon, the time has long since passed for us to embrace the Law of Seven Generations if we wish to survive this modern-day Ragnarok.

Yet the earth is not as doomed as we think. Human civilization as we know it? Probably, since the evidence makes it clear that we cannot continue as we have been. But the earth is involved in telling deeper stories that we can scarcely comprehend, sagas so large they spill out of our antlike heads and work their way through the sandstone of geologic time and the swells of oceanic currents. Yes, there will be cataclysms, collapse, extinction, and unfathomable loss. Surely by now most of us have felt the immensity of the situation before us.

And yet, and yet, and yet . . .

The earth is not evil. Fierce, chaotic, even uncaring, yes. Giantlike in its intensity, ultimately powerful. But what if the earth longs for us just as much as we long for her? What if she grieves for what has become of us just as much as we do for what has become of her? What if the terrors of our changing climate are actually grief shudders of a being who's known us longer than we've known ourselves? How might our lives change if we can begin to see each new ecological disaster as a plea demanding our attention, a Giant-like visitor come to call, rather than an attempt to destroy us?

The myth of Ragnarok is a cautionary tale full of looming consequences. But like all stories of apocalypse, there's a twist. Two humans survive and take refuge inside Yggdrasil's hollowed trunk, clinging tightly to each other as the fires of Ragnarok ravage the world. There's no mystical secret here, no esoteric truth, other than this: only by being inside the Tree of Life, only by experiencing ourselves as already within this animate, conscious, living world, can humanity find its way through the gathering storm.

As they sheltered in the tree, only their embrace gave them warmth and comfort, carrying them through the long, dark night. If we're going to survive this, we must be kind to one another. We must support each other. We must hold on to love.

Each new catastrophe, each new tendril emerging from char-blackened soil, becomes an opportunity: to breathe air that carries the exhalations of every ancestor who's ever walked the earth, to absorb into our bloodstream molecules of water that have spent a thousand lifetimes as glaciers and clouds, to open the green door of our hearts, and to step fully into the only home we've ever known.

X

The Journey Home

Integration, Community, and Dancing with the Village

The traveler has to knock at every alien door to come to his own, and one has to wander through all the outer worlds to reach the innermost shrine at the end.

—RABINDRANATH TAGORE

The Half Girl

*O*nce upon a time, in a village on the banks of a river, a baby was born. She *cried like a normal baby, crawled like a normal baby, and did everything else that normal babies do. And as she grew, she was just like every other child in the village. For a time.*

But one day, around that age when we all start to change our shape and sprout new patterns of hair and flesh, the girl looked down at herself and saw something she had never noticed before. Where other children had two legs, she only had the left leg. Where other children had two arms, she only had the left arm. Left eye, left ear, left nostril, left side of her mouth. She was a half girl.

As she continued to grow, the other children of the village teased her for being only half a person. She would go around the village trying to make herself useful, but everyone turned her away. How useful can a half girl be, really? The village kids would make fun of her, exclude her, and play tricks on her. She started asking questions about why she was only a half girl, but she received no good answers. She began to feel like she would always be seen as a half person and would only be half of what she could be. She felt like her left hand and left foot would never be enough for the village. Eventually, she couldn't stand it any longer, and one morning she packed up her few possessions and dragged her way to the village gates. She looked around and found herself completely alone. She crossed the line and left.

The Half Girl wandered from village to village, looking for somewhere that might be a refuge in a world of people who all seemed to be whole. But everywhere she went, she found herself facing fearful glances that whispered discomfort. After a long time of looking for home and never finding it, she went deep into the forest.

As the years went on, she became something of a feral creature. She continued to wander through the forest, self-reliant and utterly alone. Until one day she came upon a river.

As she went down to its banks to wash, she saw movement out of the corner of her left eye. Far down the riverbank, she saw another girl. But there was something strange about her. This girl had a right leg, and a right arm, and a right eye, and a right ear. She moved closer down the river bank. Then the new girl suddenly began to run, and finally lunged at her, as if to attack her. The Half Girl found herself running at full speed toward the other as well, and in a spectacular clash, they flung their bodies into each other and fell into the river. The waters frothed and churned as the two girls fought one another beneath the current. An arm sticking up here, a leg there, water roiling like a cauldron.

Finally, after the waves and splashing settled down, what came out of the river was not two girls, but one. Disoriented, disheveled, unable to tell right from left, she was completely turned around. Had she crossed the river? Was she carried miles downstream? She had no idea where she was. And truth be told, she looked a little wonky. One eye looked up, the other down; one ear cocked left, the other right, and one side of her mouth smiled while the other frowned. She felt awkward. But at least she was whole.

For the first time, the girl found herself walking with two legs, and she began to enjoy the sensation and rhythm of it. She wandered away from the river and down a new road she had never seen before. As she walked, her eyes slowly began to point in the same direction, her mouth slowly began to level out, and her entire body gradually came into a comfortable alignment.

After some time—we can't be sure how long—she came to a village. There, at its gates, she saw an old woman sweeping the threshold with her broom. As the elder swept, she had one foot inside the territory of the village, and another in that of the forest.

Exhausted, the Half Girl approached the elder and said, "Please, I've been on a long journey and just recently climbed out of the river. I have no idea where I am. Can you help me?"

The elder smiled, and said, "Yes, my child, I can help you. You've arrived at the village where you began, the village of your birth. And I'm sorry to say that no one has been dancing since you went away. But I have a feeling that if we enter the village dancing together, then something good will happen."

And dance they did. The Half Girl and the elder crossed the village boundary together, dancing. And soon enough the village began to join them. Children, elders, adults, and finally, the adolescents, who were all feeling a bit like half people themselves. Some say that the village has continued dancing to this day. Others say that the next morning the dancing stopped when the shrill cries of a newborn baby met the rising sun. In fact, they say that the baby born that morning was also a half child, crying out loudly to a village that didn't know how to receive it, and that in time, people began to avoid the child, beginning a long story that had all happened before.

But there are others who say that the girl became known as a powerful healer and storyteller—a Wise Elder whom people came to when they were in pain or lost on their own road of life. At the place where she died, a great tree grew under which people would gather and tell stories. It is said that the great tree still stands there, in the heart of the village, and if you go there and sit silently under its branches, it will tell you stories about the exact things that you need, stories about the things the village couldn't give you. Stories that will make you whole.

Perfectly Imperfect

What does it mean to come home to ourselves? There is an elegant longing in this story that cut me right to the core the first time I heard it told. Michael Meade, whom I first heard it from, told me he stumbled upon it while wandering in New York, when he found an out-of-print book on Borneo folktales. This version also integrates elements from Martin Shaw's telling, which I heard under a big tent one spring day on Vancouver Island. The potent simplicity of this tale brings us directly to a collective dilemma that I think about every day, which is the radically disjointed state of my culture and communities. It also begins with an honest fact that is the foundational drive toward healing: that there are parts of ourselves that we do not fully know, which appear as incomplete or unwanted and require us to reclaim them.

The modern world is increasingly image-obsessed, as modified facial structures and body types are mediated through digital filters on smartphones, and AI-generated models project unattainable standards of beauty. Images of perfection are wreaking havoc on the psyches of young people, especially young women. This has been the case for a long time. Perhaps humans have always been fixated on images, since the psyche's first language is imagery itself. Regardless, "The Half Girl" begins with the sobering, universal confrontation that all of us are, in some way, woefully incomplete.

The will to change, the quest for self-knowledge, the desire to heal, are at heart the lonely wanderings of a half person seeking something that the village couldn't give them. The core of Jungian psychology revolves around this quest for wholeness, which Jung saw as the driving force behind all healing, whether arising in dreams or pathologies. The psyche has an innate desire to seek wholeness and to integrate its disparate parts, whether they reside in the unknown dark of the shadow or are projected outward onto an idealized other. Even in his psychotic patients, of which he had many, Jung viewed the fantasies and hallucinations they suffered from as emerging from the psyche's foundational desire to be whole. Over the course of a person's lifetime, our psyche demands that we journey outward in order to become whole. Jung called this the process of *individuation.*

James Hillman, on the other hand, was skeptical of the idea that we are ever truly whole. "If there is only one model of individuation can there be true individuality?" he asked (1989, p. 40). Embracing what he called a *polytheistic psychology,* Hillman compared the Jungian bias of wholeness over multiplicity to modern Western civilization's obsession with monotheism over polytheism, which has had disastrous results both in world history and in the inner world of individuals. The soul is endless, according to Hillman, and when one encounters it, one is only pointed onward toward its infinite dimensions. We emerge from an encounter with the soul, whether facilitated by psychedelics or not, even more in touch with our fractured or unwanted parts, but often with a different perspective. We find the parts of ourselves that are missing, and we fall into the rushing river of transformation. We cannot help but emerge a different version of ourselves.

The journey home cannot take place without a journey into the vast terrain of the inner or outer world. In myth, the outward journey is paradoxically an inward journey, something that brings us across the threshold of the known, beyond the gates of the village. To Hillman, any encounter with soul illuminates our fractured, incomplete nature. Echoing the lessons of the underworld from chapter 3, Hillman said, "I think too that the underworld teaches us to abandon our hopes of achieving unification of personality. . . . A psychotherapy that reflects these depths can therefore make no attempt at achieving undivided individuality or encouraging a personal identity as a unified wholeness" (1979, p. 11). What does all of this mean for us? Simply that we are never fully whole or healed. Healing is a process of wrestling with our incompleteness until we find the blessings therein. This might take years, or a lifetime. We don't know how long the Half Girl spent in the forest, but when she emerges, she is a new person.

To approach psychedelic integration with this understanding brings a level of emotional honesty that questions the idea that some-day we will finally "be healed." The suspiciously puritanical urge to always become better versions of ourselves, whether through mate-rial wealth or moral superiority, forever ascending into some ideal-ized way of being, is a trap. Just do enough yoga, or drink enough ayahuasca, or go to enough therapy, and you'll be healed. In fact, one could say that the entire industry of "self-growth" and "healing" has become a labyrinth of perpetual aspiration that only fuels the machinery of capitalism. By its very nature, capitalism requires that you depend on it as your sole source of satisfaction, survival, and validation, selling you visions of happiness while continually demand-ing its relentless pursuit. In the eyes of capitalism, you will never be enough.

The rugged contours of our body, the locked boxes and fractured idols that adorn the shrines of our inner world, want to be related with. Yes, we can seek to repair them, but healing at its core has nothing to do with expelling or exiling. It has even less to do with whatever wellness charlatans or religious leaders attempt to sell us as indications of our spiritual inferiority or original sin.

Even after the Half Girl's long years spent wandering the forest, even after the churning union with her other half in the river, she emerges only a slightly better version of herself. Her transformation is incremen-tal at best, and it takes time as she staggers home, a humbling reminder of the pace at which true change occurs. When she reenters her village, she returns the only way any of us ever need to be: authentically incom-plete. Perfectly imperfect.

The Eternal Return

It's a beautiful thought, that after all our long years spent wandering the wilderness, we will be greeted by loving elders when we finally return to the village of our origins. In his account of the culminating act of the "hero's journey," Joseph Campbell famously spoke about "bringing back the boon" and returning as a triumphant, transformed being with gifts and wisdom to share with the tribe. I hate to break it to you, but most returns do not go according to Uncle Joe's plan. In reality, most of us are never fully able to return because, culturally speaking, there is nowhere to go back to.

Returning to society and integrating what we've learned is where psychedelic healing gets real. Traditionally, one was expected to come down from the Sacred Mountain with something to offer the people below. The perilous journey through the Underworld was undertaken to serve those living above. Drinking from the Well, entering the Temple, shedding one's skin, facing the Monstrous, dancing with Trickster, and inhabiting the Tree of Life are experiences that are meant to enliven not just you but everyone around you as well. There is much more going on in these stories than simply tending to our personal well-being.

But here's the dilemma: if the culmination of initiatory rites and psychedelic journeys is to return with some renewed vision for the tribe, what does it mean when there is no village to return to, no elders to sing one back into the fold of family, work, community, and culture? Who is waiting for us when we wander back through the village gates?

It is easy to strike out into the abyss, take the plunge into the unknown, and claim what may or not rightfully be yours to claim. Entire nations were founded on that principle, and if the current fragmentation of North American identity is any indication, it is a flimsy foundation to build upon. Anyone can eat psychedelics and still not actually do any real work because the effects of the medicine do not reach beyond one's self. The story of the Half Girl makes it clear: individual healing is only half the picture. And until we can transmute our individual process and sense of self into something that tangibly benefits others, we will all remain half people.

For most modern individuals, the old tribal mechanisms of initiation and return no longer suffice, as Westerners have become culturally addicted to what Shaw calls "faux-Severance . . . [where] we separate from family, lovers, jobs, and countries with greater speed than ever, but are adrift at the Return" (2011, pp. xxiv–xxv). This perpetual state of movement and severance is actually fetishized within the hyper-individualized framework of Western culture. It is also, I believe, a primary source of its many maladies.

During an extended trip in Thailand during my late twenties I fell into a crowd of "digital nomads" and other expats who frequented the hipster neighborhood in Bangkok where I was staying. Many of them had salt-and-pepper hair and exciting jobs that regularly took them around the world. They were all about to imminently depart for Hong Kong, New Delhi, São Paolo, London, wherever, after which they would peregrinate back to Bangkok for another month or so and repeat the cycle. Some had apartments, but many simply opted for the more pro-social environment of an upscale hostel.

This was the life I had pined for, worked toward, and admired for years. It was the pedestaled existence that I thought would most align with who I thought I wanted to be and what I thought I wanted. In Thailand, I realized that I had finally "made it" as a travel writer and guide. I was offered my first all-expenses-paid writing gig, which took me to Burma, and I was rapidly expanding my network in the world of international media and remote work. Having worked for National Geographic Student Expeditions and other travel organizations, I crested toward the pinnacle of everything I thought would make me happy.

As I sat next to a charcoal grill sizzling with gai yang chicken one night in a narrow Bangkok alleyway, though, some lingering thought began to make its way into my consciousness. This thought was germinated by getting to know some people who had already been down this globetrotting path for a decade or more. Although their lives looked fun, I began to feel what I can only describe as a profound loneliness, a relational impoverishment, that emanated from them. Now, it's possible that they were actually content, and I was simply projecting my own unrealized values and needs onto them. But the fact remained: many of their intimate relationships were either nonexistent or in tatters. They perpetually lived a world apart from family or friends. And any friendships they did have were characterized by short spurts of out-on-the-town, alcohol-fueled camaraderie, followed by months of distance. I began to think that, for some of them, those nights were all they had.

One humid evening at a ramshackle pirate ship of a bar in downtown Bangkok, the chainsaw roar of tuk-tuk engines and the dissociated sing-song of Thai music engulfing my senses, I was drinking a Leo beer with a grayer-haired version of my future self. Having just achieved a level of success that I had long been working toward, I suddenly realized that I actually didn't want it anymore. I didn't want the one-off writing gigs, the global lifestyle, or the exciting (yet underpaid) guiding jobs.

I didn't know what I wanted, but did know that something in my life needed to change. Some seed was planted there, in the bowels of that labyrinthine city. I knew that I needed to reorient my life toward something bigger than my own self-indulgent experiences, something that might eventually serve my larger community. Six months after returning stateside, I enrolled at Pacifica Graduate Institute to study depth psychotherapy, which in turn led to my work in psychedelic therapy, culminating with the book you are reading now.

Community and Ritual

In the story, after the two Half Girls converge, one girl staggers out of the river, just barely put back together. It's about as far away from a Cinderella moment as possible. There are no knights, no charming princes, no wise women emerging from the trees. It's just her. When she finally comes to the village, she is greeted by an elder who immediately knows her face, even though it may have been years since she saw it last. As she steps back inside the village bounds, she and the elder dance, and the entire community joins in.

The great west African ritualist and teacher Malidoma Somé viewed ritual as the central pillar of community, and he saw the West's lack of community ritual as indicative of its individual and collective ills. Somé said: "Without a community you cannot be yourself. The community is where we draw the strength needed to effect changes inside of us. Community is formed each time more than one person meets for a purpose. . . . What one acknowledges in the formation of the community is the possibility of doing together what is impossible to do alone. This acknowledgement is also an objection against the isolation of individuals and individualism by a society in service of the Machine" (1993, p. 66).

At the risk of being dogmatic, I will say this: I believe that psychedelic healing is meant to be done in community. The modern practice of individualized psychedelic therapy was established under two notable conditions: scientific research, and legal prohibition. The first condition of research served as a way to minimize variables in clinical trials, thereby conforming to the scientific method of experimentation and observation. The desired outcome was to measure effects in the most efficient way possible, but not necessarily to heal in the deepest way possible. There is immeasurable value in research and clinical trials, to be sure. But is it an effective template for healing as it relates to one's wider community? Do fluorescent lights, hospital corridors, and small, sterile treatment rooms seem like the most ideal conditions for the sort of transformation psychedelics can inspire? I'd say no.

The second condition of prohibition was a result of a hostile legal environment that meant anyone caught administering or taking psychedelic medicines would be thrown in jail or heavily prosecuted by the government. At the time of this writing, the war on drugs is in its fifty-second year, at least in the United States; and while there are glimmers of hope for its abatement, I believe we are a long way off from a total truce. The implications of the drug war must not be overlooked in the study of modern psychedelic healing, as most early pioneers of this field were, and still are, working in secrecy. Some have paid for it dearly. Others, especially Indigenous people, have paid for it with their lives.

Indigenous healing traditions, by contrast, have long-established methods of working with psychedelic medicine in community contexts.

During a Native American Church ceremony I attended, one man was having a particularly hard time. It was the winter solstice, and bitterly cold outside. Moaning and writhing all over the floor, this man was unable to sit up and participate in the ceremony as is expected of people in a traditional "tipi meeting." I felt my own nausea begin to surge in response to the overwhelming energy emanating from this man and his display of suffering. A sharp voice within me was desperate to get him out of the tipi and as far away from me as possible.

After what seemed like an eternity, the road man stopped the ceremony and addressed the man by name, in front of everyone. "I know you're having a hard time. But we're not going to kick you out in the cold. That's not what we do with our community. We don't kick people out when it's inconvenient for us. We take care of our community here. So I'm going to take care of you."

After a quick break out in the cold to wake him up, the man was given several more doses of peyote, which the road man took as well, according to custom. For the rest of the night the man was quiet, witnessed in his vulnerability and supported by those who had the strength to make it through the night.

I've seen children in tipi meetings take small sips of peyote tea offered by their parents. Many of those children are now strong, radiant young adults who take pride in their community. Babies and aunties and mothers are welcomed in with the "morning water," bringing in new life along with them. In the Amazon, it was not uncommon for the maestro's father, son, wife, sister, brother, and neighbor to come for a night of ceremony. For the Mazatec people, entire families come to a velada, or nighttime mushroom ceremony, in order to find the source of a particular sickness or problem that is plaguing them. I'm not saying we should start giving psychedelics to children; but in the Indigenous world, healing is rarely ever done in isolation or through excluding community or family members.

In my own work, I've seen the group dynamic become a healing force all its own. People support and encourage one another, rallying around someone when they're struggling and celebrating them when they share some long-sought insight or moment of relief. There is a rare level of camaraderie that can happen in group psychedelic work. I've often heard people share about how they found perspective on their own suffering by hearing someone else's story. When we are deep in a depression, for instance, it's easy to believe that we're the only one there. Suffering, especially depression and anxiety, creates isolation, as does the modern world, which is why group work can be so powerful. One witnesses others in their healing and is witnessed in their own.

None of this means that non-Indigenous people should simply replicate Indigenous-style group ceremonies. Nor does it mean that people are effecting meaningful change in the world simply by tripping together. But I will say that approaching psychedelic healing as if building a temporary village can be a radical act of remembrance. The experience of "sudden community," as Michael Meade calls it, can be a balm for the radically disconnected and terminally lonely existence that so many people grapple with today.

In certain cases, individualized work is necessary. When someone feels they might not be able to let go or feel safe in a room full of people, that is a good enough reason to begin with individual work. Sadly, some people have too much trauma to participate comfortably in group ceremonies, and some particular personalities are simply not conducive for group work. But for the most part, group psychedelic work is a powerful experience that, if held safely and ethically, can create exponentially more avenues of healing than simply taking these medicines alone or in a modern "clinical" context.

The Spiral Road

Carl Jung once wrote, "I felt that at some time or other I had passed through the valley of diamonds, but I could convince no one—not even myself, when I looked at them more closely—that the specimens I had brought back were not mere pieces of gravel" (1961/1963, p. 104). This is a relatable sentiment to almost anyone who's entered the "valley of diamonds" that psychedelic medicine can open within us, as is the feeling of those precious gems of wisdom slowly turning to gravel in your hands.

Psychedelic integration is a process that asks us to continue relating with whatever we experienced atop the Mountain long after we've descended from its peak. Integration isn't something we check off the list and move on from. It is never complete. Rather, once we set one foot upon this spiral road, we are forever located, as Victor Turner put it, "betwixt and between." Our lives become translucent, liminal, and paradoxically oriented toward this world and the other. Integration asks us to become travelers of this spiral path that eventually brings us right back to our roots, to the ground beneath us, to the metaphorical village of our origins. We return the same, yet entirely changed.

Rilke said:

Take your well-disciplined strengths
and stretch them between two
opposing poles. Because inside human beings
is where God learns.
    (1992, p. 236)

The challenge of the journey home lies in navigating the tension between these "two opposing poles." Like the Half Girl encountering her other side at the riverbank, the return stretches our being to encompass many truths and realities at once. Upon our return, all of us are faced with navigating multiple crossroads as we confront the dualities that permeate our world and psyches.

Something sacred takes root within us as we navigate this twisting path where "God learns." This is the same tension that the zen monk sits in while staring at the wall in *zazen* meditation, the same intensity the road man navigates in the sweltering darkness of the sweat lodge. It is the tension of the artist facing the blank page or canvas. I feel it every time a client sits down in front of me, preparing to spill their soul. It is also the tension we navigate when we attempt to share an experience that changed some fundamental aspect of who we are. There may be people in our lives who cannot, or will not, understand. There may be external realities that do not easily match with the path we've found ourselves walking.

A great many things will have to change.

At the end of the story, the dancing is interrupted by the newborn cries of another half child, destined to grow up in the shadow of a community that did not know how to hold them either. The former Half Girl becomes a Wise Elder who likely becomes the very grandmother who greets the wayward youths as they return to the village gates. And the tree that sprouts from her body becomes a gathering place for the entire village, a place of celebration, a place of healing, a place where stories are told that heal the soul.

Skills

Sudden Community

A "sudden community" or temporary village constructed around group psychedelic work can look many ways, but on its most basic level it consists of:

- ▼ A group commitment to the work and what emerges
- ▼ Group agreements around what sort of behavior is welcome and what is not
- ▼ Ritualized severance from the everyday or "profane" world
- ▼ Closer proximity to nature (ideally)
- ▼ An intimate but temporary experience of community living, such as cooking and eating together
- ▼ Group processing through either facilitated or peer-led sharing/integration circles before and after the ceremony
- ▼ Ritualized transitions into and out of sacred/intentional space that honor the process of healing, the land, the medicine in question, and the dignity of each participant

▼ A clear beginning and end to the experience

▼ Methods of staying connected with the entire group, if desired

No, these are not instructions on how to start a cult. They are simply some basic guidelines that I have seen be supportive of group work, with or without psychedelics. Usually, this works well with a knowledgeable or trained individual(s) running the show. Though having a leader is by no means required, communities, temporary or not, inherently imply certain roles and hierarchies that ideally serve the whole. That said, I encourage people to find their own ways of navigating power and hierarchy within the context of group work.

Three Spheres of Integration

In the words of Lakota scholar, activist, and writer Vine Deloria Jr., "The theory of relativity, in this sense, hardly means that all things are relative. It rather means that all things are related" (1973, p. 299).

When I first read Deloria's words, they completely rearranged my understanding of psychedelic integration, speaking to a fundamental truth that I knew but could not yet express. My conceptual approach to integration, how I practice it with my clients, and how I try to embody it in my own life are all based on the underlying principle that integration is a reflection of relational health, and vice versa. The word *integrate* comes from the Latin *integrare*, which means "to make whole, to renew, or to begin again." The word *relationship* stems in part from the Latin *relatio*, which interestingly means "to bring something back or to restore," which is what we do every time we try to make sense of a psychedelic experience.

Based on elements from my master's thesis and from time spent working with clients, I have developed what I call the Three Spheres of Integration framework. The three spheres, and the subcategories contained within them, represent three ways to engage with the integration process from a relational perspective. Integration is a spiral, not a line. This path is not about perfection or even "self-growth." If anything, this framework acts simply as a mirror that, when engaged honestly, can help us approach new pathways for how we relate with these three spheres: the outer world, our inner selves, and the imaginal-creative spirit.

Please see the appendix for a corresponding question inventory designed to support you in navigating this framework.

Relationship to the Outer World

Integration asks that we revitalize our relationships with all other forms of life, including the plants, animals, and people upon whom we depend. Returning from liminal space offers us an opportunity to reevaluate or renew our appreciation for all life and those whom we share it with. This takes the form of revivifying one's connection with our human relationships and community, our relationship to place and nature, and our relationship to diet and consumption.

Human Relationships and Community

Psychedelic experiences help one appreciate and come into greater alignment with the figures that play important roles in one's life: partners, parents, siblings, teachers, and friends. If one has been stuck in a toxic or abusive relationship, psychedelic experiences can often create the perspective or fortitude needed to confront that person or leave them. Alternatively, a psychedelic journey can clarify where we might have wronged others. When one is in a place of power or leadership, as discussed in chapter 7, the journey can help clarify one's responsibility to their wider community. Our relationship to our sexuality and intimacy, including any associated shame or traumas, plays a role here here as well.

Place and Nature

Seeing nature as an inherent element of integration transcends our individualized understanding of "mental health" and reorients our awareness to the living ground upon which we walk. As discussed in chapter 9, one's relationship to the natural world supports a holistic vision of health, and of "self," that is far more vast than our anthropocentric understanding. Embracing the historical legacies associated with our place on the earth is pivotal here as well. For people living in the Americas, a sobering look into the histories of genocide, slavery, and colonization will likely play a large part in this process. People living in other parts of the world have their own land-based stories to engage with and understand.

Diet and Consumption

People often change their diets after a psychedelic experience. One realizes that the food one eats does not come from a supermarket shelf but from a living animal or patch of earth. Reevaluating one's relationship to consumption in general—whether of certain types of food, news and social media, substances, or psychedelics themselves—can become a central part of one's integration. Sometimes integration requires that we step away from psychedelics altogether in order to fully process and enact how we must change. Perpetually embarking on the spiritual quest without time for integration simply leaves the gifts atop the mountain.

Relationship to the Inner Self

The hard work of psychedelic healing is that one is exposed to one's shadow and other exiled parts of the psyche. Remembering many of the mythic beings we've encountered throughout this book, how might we begin to view our fragmented parts and shadows not as demons to conquer, but as ancient deities that inhabit neglected areas of the soul? The inner self also relates to our unknown vastness and the expansive, infinite nature of the soul. Cultivating our relationship with the inner self can be broken down into three domains: creating space for the self, courting the shadow, and viewing all things as medicine.

Creating Space for the Self

How will integration ever occur unless one creates space for it? This is especially relevant for those of us who lead increasingly busy lives. Creating space for the self relates directly to all other aspects of integration and even may be viewed as the core pillar upon which all the others depend. Integration takes time—days, months, or years—and without consciously creating time for one's self, it won't occur. Creating daily space and time to reconnect to the inner world is essential. Those in the healing professions may call this self-care, though its implications reach much deeper than simply feeling better. This can take the form of a quiet morning alone, a walk in the woods, or a meditation practice, for instance.

Courting the Shadow

As Jung wrote, doing the work to face and integrate one's shadow material was the "essential condition for self-knowledge" (1959/2014, p. 8). If one is faced with a difficult experience of one's shadow during a psychedelic experience, this is the opportunity to lean into that discomfort rather than continuing to bury it in shame. And while this work can be excruciating, doing it in a supportive community can be the precise medicine that these wounded parts of ourselves need most. As discussed in chapter 5, facing one's traumas is also an uncomfortable but sometimes unavoidable element of psychedelic healing. Like the Lindworm serpent, these parts of ourselves can be successfully courted back into the warmth and light of our psychic home.

Finding the Medicine

In many Indigenous cultures and Eastern traditions, nothing is seen as occurring by accident. Malidoma Somé wrote, "Visible wrongs have their roots in the world of the spirit" (1993, p. 43). To view life's challenges and hardships as devoid of greater meaning drains all significance out of one's life. This isn't to say that bad things happened to someone because they were "needing it," "calling it in," or some other New Age cliché meant to bypass or explain away suffering. Some things are simply awful and are deserved by no one. Yet as Viktor Frankl described in his book *Man's Search for Meaning*, we give our power away when we choose not to find meaning in unthinkable circumstances (2014). Finding the medicine dwelling *within* undeniably painful situations is often the only way *through* them.

Relationship to the Imaginal Spirit

The imaginal spirit is a domain outside human control; it is the realm of inspiration, awe, and the spirit. It is a realm that some people might consider sacred or divine, or a level of ultimate reality. I'm talking about forging a relationship to something much larger than ourselves. This can manifest in three ways: cultivating practice, creative flow, and service.

Cultivating Practice

Shaw (2011) wrote that after initiatory experiences, one must cultivate a "defined practice to travel back and forth to the kind of perception you want to inhabit" (p. 17). Throughout this book we've explored myths that speak about apprenticeship and learning. As we discussed in chapter 8, discipline means being a disciple of something greater than oneself. Without a practice of some kind, one's capacity to use their gifts remains only partially realized. One's practice might take the form of a simple morning ritual, a monthly act of reflection, any variety of physical or creative practices, or any combination of the above. For others, one's vocation can become a practice, such as psychotherapy or other healing professions. What matters is that we take seriously the work we choose to commit to.

Embracing Creativity

Creativity requires us to bring something from the inner world to the outer. "Soul is imagination," according to Hillman (1992, p. 69). Embracing creativity and imagination means reconnecting to one's soul and expressing that unique, sacred part of one's self into the world. It's a vulnerable thing. Whether painted upon the walls of the Lascaux cave in France or built into an Islamic mosque, human beings have used art and creativity to express their relationship to the divine since time immemorial. Making music; dance; writing and poetry; theater; visual art; and even building a house can be powerful outlets for creativity.

Being of Service

Service is the apex of integration, wherein one gives the fruits of one's experience away to one's larger community. In order for these fruits to become real, they must be shared. The vision atop the Sacred Mountain means nothing if it does not inspire us to make the world a better place. Whatever you find *down there, out there,* or *in there,* give it all away.

Afterword

Winter Solstice

I'm pushing a wheelbarrow under heavy clouds that hang above the wet Cascadian forest. The impersonal presence of the wild is breathing down my neck, seeping down through the imposing gray-green hills. Though not far from the city, this forest, thick with mossy Douglas fir and old-growth cedars, continues south until all boundaries dissolve into the untamed vastness of the Mt. Hood wilderness.

I've arrived at the tiny one-room cabin where I'll spend the night. Now it's just me and the rapidly encroaching darkness. But here in this little hut I will make an oasis of prayer.

I've always liked undertaking a psychedelic journey on the winter solstice. It feels like something my northern European ancestors would understand implicitly. Traditionally celebrated as a return of the light, to me this night has always been a potent doorway into the dark. It's a time I can reliably look toward for my own (often postponed) inner work.

It is especially needed this year, as I've been working myself to the bone. The burnout crept in slowly. My focus scattered, creativity drained, confidence shaken, barely able to respond to emails. I was burned out. The old frog in the pot. I should have known.

Mushrooms have always been a reliable ally in such situations. It's been nearly a year since I've ventured into their world, and I feel a lingering sense that, once again, it's time. I need a good talking to, or a purge, or better yet, an all-out cry. It might not be fun, and it certainly won't be easy, but a complete psychospiritual reset is what the doctor ordered. I need this.

Now the woodstove is lit, iron slowly groaning as it wakes up to the unfamiliar heat. Cedar, copal, *palo santo*, Agua de Florida, and an Amazonian plant salve are arrayed around the altar with certain items of ceremonial significance to me. I roll some of my teacher's prayer tobacco into three smokes for three purposes. My deer-hide drum and flutes lay upon the sheepskin, and blankets neatly cover the simple pad that will serve as my bed. It's actually looking pretty cozy. I feel proud of myself.

The night is starting later than planned, as usual. But the ceremony cannot be rushed. After all, good preparation usually means a good journey. What you put in, you get out—words I've uttered to clients countless times.

It feels good to be back in my solitary element. I am silent for the first time in what feels like months. There are no words except the prayer I offer outside with my tobacco, speaking aloud to the flowing creek and the spirits of the land my request for permission and my intentions for this night. All is said and done. I am ready.

I consume seven grams of dried *Psilocybe cubensis* mushrooms of a notably potent genetic variety. I've had microdoses of this batch that left me almost unable to walk before. I'm nervous about taking this dose. But I know what I need, and that is to be melted down, tempered by the hand of God, and refined into some new form that will better serve me and everyone in my life. That's the prayer, at least. So seven grams it is. I take a breath, and down it goes.

The crackle of the fire fills my soul with a warm glow. I think about the stories and deep reverence I've heard from one of my teachers—a Native elder and medicine man—about this primordial element. I acknowledge the flames as the inner heat of my metabolism starts to break down the mushrooms I've just consumed. Soon, I tell myself, everything will change.

Sitting in silence, I can feel the subtle creep of the medicine undulate from my belly. It's beginning to come on, and from what I know of this variety, it's going to hit me hard. I pick up my drum and begin to play.

The deep bass tones of this ancient instrument saturate my body. I lose track of time. I imagine horned gods and cedar spirits and ambiguous Trickster beings descending on my little hut. I can feel them subtly poking and prodding me. I am being sussed out and inspected. I try to relax and breathe, welcoming whatever alien sentience seems to be scrutinizing me from within.

Finally, I check the clock. It's been an hour and a half since I consumed the medicine. And yet, I am still strangely coherent. I lie down and try to surrender more deeply, allowing the mushrooms to do their work. Relaxing my body, allowing the medicine to unfurl, welcoming it, talking to it.

Another hour passes.

Suddenly, in a dreamy flash, I see a Hopi kachina-like being above me with a rattle. I sit up, and a wave of nausea shudders through me. *All right, here we go,* I think to myself. A good purge might clear the way for my nervous system to reset, which could allow the medicine to finally move through me. I reach for my rattle, and the nausea vanishes. I find myself trying to conjure it back, like a dog I've shooed away, only to miss it later. I laugh to myself at the irony of actually wishing my nausea would return—an indication of how desperate I am to just feel *something*.

Now midway through what should be an earth-shattering psychedelic journey, I am sitting with the confronting reality that I don't feel a thing.

I put more wood on the fire, take a drink of water, and go outside to smoke another prayer tobacco in the cold, silver night air. I stare at the oblong moon through the swaying cedar branches, contemplating the utter strangeness of this experience. I feel alone, confused, and frustrated. I exhale steam and herbaceous tobacco smoke into the night, asking for guidance, praying for some fucking direction: "Please help me. Please guide me. Please show me what I need to do." Nothing.

I remember the words I once heard a Native woman share in a peyote meeting. She was angry, and she took it upon herself to chastise the casual attitude that many of the participants had before entering the tipi. Some were smoking weed, while others just laughed and joked a bit too much for her liking. "Our elders told us, if you disrespect this medicine, it will leave you," she said. "Suddenly it'll be gone, and you'll be all alone." I've heard similar sentiments echoed from other Indigenous teachers I've known. If we disrespect the medicine, then one day it will disappear.

Had I disrespected the mushrooms? Had I somehow misunderstood or damaged my relationship with them? Had I grown too familiar, too casual with something far above my pay grade? Had my work in the unfolding "psychedelic renaissance" actually taken me further away from the lessons that this medicine wanted me to receive? Had I really learned anything at all?

Finally it's 4:30 a.m. and I'm staring into the coals, contemplating how seven grams of undeniably potent mushrooms had no effect. I am running through the possible mechanistic causes—human errors in preparation or measurement, SSRI medications, old or impotent mushrooms—and realize that none of them apply, whatsoever. They simply did not affect me.

I've seen this happen before with certain clients. But I've never been the one to experience it. I feel a strange cocktail of curiosity and desperation. *Why hast thou forsaken me?* I think to myself, half joking, half gravely serious.

I prepared as well as I could for the journey, barring a rather rushed arrival. I asked permission, I offered tobacco, I did my ritual, and I set my container. And against all my best efforts, the mushrooms had other plans.

What did this mean? What was I supposed to learn? What were the mushrooms trying to tell me? Had I failed? Was I broken? I steep in these questions until sleep finally takes me.

It's morning now. The rain is falling, and the fire's gone out. I roll up my sheepskins and instruments and pack my bags, which I place into the soaked wheelbarrow from the day before. I say my beleaguered thanks to the land and to the mushrooms, despite my frustration with them.

But deep down, I know that what transpired last night has nothing to do with the mushrooms and everything to do with me.

I heave my belongings up the steep, muddy hill. Finally I arrive at the earthen dwelling of an old friend who owns the land. He's a devout Tibetan Buddhist, and I doubt I'll see him again until he emerges from his next three-month retreat. He invites me in for tea.

To this day, I'm still contemplating this experience and the questions it provoked. I don't have any answers. Despite all the study, the exploration, and hands-on experience in the trenches of psychedelic therapy, these medicines remain the most foreign, feral creatures I have ever encountered. To say that we know anything about psychedelics is like saying that we know anything about a snow leopard, a yew tree, a cloud formation, or an octopus. Sure, we might have data points. We might even be able to get close to them. But ultimately, they are autonomous beings playing by a set of rules that our human psyche will never fully grasp.

And maybe that's a good thing. Maybe it does us good as a species to engage with something that refuses to conform to our will, that bucks our domestic urges to such a degree that they can seemingly, at will, pack up the whole show and leave town. With few truly wild things left in this world, maybe it's good if psychedelics remain that way, just slightly beyond reach of civilization's devouring grasp.

Perhaps it was all just a trick of the mind, a cosmic joke, revealing my ignorance, checking my humility, reminding me of how much I truly don't know. By refusing to let me feel or see or experience anything of their world, perhaps this medicine performed the ultimate aikido move on my psyche. Maybe it did work, but not in the way I wanted. Trickster always has the last laugh. Because the joke's on me, as it is on all of us who seek to bend these Otherworldly substances to our will. We will continue to try to contain these feral beings, and they will continue to slip through our hands, running back to the liminal forest, begging us to follow them. And so the old story begins again.

As psychedelics become the magic pill that a wounded world looks to for its healing, they might just perform the greatest magic trick of them all. It's something these medicines and those who've guarded them have done for centuries in the face of colonization and conversion, a dance move mastered under the grip of draconian drug war policies, a final act replicating an eternal pattern that echoes out of the unending cycles of nature and the earth itself: to disappear, and then be everywhere.

Appendix

Three Spheres of Integration: Question Inventory
Relationship to the Outer World

Human Relationships and Community

1. Who and what do you define as your community?
2. What kind of community do you want to be a part of?
3. What is your relationship like with your blood family/family of origin?
4. What are your close/intimate relationships like?
5. Are you in any form of a romantic relationship(s)?
6. If not, what do you envision in a romantic relationship?
7. What do you hope to give?
8. What do you hope to receive?
9. How do you relate with your sexuality and the sexuality of others?
10. Who do you need to forgive?
11. Who needs your forgiveness?

Place and Nature

1. What is the story of the land you walk upon?

2. What is the story of your family, ancestors, and ancestral lands?

3. Who are the Indigenous people who live/lived where you call home?

4. Where do you consider sacred?

5. Where do you feel most at home?

6. What can you do to nurture, relate with, and protect the place you call home?

Diet and Consumption

1. What is your relationship to food and larger food systems?

2. What does your diet consist of?

3. What feels comforting to consume?

4. What feels shameful or out of balance to consume?

5. What feels intrinsically right to consume?

6. How do you want to change your consumption habits?

7. What is your relationship to substances, including psychedelics?

8. Do you have any addictions? If so, what are they?

9. What is your relationship to news and social media?

Relationship to the Inner Self

Creating Space for the Self

1. How much time do you allow for yourself each day?

2. What form does your "self time" take?

3. What gets in the way of this time?

4. How do you spend your mornings? Do you have a morning routine?

5. How do you spend your evenings? Do you have an evening routine?

6. What rejuvenates you?

7. What drains you?

8. What do you need to do for yourself but have been avoiding?

9. If you get very quiet for a moment, what does your inner self have to say right now?

Courting the Shadow

1. What is your sense of your own wounding?

    a. Can you locate it on/in your body?

    b. Can you locate it in time?

    c. Can you locate it mythically or archetypally?

2. Where and how does your shadow reveal itself?

3. List three qualities of your wounds and shadow and how they express themselves.

4. How do you normally respond when this wound is touched?

5. How would you like to respond differently?

6. Where do you see this playing out most frequently in your life?

7. What makes you angry?

8. What are you grieving for?

Finding the Medicine

1. What helps you find a new perspective?

2. What are you learning from your current situation?

3. How will you be different on the other side of this situation?

4. Is there a myth or archetype in your current situation? If so, what is it?

5. What part are you playing?

6. What new roles do you want to play in this dynamic or situation?

7. What new stories want to be told after this one?

Relationship to the Imaginal Spirit

Cultivating Practice

Which of the following do you currently practice?

1. Meditation
2. Physical practices (yoga, qigong, running, weight training)
3. Journaling/writing
4. Poetry
5. Music
6. Art
7. Breath work
8. Gratitude
9. Nature-based practices (hiking, gardening, hunting, fishing, etc.)
10. Crafting (pottery, knitting, crocheting, wood carving, etc.)
11. Other

How often do you engage in this practice? Is it enough?

What is a practice you've been curious about or wanting to learn?

Embracing Creativity

1. What is your relationship to your inner life/imagination?
2. What did you like to do as a child for play?
3. What forms of creativity feel safe or easy?
4. What forms of creativity feel scary or hard?
5. What does your inner creative self want to express?
6. What can you do today that is creative?
7. How can you invite more creativity into your life?

Being of Service

1. How do you want to grow?

2. How do you want to contribute?

3. What do you want to learn?

4. What brings you joy?

5. What is something you can offer that no one else can?

6. How do you relate to power and leadership?

7. Why do you do what you do?

8. What are your unique gifts?

Acknowledgments

This book was written on the ancestral homelands of the Chinook, Multnomah, Clackamas, S'klallam, Paiute, Cowichan, Ute, Nahua, Taino, and Zapotec peoples.

Thank you to my parents, Rick Yugler and Chris Tarpey, for your unwavering support throughout my life and for your unfathomable ability to remain calm as I routinely embarked on questionable journeys into unknown lands, both inward and outward. Thank you, Tim McKee and Margeaux Weston, for saying yes to this book, and the NAB team.

Thank you, Chief Alex Turtle and Chenoa Egawa. Gracias a mis maestros Shipibos, Don Enrique y Don Miguel Lopez. Thank you, Timothy White, Erica Gagnon, Claudia Cuentas, Martin Loarte Valenzuela, Forward Kwenda, and so many others who have taught me along my path. Thank you to the ancient ones: the *niños santos* mushroom beings, madre ayahuasca, chief peyote, abuelo huachuma. Thank you to the Indigenous peoples who have protected and fought for the preservation of these sacred medicines and ceremonies.

Thank you, Michael Meade, for your guidance during the crafting of this book. Thank you, Martin Shaw, Tom Hirons, Sophie Strand, Bayo Akomolafe, and all the feral storytellers. Grá Mor to Manchán Magan, for your generosity of heart and for initiating me into the humbling tradition of Irish literary critique. Thank you to Kirsten Webb, for your impeccable editing, mythopoetic insights, and the care in which you held and stewarded me and this book.

Infinite mantras of mango love to Devendra Banhart—thank you for your friendship and for supporting this little cookbook since the beginning. Thank you, Dr. Robert Stuckey, Pacifica Graduate Institute, and all of my Jungian mentors. Big thanks to David Bronner and Astarae Metcalf, for all you do to increase legal access to psychedelic healing. Ian MacKenzie and the School of Mythopoetics. Justin Townshend and the MycoMeditations team. Bows of gratitude to Harvey Schwartz, Jamaica Stevens, Diana Quinn, Daniel Shankin, Laura Mae Northrup, Tom Eckert, Nate Howard and the Inner Trek team, Mario "Onieros" Martinez, Mariel Pastor, and the Rhizome PDX community. Thank you to my clients and students, past present and future. Bless you all.

And finally, thank you to the stories themselves, without whom we'd be lost.

References

Abram, D. (1996). *The spell of the sensuous.* Random House.

Akomolafe, B. (2018, October 16). When you meet the monster, anoint its feet. *Emergence Magazine.* https://emergencemagazine.org/essay/when-you-meet-the-monster/

Allione, L. T. (2008). *Feeding your demons: Ancient wisdom for resolving inner conflict.* Little, Brown Spark.

Branston, B. (1980). *Gods of the north.* Thames and Hudson.

Buber, M. (1958). *I and thou.* Charles Scribner's Sons.

Carhart-Harris, R., Leech, R., Hellyer, P. J., Shanahan, M., Feilding, A., Tagliazucchi, E., . . . Nutt, D. (2014). The entropic brain: A theory of consciousness states informed by neuroimaging research with psychedelic drugs. *Frontiers in Human Neuroscience, 8*(20). http://dx.doi.org/10.3389/fnhum.2014.00020

Crawford, J. (2015). *The Poetic Edda: Stories of the Norse gods and heroes.* Hackett Publishing Company.

Deloria, V. (1973). *God is red.* Dell.

de L. Osório, F., Sanches, R. F., Macedo, L. R., dos Santos, R. G., Maia-de-Oliveira, J. P., Wichert-Ana, L., . . . Hallak, J. E. (2015). Antidepressant effects of a single dose of ayahuasca in patients with recurrent depression: A preliminary report. *Brazilian Journal of Psychiatry, 37*(1), 13–20. https://doi.org/10.1590/1516-4446-2014-1496

Eisler, R. (1988). *The chalice and the blade: Our history, our future.* HarperOne.

Eliade, M. (1957). *The sacred and the profane.* Harcourt.

Eliade, M. (1995). *Rites and symbols of initiation: The mysteries of birth and rebirth.* Spring Publications.

Frankl, V. (2014). *Man's search for meaning*. Beacon Press.

Garcia Romeu, A., Griffiths, R., & Johnson, M. (2015). Psilocybin-occasioned mystical experiences in the treatment of tobacco addiction. *Current Drug Abuse Reviews, 7*(3), 157–164.

Gilbert, J. (2013, July). A brief for the defense. *The Sun*, 451. https://www.thesunmagazine.org/issues/451/a-brief-for-the-defense

Graves, R. (1960). *The Greek myths: Volume one*. Penguin Books.

Hamill, J., Hallak, J., Dursun, S. M., & Baker, G. (2019). Ayahuasca: Psychological and physiologic effects, pharmacology and potential uses in addiction and mental illness. *Current Neuropharmacology, 17*(2), 108–128. http://doi.org/10.2174/1570159X16666180125095902

Harvey, G. (2006). *Animism: Respecting the living world*. Columbia University Press.

Hillman, J. (1979). *The dream and the underworld*. Harper & Row.

Hillman, J. (1989). *A blue fire: Selected writings by James Hillman*. HarperCollins.

Hillman, J. (1992). *Re-visioning psychology*. HarperCollins.

Hollis, J. (1996). *Swamplands of the soul: New life in dismal places*. Inner City Books.

Hyde, L. (2007). *The gift: Creativity and the artist in the modern world*. Vintage Books.

Hyde, L. (2010). *Trickster makes this world: Mischief, myth, and art*. Farrar, Straus, and Giroux.

Intellectual Deep Web. (2017, August 24). Why study Greek mythology—James Hillman [Video]. Youtube. https://www.youtube.com/watch?v=blF0NdSm1lQ

Jung, C. G. (1963). *Memories, dreams, reflections* (A. Jaffé, Ed.) (R. Winston & C. Winston, Trans.) (Rev. ed.). Vintage Books. (Original work published 1961)

Jung, C. G. (1970). The structure and dynamics of the psyche (R. F. C. Hull, Trans.). In H. Read et al. (Eds.), *The collected works of C. G. Jung: Complete digital edition* (Vol. 8, pt. 3, p. 158). http://www.ebscohost.com/ (Original work published 1959)

Jung, C. G. (1972). Two essays on analytical psychology (R. F. C. Hull, Trans.). In H. Read et al. (Eds.), *The collected works of C. G. Jung: Complete digital edition* (Vol. 7, pt. 110, pp. 70–71). http://www.ebscohost .com/ (Original work published 1953).

Jung, C. G. (2001). *Modern man in search of a soul* (C. F. Baynes & W. S. Dell, Trans.). Routledge.

Jung, C. G. (2014). Archetypes and the collective unconscious (R. F. C. Hull, Trans.). In H. Read et al. (Eds.), *The collected works of C. G. Jung: Complete digital edition* (Vol. 9). http://www.ebscohost.com/ (Original work published 1959)

Kalsched, D. (1996). *The inner world of trauma: Archetypal defenses of the personal spirit*. Routledge.

Kalsched, D. (2013). *Trauma and the soul: A psychospiritual approach to human development and its interruption*. Routledge.

Kerenyi, K. (1980). *Gods of the Greeks*. Thames & Hudson.

Kerenyi, K. (2020). *Hermes: Guide of souls*. Spring Publications.

Kettner, H., Gandy, S., Haijen, E. C. H. M., & Carhart-Harris, R. L. (2019). From egoism to ecoism: Psychedelics increase nature relatedness in a state-mediated and context-dependent manner. *International Journal of Environmental Research and Public Health, 16*(24). http://dx.doi.org/10.3390/ijerph16245147

Kimmerer, R. W. (2015). *Braiding sweetgrass: Indigenous wisdom, scientific knowledge, and the teachings of the plants*. Milkweed Editions.

Kübler-Ross, E. (2014). *On death and dying: What the dying have to teach doctors, nurses, clergy, and their own families*. Scribner.

Love, S. (2021, February 9). Can a company patent the basic components of psychedelic therapy? *Vice*. https://www.vice.com/en/article/93w mxv/can-a-company-patent-the-basic-components-of-psychedelic -therapy

Magan, M. (2020). *Thirty-two words for field: Lost words of the Irish landscape*. Gill Books.

Marshall, W. (2012, September 21.) The therapeutic experience of being suspended by your skin. *The Atlantic*. https://www.theatlantic.com

/health/archive/2012/09/the-therapeutic-experience-of-being
-suspended-by-your-skin/262644/

McKenna, T. (1987, September 12). Nature is the center of the mandala [Speech audio recording]. The Library of Consciousness. https://www.organism.earth/library/document/nature-is-the-center-of-the-mandala

McKenna, T. (1993). *Food of the gods: The search for the original tree of knowledge.* Bantam.

McKenna, T. (2015, January 7). The danger is madness [Audio podcast episode]. In *Psychedelic salon.* https://psychedelicsalon.com/podcast-430-the-danger-is-madness/

Metzner, R. (1998). *The unfolding self.* Origin Press.

Metzner, R. (2005). *Sacred mushroom of visions: Teonanácatl: A sourcebook on the psilocybin mushroom.* Park Street Press.

Mithoefer, M. (2015, August 19). *A manual for MDMA-assisted psychotherapy in the treatment of posttraumatic stress disorder.* https://maps.org/research-archive/mdma/MDMA-Assisted-Psychotherapy-Treatment-Manual-Version7-19Aug15-FINAL.pdf

Nayak, S. M., & Griffiths, R. R. (2022). A single belief-changing psychedelic experience is associated with increased attribution of consciousness to living and non-living entities. *Frontiers in Psychology, 13,* 852248. https://doi.org/10.3389/fpsyg.2022.852248

O'Donohue, J. (2008). *To bless the space between us: A book of blessings.* Doubleday.

Perera, S. (1981). *Descent to the goddess: A way of initiation for women.* Inner City Books.

Radin, P. (1956). *The trickster: A study in American Indian mythology.* Philosophical Library.

Rasmussen, K. (1932). *The eagle's gift: Alaska Eskimo tales* (I. Hutchinshon, Trans.). Doubleday, Dorian & Company.

Rilke, R. M. (1992). Just as the winged energy of delight. In R. Bly, J. Hillman, & M. Meade (Eds.), *The rag and bone shop of the heart: Poems for men* (p. 236). Harper Perennial.

Roszak, T. (1992). *The voice of the earth: An exploration of ecopsychology.* Simon & Schuster.

Rotterdam, L. C. Z. (2021, January 12). Cutting through views: Three practice verses by Machig Labdrön. *Lion's Roar.* https://www.lionsroar.com /cutting-through-views-three-practice-verses-by-machig-labdron/

Rumi, J., & Barks, C. (1995). *The essential Rumi.* Harper.

Schrei, J. (Host). (2022, October 24). Embodiment means being torn apart and flying away [Audio podcast episode]. In *The Emerald.* https://podcasts.apple.com/gb/podcast/embodiment-means-being -torn-apart-and-flying-away/id1465445746?i=1000583720432

Shaw, M. (2011). *A branch from the lightning tree: Ecstatic myth and the grace in wilderness.* White Cloud.

Shaw, M. (Director/performer). (2023, May 15). *Codes from the old world* [Theater production]. Sunset Labs, Victoria, BC, Canada.

Singer, J. (1994). *Boundaries of the soul: The practice of Jung's psychology.* Anchor Books.

Somé, M. P. (1993). *Ritual: Power, healing and community.* Swan/Raven & Company.

Starhawk. (1987). *Truth or dare: Encounters with power, authority, and mystery.* Harper & Row.

Strassman, R. (2000). *DMT: The spirit molecule.* Park Street Press.

Taylor, K. (2017). The ethics of caring: Finding right relationship with clients. Hanford Mead Publishers.

Turner, V. (1995). *The ritual process: Structure and anti-structure.* Aldine de Gruyter.

Valdez, C. (2022, May 31). Archaeologists discover passageways in 3,000-year-old Peruvian temple. Reuters. https://www.reuters.com /world/americas/archaeologists-discover-passageways-3000-year -old-peruvian-temple-2022-05-30/

Van Gordon, W., Shonin, E., Diouri, S., Garcia-Campayo, J., Kotera, Y., & Griffiths, M. D. (2018). Ontological addiction theory: Attachment to me, mine, and I. *Journal of Behavioral Addiction, 7*(4), 892–896.

von Franz, M. L. (2020). The collected works of Marie-Louise von Franz, volume 1: Archetypal symbols in fairytales. Chiron Publications.

Wasson, G. (1980). *The wondrous mushroom: Mycolatry in Mesoamerica.* McGraw Hill.

Wolkstein, D., & Kramer, S. (1983). *Inanna: Queen of heaven and earth.* Harper & Row.

Yalom, I. (2012). *Love's executioner: And other tales of psychotherapy.* Basic Books.

Zimmerman, J., & Coyle, V. (2009). *The way of council.* Bramble Books.

Index

V

valley of diamonds, **238–239**
Veronique case study (depression and grief), 67–69
vicarious trauma, 147–148
Vietnam veteran, 118
vine of the soul. *See* ayahuasca
Vishnu, 113
vision
  narcissistic inflation, 217–218
  price of vision, 206–208
  shadows of ecstasy, 219
  Völuspá (prophecy of Ragnarok), 225–229
  climate change and the new gods, 229–230
  desouled world, 232–233
  Nordic kinship with natural world, 231
  skills for navigating the Tree of Life, 241–245
  twilight of the gods, 230–231
  witch's pyre, 233–235
völva, 230
vomiting, 117
  catharsis, 97
  midwifing the purge, 123–124
von Franz, Marie Louise, 208
vulnerable uncertainty, 175

W

WAIT (Why Am I Touching/ Talking?), 59
war on drugs, 256–257
warmth, skin shedding, 124–125
Wasson, R. Gordon, 43, 50, 120
water, skin shedding, 124
Watts, Alan, 165
The Way of Council (Zimmerman and Coyle), 60
We Will Call It Pala (McGaughey), 171
weather, 229–230
Weather Underground, 166

the Well, 15
amplification (collective unconscious), 35–38
association (individual unconscious), 34–35
collective unconscious, 21–23
Connla's Well, 15–17, 18, 20–21, 23–28, 31, 38, 40
cosmic fisherman, 25–28
language of psyche, 30–31
layers of myth, 28–30
Mythopoetic Integration, 31–40
mythos (story), 32–33
Otherworld, 17–21, 26
pathos (feeling), 33–34
personification (imaginal-animistic psyche), 38–40
Salmon of Knowledge, 23–25, 38
wells, 18–19
Welwood, John, 221
wielding the shield, 147–148
wilca snuff, 53, 64
winter solstice journey, 267–272
Wise Elder archetype, 36–37, 39, 191–192
witch's pyre, 233–235
witchcraft, 232
Wounded Healer archetype, 188–191

X

Xochipilli, 120

Y

Yalom, Irvin, 63
Yggdrasil, 98, 226, 228, 230, 234, 242, 245
Yoda, 37
Yoruba people, 159–160

Z

Zeus, birth of Hermes, 153, 156
Zimmerman, Jack, 60